# Wild Things 2

Further Advances in Palaeolithic and Mesolithic Research

*edited by*

James Walker and David Clinnick

Oxford & Philadelphia

Published in the United Kingdom in 2019 by
OXBOW BOOKS
The Old Music Hall, 106–108 Cowley Road, Oxford OX4 1JE

and in the United States by
OXBOW BOOKS
1950 Lawrence Road, Havertown, PA 19083

© Oxbow Books and the individual contributors 2019

Paperback Edition: ISBN 978-1-78570-946-3
Digital Edition: ISBN 978-1-78570-947-0 (ePub)

A CIP record for this book is available from the British Library

Library of Congress Control Number: 2019949795

All rights reserved. No part of this book may be reproduced or transmitted in any form or by any means, electronic or mechanical including photocopying, recording or by any information storage and retrieval system, without permission from the publisher in writing.

Typeset in India for Casemate Publishing Services. www.casematepublishingservices.com

For a complete list of Oxbow titles, please contact:

| UNITED KINGDOM | UNITED STATES OF AMERICA |
|---|---|
| Oxbow Books | Oxbow Books |
| Telephone (01865) 241249 | Telephone (610) 853-9131, Fax (610) 853-9146 |
| Email: oxbow@oxbowbooks.com | Email: queries@casemateacademic.com |
| www.oxbowbooks.com | www.casemateacademic.com/oxbow |

Oxbow Books is part of the Casemate Group

*Front cover:* Body shape and relative size of male and female Alces alces, Cervus elpahus and Capreolus capreolus. Drawing by Ben Elliott.

# Contents

List of contributors ................................................................................................................ v

1. Introduction: More wild things ........................................................................................ 1
   James Walker and David Clinnick

2. A view from the tops: Combining an assemblage analysis and a Geographical
   Information Systems approach to investigate upland site function and
   landscape use in the Lower Palaeolithic of Britain ......................................................... 9
   Helen C. Drinkall

3. Clovis and the implications of the peopling of North America ................................... 35
   Alan M. Slade

4. Experimental magnetic susceptibility signatures for identifying hearths
   in the Mesolithic period in North East England, UK .................................................... 55
   Lisa Snape and Mike J. Church

5. In the fringes, at the twilight: Encountering deer in the British Mesolithic ............... 81
   Ben Elliott

6. Man's best friend? A critical perspective on human-animal relations from
   Natufian and Pre-Pottery Neolithic mortuary practices ............................................... 97
   Gabrielle Borenstein

7. Empathy, cognition and the response to death in the Middle Palaeolithic:
   The emergence of postmortemism ............................................................................... 109
   Suzi Wilson

8. Seeking the body: The nature of European Palaeolithic cave art and
   installation art ............................................................................................................... 123
   Takashi Sakamoto

9. Reflecting Magdalenian identities: Considering a functional duality for
   Middle to Late Magdalenian antler projectile points .................................................. 137
   Michelle C. Langley

10. Concealing traces of 'untamed' fire: The Mesolithic pottery makers and
    users of Japan ............................................................................................................... 155
    *Makoto Tomii*

11. Naming *neanderthalensis* in Newcastle, 1863: The politics of a
    scientific meeting ........................................................................................................ 171
    *Miguel DeArce*

12. George Busk and the remarkable Neanderthal .................................................... 191
    *Paige Madison*

# List of contributors

GABRIELLE BORENSTEIN
Department of Anthropology
261 McGraw Pl
Ithaca
New York
14853, USA
gbb47@cornell.edu

MIKE J. CHURCH
Department of Archaeology
Durham University
South Road
Durham
DH1 3LE
UK
m.j.church@durham.ac.uk

DAVID CLINNICK
National Heritage Board of Singapore
61 Stamford Road #03-08
Singapore 178892
davidclinnick@gmail.com

MIGUEL DEARCE
Smurfit Institute
Department of Genetics
Trinity College Dublin
Ireland
mdearce50@gmail.com

HELEN C. DRINKALL
Department of Archaeology
Durham University
Durham
DH1 3LE
UK
h.c.drinkall@durham.ac.uk

BEN ELLIOTT
School of Archaeology
University College Dublin
Belfield
Dublin 4
Ireland
benjamin.elliott@ucd.ie

MICHELLE C. LANGLEY
Australian Research Centre for Human Evolution
Environmental Futures Research Institute
Griffith University
Nathan
Australia
m.langley@griffith.edu.au

PAIGE MADISON
Arizona State University
PO Box 874601
Tempe
Arizona
85287, USA
pamadiso@asu.edu

ALAN M. SLADE
Texas Archaeological Research Laboratory
University of Texas at Austin
Austin
Texas
78758, USA
alan.slade@austin.utexas.edu

LISA SNAPE
Department of Geography & Geology
Paris-Lodron-Universität Salzburg
Hellbrunnerstrasse 34
5020 Salzburg
Austria
lisa.snape@sbg.ac.at

TAKASHI SAKAMOTO
Department of Archaeology
Durham University
South Road
Durham
DH1 3LE
UK
takashi.sakamoto@durham.ac.uk

MAKOTO TOMII
Centre for Studies of Cultural Heritage and
Inter Humanities,
Graduate Schools of Letters,
Kyoto University,
Yoshida-Honmachi,
Sakyo, Kyoto,
606-8501
Japan
tomii.makoto.2e@kyoto-u.ac.jp

JAMES WALKER
School of Archaeological and Forensic Sciences
University of Bradford
Bradford
BD7 1DP
j.walker17@bradford.ac.uk

SUZI WILSON
Department of Archaeology
Durham University
Durham
DH1 3LE
UK
suziwilson@protonmail.ac.uk

# Chapter 1

## Introduction: More wild things

*James Walker and David Clinnick*

The first Wild Things volume was a compilation of papers given at a conference held at Durham University focused on all things Palaeolithic and Mesolithic. The conference was a great success, bringing together researchers from various different career stages, from postgraduate through to emeriti. Additionally, with a wide and eclectic array of subject matter being covered, the event fostered dialogue between researchers that might not have otherwise been exposed to one another's work. Recognition of this fact was a key theme emphasised in the first volume: the amount of commonality – things to be learned, in spite of the wide variety of topics being discussed (Foulds *et al.* 2014). Perhaps traditionally isolative categories of research, be they spatial or temporal, are more arbitrary than we have sometimes thought to admit. One of the keynotes (perhaps better left anonymous!) was heard to remark – tongue in cheek, we are sure – that they were 'unaware and slightly jealous at how much interesting stuff you lot [sic] have and are doing in the Mesolithic'. The feeling was (we are also sure) quite reciprocated.

The success of the first conference and accompanying volume prompted a second meeting, this time tied to the broader circulation of similarly themed conferences that, with semi-regularity for a time, migrated annually around different institutions up and down the UK. This second volume, however, is not a straightforward conference proceedings – although various contributions were indeed included from the meeting. With the first Wild Things volume, we were impressed with the diversity of research showcased. Realising that this was an asset to be celebrated, the second volume serves as a taster to highlight some of the many aspects of prehistoric research that are, in varying ways, related to prehistoric research themes at the archaeology department in Durham. Some contributions are directly related, coming from current or former students, while for others the link is more tenuous – an overlap in research interests, sometimes as colleagues or friends. We hope that the volume showcases the variety of research connected to the department in some way, and, like its predecessor volume, highlights the value of engaging with researchers from beyond the insulative spheres of our own work.

In the first Wild Things volume, it was clear that there was much to be gained from pushing researchers to go beyond traditionally limiting research frameworks such as Mesolithic and Palaeolithic, and the diversity of this second volume partly reflects a desire to push even further. This artificial divide has continued to erode, but we also sought to include subject matter and authorship from further afield (Americas, Near East and East Asia), in part as a reflection of the fact that terms such as Palaeolithic and Mesolithic are often themselves used as geographic denominators, and are thus restrictive terms spatially as well as chronologically. Some of the papers in this volume deal with early hominins and human evolution, while others are firmly rooted in AMH hunter-gatherer and early farming societies. Still other contributions – the last two chapters – highlight the importance of reflexivity, and engaging with the history of our discipline in order to better understand our current state of knowledge.

The ordering of the volume, explained below, provides a general route of progression, but to retrospectively shoehorn a theme or narrative would be both self-defeating and disingenuous; we prefer to let each entry stand alone, and, save for some of the connecting links discussed here, for the reader to see some of the many novel and different ways there are of grappling with various different questions of the deep past, from early hominins to recent hunter-gatherers. If nothing else, they show the field to be in a state of rude health.

## Where the things are

Landscape-based studies are a vital component of ancient prehistoric archaeology, and our volume opens with three studies that, among other things, could fairly be described as innovative landscape-based approaches to the past. We have to think beyond the discrete site-unit resolution that frames much of the material record if we are to attempt to understand the various different ways in which hunter-gatherers perceive, interact with and live in the landscape (Zvelebil and Moore 2006). If reconstructing human landscapes from the early Holocene was not challenge enough, delving further back in time entails working with an increasingly disparate and depauperate material record, and a much greater time-lapse of landscape taphonomy, with multiple instances of glacial advance and retreat. As the cover-art of Fairweather Eden – the popular account of the Boxgrove excavations (Pitts and Roberts 1998) – evocatively portrayed, with a scene from ancient Britain with humans and proboscideans living alongside one another, the world must, at times, have been a very different place. It is not far off from this particular different time and place that our volume begins.

We open with an innovative marriage of GIS landscape approaches and traditional lithic-based analyses of Lower Palaeolithic assemblages from the south-east of

Britain. Relating differences in assemblage to particular places within the prehistoric landscape is a crucial part of understanding variability and structured use of space. In this respect, this chapter (*Drinkall*) provides a timely contribution to an area that has undergone much development recently (see Coward *et al.* 2015) that assesses broader questions of hominin evolution and human development from a landscape-based perspective. Drinkall elicits a connection between site location, assemblage composition and intervisibility that has previously been lacking from many accounts of archaic hominins in northern Europe.

Moving on in time and place to the early prehistory of the Americas, our next chapter (*Slade*) reflects upon diversity of environment and group interactions as a factor in explaining assemblage patterns – in this case, the iconic Clovis technocomplex. Although no longer regarded as the first Americans, the questions of where the Clovis came from and how this relates to earlier, contemporary and later technologies in the Americas remains at the fore of New World prehistory (Waters *et al.* 2018). Using dated sites and associated faunal assemblages, Slade posits that rather than a homogenous spread, as has sometimes been portrayed, the Clovis industry comprises multiple regionalised developments within the broader bracket of the famous fluted-point tradition.

Our fourth chapter (*Snape-Kennedy and Church*) takes us back across the Atlantic to Britain once again, but this time to the Mesolithic of North East England, and the question of settlement use. A number of Mesolithic structures have been uncovered in recent decades (*e.g.* Waddington 2007), but the question of what constitutes settlement evidence and how we recognise or interpret it has remained, since the 1970s (Newell 1981), something of an enigma. Evidence of hearth-places, long recognised as evidence of at least temporary settlement placement, offer some routes forward for new analytical approaches. Here, Snape-Kennedy and Church have developed one such approach built around complementing magnetic susceptibility signatures with microcharcoal analysis in order to assess the archaeological visibility of hearths. In doing so, they are able to highlight some of the drawbacks and potential for archaeologists seeking to identify and interpret hearth remains from this period using magnetic susceptibility – a vital contribution to a field that has long struggled with questions of settlement and placing people and their archaeological signatures within the landscape.

While the first three contributions, in very different ways, showcase various different ways in which prehistorians are able to grapple with questions of land use and landscape, the fifth chapter (*Elliott*), while staying in Mesolithic Britain, focuses on a particular socio-ecological subject that has been at the heart of Mesolithic studies in north-west Europe since the pioneering work of Grahame Clark (1936): the relationship between people and deer. Using analogues from studies of modern-day animal ecology and behaviour, Elliott highlights how it is possible to develop a far more nuanced approach to human/animal relations than has typically been shown in Mesolithic research. Chapter 6 (*Borenstein*) follows on from this by also exploring human-animal relationships from a 'Social Zooarchaeology' perspective. This particular approach has become popular in recent years for helping reconcile a tension between mutually exclusive interpretations of economic and symbolic significance when discussing prehistoric faunal assemblages (Russell 2014). Borenstein contrasts mortuary contexts from the Natufian Epipalaeolithic and Pre-pottery Neolithic where both humans and animal remains have been interred. Various differences and continuities hint at shifts in behaviours and attitudes to the dead across this transition that run deeper than a mere change in economic status of the sort typically associated with the shift to farming.

Continuing with the question of what the treatment of the dead can tell us about the living, the next chapter (*Wilson*) also looks at the importance of these attitudes. Unequivocal evidence of mortuary practices, and particularly burials, has long been the subject of intense debate in studies of the Palaeolithic, largely due to the presumed significance of these behaviours as an indicator of cognitive development, and an emergent capacity for understanding symbolism and religious thought (Pettitt 2010). Wilson injects new life into the debate by approaching the subject from a very different perspective: what if attitudes towards the dead initially revolved around the living and the corpse rather than a belief in some sort of afterlife? Coining the term 'postmortemism', Wilson cogently outlines a theory that roots early mortuary practices in embodied practices; borne from expressions of closure and cohesion in the wake of loss, before eventually birthing what we might recognise as spiritual beliefs.

While Wilson explores how fields such as psychology can inform our interpretations of behaviours in the past, our eighth chapter (*Sakamoto*) takes a similarly refreshing perspective on an age-old debate, but this time by using concepts from the philosophy of art to reorient our view of Palaeolithic cave art. By invoking the analogy of installation art, whereby the venue and place is an intrinsic part of the artistic experience, cave art researchers have long held that the reduced visibility of cave interiors must have impacted upon the perception of the art (Lewis-Williams 2002), but Sakamoto goes further, suggesting that the location of much cave art deep within sometimes difficult to access cave interiors was a deliberate choice to heighten the senses and demand bodily engagement as part of a multi-sensory experience. As with the preceding chapter, by adopting aspects from schools of thought from other disciplines, Sakamoto is able to help us review a familiar topic in a new and revealing light.

Our ninth contribution (*Langley*) moves out of the cave to consider the artefact, specifically, the significance of artistic expression in its application to objects – the barbed antler projectile points of the Magdalenian – that may be encountered at different times and places within a landscape, and thus also harking back to our opening chapters. In this manner, Langley follows in the footsteps of a grand tradition in the ethnoarchaeology of prehistoric hunter-gatherers that seeks to make sense of stylistic variation among artefacts (Weissener 1983). The Magdalenian antler projectile points – ostensibly, components of a hunting toolkit

– have long enamoured prehistorians with their aesthetic sensibility. In this manner, Langley argues that these points neatly reflect a clue as to the broader social identities of the makers and users of the sort that is rarely so clear in Palaeolithic contexts. The points exhibit dual functionality, serving to procure prey, but also to signify the group identity of the users, while recalling, perhaps, a broader social identity that which we recognise archaeologically as the Magdalenian.

It is clear from Langley's work that craftsmanship was of just as much importance to prehistoric peoples as it is to people around the world today – our tenth chapter (*Tomii*) reinforces this point with an innovative approach to contextual examinations of the ornate pottery associated with the Jomon hunter-gatherers of Japan. Tomii stresses the importance of the place(ment) and the artefact – a sort of half-way house between the subject matters of Sakamoto and Langley. The manner in which these pots were placed into the pits from which they were recovered was clearly intentional. Combining a detailed photographic record of each vessel with contextual photographs and drawings of the artefacts from where they were uncovered *in situ*, it seems that many were placed in such a way as to obscure the most discoloured surfaces – these traces of discolouration having resulted from the less easily controlled aspects of the firing method used in their creation. The motivation for this is a matter for debate, but perhaps it shows a pride in craftsmanship?

The final two chapters of our volume provide neatly complimenting insights into what might fairly be described as a pivotal moment in the birth of palaeoanthropology, and certainly research into the as-yet unnamed Palaeolithic. The first of these, our eleventh chapter (*DeArce*), concerns the naming of *Homo neanderthalensis*, and specifically the politics of the various interested disciplines that led to the marginalisation of its name-giver. When William King proffered the name for the specimen in 1863, it was the first time a new species of human had been formally recognised; except that King's view was not well received, and the name fell into obscurity until after his death. The general consensus at the time was that whatever the Feldhofer 1 specimen was, it was not worthy of recognition as a separate species, despite the eventual acceptance of the status (Madison 2016). While the multi-talented but oft-overlooked King has enjoyed some attention in recent years (DeArce & Wyse Jackson 2015), this paper represents a landmark contribution to the history of our discipline by providing an in-depth insight into the various movers and shakers in the nascent field, and how events at the crucial 1863 meeting of the BAAS in Newcastle, where King's views were presented, unfolded in such a way as to hamper any impact he might have hoped to have had. It presents a wonderfully insightful piece into the fractious politics (personal, professional and racial) of the time, and how King and his work fell between the cracks.

Whereas King was a relatively peripheral character relative to some of his peers in the academic elite of Victorian Britain, George Busk most certainly was not. A respected surgeon and scientist who associated with the likes of Darwin, Huxley, Falconer and other intellectual heavyweights of the time through his membership of the

X Club, Busk was at the fore of many prominent scientific discussions in his later years, and was a key figure in bringing the Feldhofer and Gibraltar Neanderthal specimens to the attention of the English-speaking scientific community. In this, our twelfth and final chapter (*Madison*), which also concerns the early study of the Feldhofer specimen, an intriguing account is given of Busk's career history and academic interests, before exploring how these informed his position on the Neanderthal skull. Busk's time as an early pioneering excavator of prehistoric archaeological sites meant that, while he acknowledged the assessment of Charles Lyell, the pre-eminent geologist of the time, that the specimen was 'old', he nevertheless recognised the lack of conclusive evidence for the fossil's antiquity. Madison posits that it was perhaps this, as much as the question of human variability, that predisposed him to the idea that the skull was human, rather than not.

These final two chapters conclude the Second Wild Things volume with a reflection upon the history of prehistory – a field which many Durham researchers have been focused upon (*e.g.* Rowley-Conwy 2007; White 2017). Increasingly, it behoves us as a discipline to take pause to consider our roots and the intellectual history from which many 'new' ideas come. The chapters within the pages of this volume span a wide gamut of ideas and approaches. Ethnoarchaeology, neuropsychology, philosophy, art-theory, GIS-based modelling, anthracology and magnetic susceptibility … the many and varied approaches explored here show that there is no shortage of ways in which prehistorians are able to make better sense of the deep past. It is a truism to say that much of the most important parts of human history happened (ironically) in prehistory, and therein lies the fun and challenge of working in an area that is often characterised as lacking in data. We are compelled to ask better questions; to think more about what we have, and how to get the most out of it. This volume, along with its predecessor publication, highlights this point, and in doing so provides a refreshing and diverse cross-section of research for the prehistorian's palate.

## A final remark

In concluding our opening preface for the book, we should also raise two final points. When the Wild Things name was initially selected for the first conference, it was done so as an amusing reference to the popular children's story of the same name (Sendak 1963). Without getting side-lined into the question of whether 'wild' is a suitable antonym for domesticated, we would simply like to make it clear that the title was a self-referential jab at the history of hunter-gatherer research – *not* some proclamation of a Hobbesian world-view. This is a point that could be discussed at length, but having made our view clear, and now explained the humour – and thus probably ruining it – all that remains on our part is to thank the various people who have made this volume possible. Our thanks, of course, go to all the contributing authors and their incredibly virtuous patience, as well as the staff at Oxbow, for the saintliness of theirs, too. We would also like to thank Paul Pettitt, Fred Foulds, Helen Drinkall and Steph Piper as fellow organisers of the second Wild Things conference, and all those who helped make the event possible. Finally, we should also thank Peter Rowley-Conwy, Mark White, Bob Layton and the various other staff in the archaeology and anthropology departments at Durham who helped with the Wild Things events, and have, more generally, fostered a strong tradition of prehistoric research here.

## Bibliography

Clark, J.G.D. (1936) *The Mesolithic Settlement of Northern Europe: A study of the food-gathering peoples of Northern Europe during the Early Post-glacial period*. Cambridge: Cambridge University Press.

Coward, F., Hosfield, R., Pope, M. and Wenban-Smith, F. (eds) (2015) *Settlement, Society and Cognition in Human Evolution: Landscapes in mind*. Cambridge: Cambridge University Press.

DeArce, M. and Wyse-Jackson, P.N. (2015) The Alternative Geologist: William King (1809–1886) and his scientific controversies. *Journal of the Galway Archaeological and Historical Society* 66, 100–124.

Foulds, F.W., Drinkall, H.C., Perri, A.R., Clinnick, D.T.G. and Walker, J.W.P. (eds) (2014) *Wild Things: Recent advances in Palaeolithic and Mesolithic research*. Oxford: Oxbow Books.

Lewis-Williams, D. (2002) *The Mind in the Cave: Consciousness and the origins of art*. London: Thames & Hudson.

Madison, P. (2016) The Most Brutal of Human Skulls: Measuring and knowing the first Neanderthal. *The British Journal for the History of Science* 49, 411–432.

Newell, R.R. 1981. Mesolithic Dwelling Structures: Facts and fantasy. In: B. Gramsch (ed.) *Mesolithikum in Europa, 2. Internationales Symposium Potsdam, 3 bis 8. April 1978*, pp. 235–284. Berlin: Veroffentlichungen des Museums fur urund Fruhgeschichte Potsdam 14/15.

Pettitt, P. (2010) *The Palaeolithic Origins of Human Burial*. London: Routledge.

Pitts, M. and Roberts, M. (1998) *A Fairweather Eden: Life in Britain half a million years ago as revealed by the excavations at Boxgrove*. London: Arrow Books, Cornerstone Publishing.

Rowley-Conwy, P. (2007) *From Genesis to Prehistory. The archaeological Three Age System and its contested reception in Denmark, Britain and Ireland*. Oxford: Oxford University Press.

Russell, N. (2014) *Social Zooarchaeology: Humans and animals in prehistory*. Cambridge: Cambridge University Press.

Sendak, M. (1963) *Where The Wild Things Are*. New York: Harper Row.

Waddington, C. (ed.) (2007) *Mesolithic Settlement in the North Sea Basin: A case study from Howick, North-East England*. Oxford: Oxbow Books.

Waters, M.R., Keene, J.L., Forman, S.L., Prewitt, E.R., Carlson, D.L. and Wiederhold, J.E. (2018) Pre-Clovis Projectile Points at the Debra L. Friedkin Site, Texas – Implications for the Late Pleistocene peopling of the Americas. *Science Advances* 4, 1–13.

Weissener, P. (1983) Style and Social Information in Kalahari San Projectile Points. *American Antiquity* 48, 253–276.

White, M. (2017) *William Boyd Dawkins and the Victorian Science of Cave Hunting*. Barnsley: Pen & Sword Books.

Zvelebil, M. and Moore, J. 2006. Assessment and Representation: The informative value of Mesolithic landscapes. In: E. Resink and H. Peeters (eds) *Preserving the Early Past. Investigation, selection and preservation of Palaeolithic and Mesolithic sites and landscapes*, pp. 151–166. Nederlandse Archeologische Rapporten 31. Amersfoort: Rijksdienst voor het Oudheidkundig Bodemonderzoek.

# Chapter 2

# A view from the tops: Combining an assemblage analysis and a Geographical Information Systems approach to investigate upland site function and landscape use in the Lower Palaeolithic of Britain

*Helen C. Drinkall*

**Abstract**
*Lower Palaeolithic sites in upland areas have often been overlooked in favour of the wealth of information contained within the lowland fluvial archive. This, combined with a site-orientated techno-typological perspective, has potentially limited our understanding of hominin organisation to only a single facet of behaviour, that represented by riverine locations. Consequently, questions still remain regarding the way hominins were utilising upland areas away from the main river valleys, especially regarding the types of activities conducted and the organisation of behaviour within these landscapes.*

*This paper seeks to demonstrate how the integration of a Geographical Information Systems (GIS) approach with more traditional artefact studies can generate a better understanding of how hominin behaviour responds to landscapes. The application of viewshed analysis and digital terrain models (DTM) on selected upland sites from Kent and the Chilterns (UK) supplements the lithic data and provides additional lines of evidence with which to interpret assemblage signatures and site function.*

## Introduction

Traditionally, studies of the Lower Palaeolithic have taken a site-orientated approach, analysing the technological and typological aspects of lithic assemblages in isolation and with little consideration of how sites integrate within wider patterns of settlement and mobility. Whilst this approach has provided a wealth of information and a strong knowledge base, attempts to look beyond single sites and their stone tools towards a broader landscape has proved problematic. In contrast to Africa, the Palaeolithic record in Europe is characterised by a patchy exposure of sediments, and a lack of chronological anchoring (Stern 1994; Diez-Martín et al. 2008). This is especially challenging for open-air surface locations, which are key components for a landscape approach. Consequently, traditional approaches are heavily site-based (Villa 1991), that deal with selective glimpses of Palaeolithic land surfaces that are isolated in time and space (Diez-Martin et al. 2008). Despite this, a landscape perspective is vital in a period where people were so closely linked to their environment, with the surrounding resource base influencing hominin behaviour and consequently the assemblage character of a site (Ashton et al. 1998; Pope 2002).

This paper presents a methodology that integrates artefact signatures with landscape context, thereby creating a better understanding of behavioural variation and choice of site. In the original research (Drinkall 2013), the combination of a traditional techno-typological analysis with a *chaîne opératoire* and experimental Geographical Information Systems (GIS) approach proved to be a powerful combination. The use of three-dimensional landscape representation and viewshed analysis was shown to aid interpretation, and understanding of site function, when applied in an upland Palaeolithic context.

The four case studies presented here are based on upland sites in Kent and the Chilterns (Figure 2.1). These, along with others from areas such as Hampshire and Surrey (Walls and Cotton 1980; Scott-Jackson and Winton 2001; Harp 2005), form a corpus of Lower Palaeolithic sites, located away from the main river valleys and associated with a particular type of geological feature termed solution hollows (or dolines). Whilst the majority of sites from this period are recovered from lowland riverine contexts (Wymer 1999), they represent a small fraction of the hominin landscape. This limits our understanding of hominin organisation to only a single facet of behaviour associated with the resource base found in the large lowland river valleys. The upland sites presented here allow behaviour in other areas of the palaeolandscape to be investigated. The selected examples demonstrate how lithic analysis can be combined with GIS techniques in an upland setting, to inform about patterns in hominin choice of site and behavioural variation.

## Suitability for a landscape approach

In contrast to the secondary disturbed nature of many of the Lower Palaeolithic sites contained within the gravels of the main river systems (Wymer 1996), the *in situ* nature of these upland sites makes them ideal for a landscape study. They are contained within solution hollows (dolines), which form in karstic landscapes characterised by underground drainage (Ford and Williams 1989). The surface depression that distinguishes these features enlarges and deepens over time, collecting and trapping sediment from the surroundings. Periodically, the drainage conduit becomes blocked,

## 2. A view from the tops

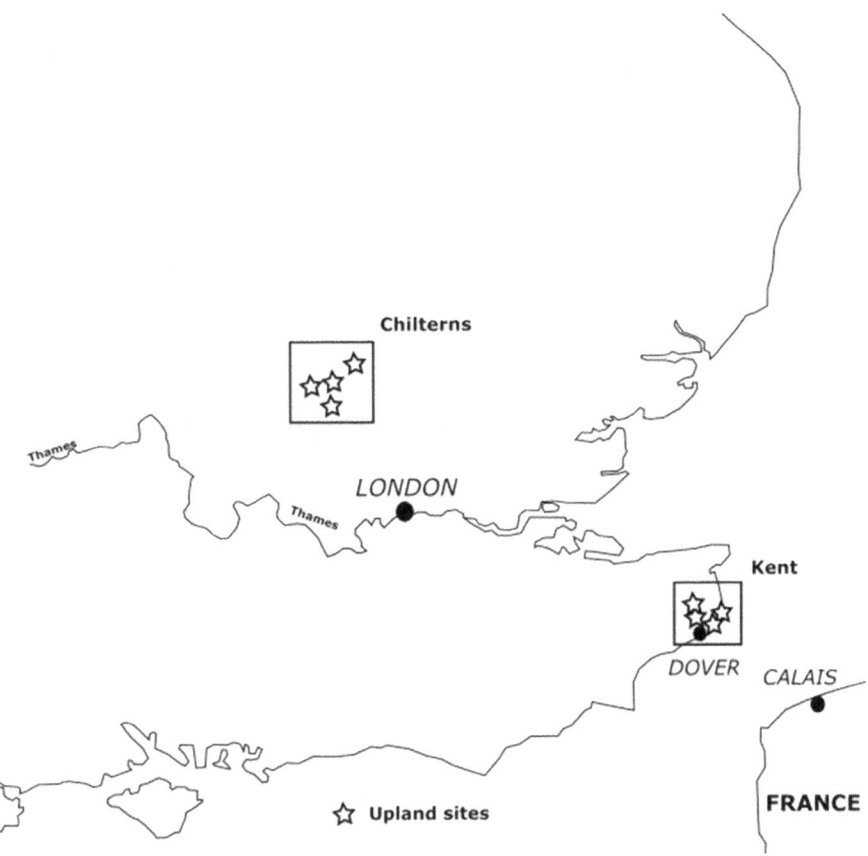

*Figure 2.1. Location of the two upland study areas.*

causing the formation of temporary ponds, which provide a variety of resources including water and easily accessible raw material (flint nodules) eroding out of the sides of the solution hollow (Catt *et al.* 1978; Ford and Williams 1989). Hominins attracted to these locations discarded artefacts on the margins of the pond, which were then incorporated as the depressions widened and deepened, trapping lithic assemblages as the ponds eventually filled in (White 1997; White *et al.* 1999). Further discussion of their formation processes can be found in Bailiff *et al.* 2013 and Drinkall 2013. Fundamentally, these solution hollows provide a sealed collection of the artefacts that hominins utilised and discarded at that point in the landscape.

An important aspect of a GIS approach that relies on modern base-maps is that no significant change has occurred in terms of the overall form of the landscape since the Palaeolithic. Using such techniques on sites in the lowland river valleys is difficult, with successive glaciations causing mass movement of sediments, which has left a landscape substantially different from that of the present day (Van Andel and Tzedakis 1996; Diez-Martín

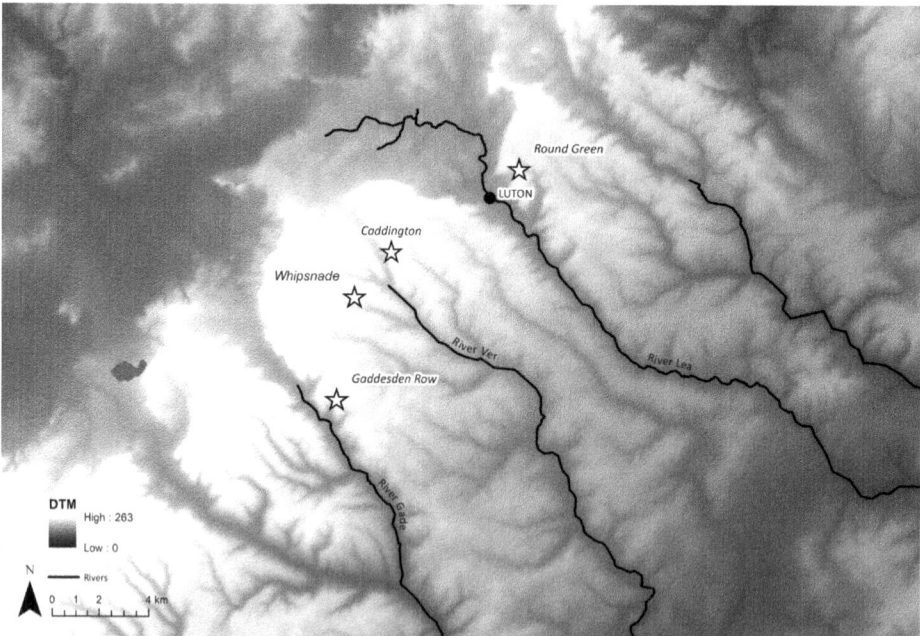

*Figure 2.2. Location of the main Lower Palaeolithic sites in the Chiltern hills used for this study.*

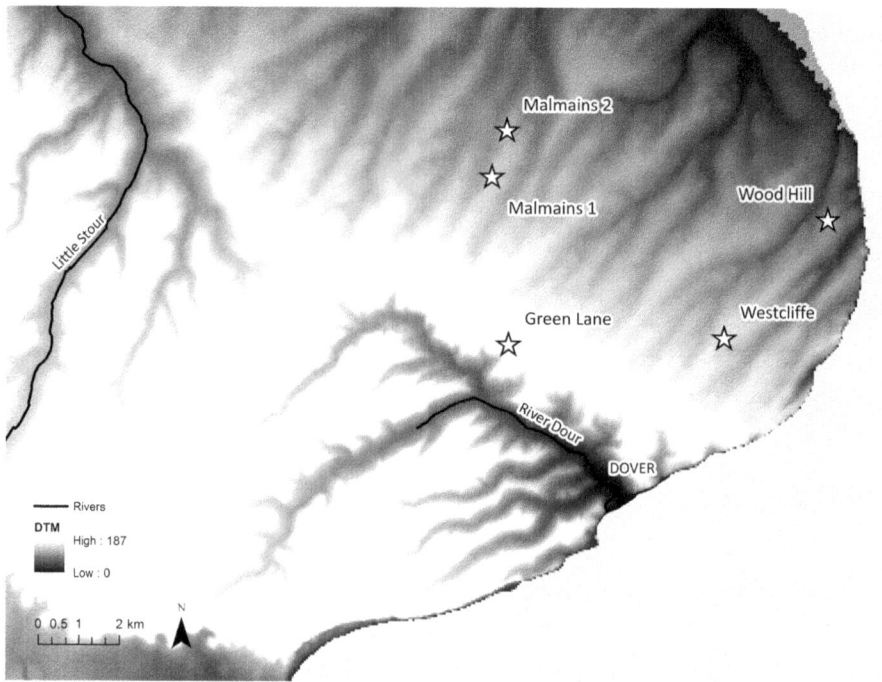

*Figure 2.3. Location of the main Lower Palaeolithic sites on the North Downs of Kent.*

*et al.* 2008; Stern 2008). One example is the assemblage from High Lodge in Suffolk, which was transported as a raft of sediments by the ice sheets of the Anglian (Rose 1992). With regards to the immense earth-shifting disturbances caused by the glacial advances during the Pleistocene, these upland locations by comparison suffered limited disturbance. The Chilterns hills constitute a discrete area that was never fully glaciated (Sampson 1978b), with the ice sheets flowing around rather than traversing the uplands (White 1997). In addition, Scott-Jackson (2000) has argued that the land-surface in Kent has remained relatively stable, with the downlands lying beyond the extent of the Anglian ice sheets. There will certainly have been some form of movement through periglacial freezing and thawing of the permafrost layer (Murton 1996; Murton and Lautridou 2003). However, despite disturbing archaeological layers, the artefacts and enclosing sediments remained within the confines of the dolines, protected and encapsulated, thereby retaining a degree of spatial integrity. Consequently, these sites are appropriate for use in a GIS model as they can be treated as primary locations, providing a glimpse of assemblages that are still in the place they were originally deposited.

## Sites

The representative sites come from two areas in southern Britain. The first is the Chiltern hills, where a cluster of upland Palaeolithic sites was discovered in the nineteenth century by antiquarian Worthington George Smith. The four main sites in the area are Caddington, Gaddesden Row, Round Green and Whipsnade (Smith 1894; 1916; Evans 1908; Smith 1918; Sampson 1978a; Wymer 1980; Bridgland and Harding 1989; White 1997; White *et al.* 1999) (Figure 2.2). A similar collection of Lower Palaeolithic assemblages come from the south-eastern end of the plateaus surrounding Dover and Deal on the North Downs of Kent. These sites were identified through an extensive fieldwalking programme undertaken by the Dover Archaeology Group. The main sites are Westcliffe St Margaret's, Wood Hill, Green Lane and Malmains 1 and 2 (Halliwell and Parfitt 1993; Parfitt and Halliwell 1996; Hoskins *et al.* 1998; Scott 1999; Scott-Jackson 2000; Parfitt 2002; Bailiff *et al.* 2013) (Figure 2.3). In this paper the integrated approach combining traditional artefact analysis and GIS techniques will be applied to four of these sites: Caddington, Gaddesden Row, Green Lane and Westcliffe.

## *The Chilterns*

Caddington in Bedfordshire (TL 050193) is the largest lithic assemblage in the area. It is situated 3 km to the south-west of Luton, on the plateaus between the River Lea and the River Ver (White 1997) (Figure 2.2). First identified in 1888, the material from Pit C, later incorporated into what was termed by Campbell and Sampson as the Cottages site, comprises over a thousand artefacts (Smith 1894; Campbell and Sampson 1978; Sampson 1978a; 1978b; White 1997).

Gaddesden Row, Hertfordshire (TL 039136) is situated 10 km south-west of Luton on the interfluves between the River Ver and the Gade (Evans 1908; White 1997) (Figure 2.2). The artefacts came from Butterfield's Pit, around 1890, and although the assemblage constitutes a primary working site, it is by no means as prolific as Caddington (Wymer 1980; Bridgland and Harding 1989; White 1997).

### North Downs of Kent

The site of Green Lane, Whitfield (TR 294450) is located on a plateau overlooking the River Dour to the south-west, with the town of Dover approximately 3 km to the south-east (Figure 2.3). A program of fieldwalking in 1991 by DAG produced a number of handaxes and flakes. This was followed by an excavation in 1992 which uncovered both Palaeolithic material and features related to later prehistoric occupation (Halliwell and Parfitt 1993; Parfitt 2002).

The site of Westcliffe St Margaret's (TR 346452) is situated 6.5 km to the north-east of Dover and 5.6 km south-west of Deal. Both this site and the nearby site of Wood Hill are located on the same chalk ridge within a deposit of Clay-with-Flints (Figure 2.3). In a comparable scenario to Green Lane, the site was discovered in 1995 through fieldwalking conducted by DAG. A borehole survey and excavation by a team from Durham University confirmed the artefacts were located around the edges of a solution hollow (Parfitt and Halliwell 1996; Scott 1999). Three seasons of work, between 2002 and 2004, were undertaken, including a program of survey, trial trenching and small-scale excavation (Bailiff *et al.* 2013; Drinkall *et al.* in prep). The lithic assemblage is similar in size to that from Caddington, with over a thousand artefacts.

## Methodology

The presence or absence of particular types and patterns of lithic discard can tell us a great deal about hominin engagements with the landscape, providing a direct link between people, the places they inhabited and the environment in which they lived (Clarkson 2008). Artefacts discarded at a site reflect the exploitation of key resources in the surrounding environment and the implementation of particular technological and land-use strategies (Binford 1980; Blumenschine 1991; Miller and Barton 2007). The proportion and different types of artefacts at each site form an assemblage signature that reflects the types of activities conducted at that particular location. The combination of these signatures with the GIS data provides a chance to investigate the correlation between a site's function and its position in the landscape.

### Artefact signatures

The assemblages were analysed using a techno-typological and *chaîne opératoire* approach, and were essentially categorised based on the presence or absence of key artefact signatures and tool types. The typological analysis consisted of identifying the main artefact types (handaxes, roughouts, flakes, flake tools, cores and core tools), as well as the types of flake tools present. The flake cortex data was split into four categories, non-cortical, <50%, >50% and wholly cortical, to give an indication of which stage of the reduction sequence the flakes came from. This is combined with a *chaîne opératoire* approach, which provides information about the different stages of manufacture present at a site. This included preliminary working (cores, cortical flakes and tested pieces), further reduction (partially and non-cortical, hard and soft hammer flakes, debitage and chips), on-site handaxe and flake tool manufacture (roughout, shaping and thinning flakes, tool spalls) and the use and discard of the finished tools (handaxes, flake and core tools).

A similar approach was used by Turq (1988; 1989) for the Middle Palaeolithic of France, where he identified four types of site, reflecting a range of activities. 'Extraction and exploitation' sites were geared towards raw material procurement and initial working, identified by the presence of flint nodules, tested nodules and a high presence of cortical flakes from the initial decortication of cores in preparation for transport. A similar type of assemblage, but also including evidence of further working to produce flakes or retouched tools, was termed 'extraction and production'. Key elements included large amounts of debitage exhibiting a high percentage of remaining cortex, broken handaxes or roughouts and the transportation of finished products away from the site. Short-term occupations linked with specialised activities aimed at exploiting specific resources were also identified. These 'episodic' sites included the working of only a few flint nodules and the use of retouched tools. The sites that displayed mixed signatures, including the procurement of flint, flaking and reduction of nodules and the production of finished tools, were classed as 'mixed strategy' locations. These included all stages of flake production and tool manufacture, with high numbers of retouched tools and highly reduced core forms. Other such examples include Clark's longer habitation, ephemeral and special purpose occupation sites (2001), and Price's extractive sites aimed at resource procurement, short-term temporary locations and base-camps (1978). Whilst the approach here builds on these studies, the site types used are more flexible, integrating typological data with specific tool functions to determine a variety of lithic assemblage signatures.

The identification of different types of flake tools has been combined with use-wear evidence collated from the literature (Keeley 1980; Roebroeks 1984; Loy and Hardy 1992; Mitchell 1995; Ashton 1998; Lhomme 2007; Ramos *et al.* 2008), to provide an indication of the types of activities for which the tools would have been used. The results suggested that scrapers could be associated with hide working, retouched flakes with carcass- or meat-based processing, whilst notches, denticulates and flaked flakes were predominantly linked to the procurement of wood- and plant-based resources. A summary of the evidence is given in Table 2.1, however a more detailed discussion and full list of examples can be found in Drinkall 2013. This association provides a more dynamic picture of the Lower Palaeolithic record, allowing sites to be categorised on

*Table 2.1. Association of tool types with usewear and activity functions from Lower/Middle Palaeolithic sites in or near the study area.*

| Tool type | Activity | Site example |
| --- | --- | --- |
| Handaxe | Butchery | Boxgrove, Sussex (Roberts and Parfitt 1999; Mitchell 1995) |
| Flake | Multi-task – due to variable edges | Hoxne, Suffolk (Keeley 1980) |
| Scraper | Hide processing | Hoxne, Suffolk (Keeley 1980) Also in the Middle Palaeolithic at Maastricht-Belvédère, Netherlands (Roebroeks 1984) |
| Flaked flakes | Wood-related activities | Barnham, Suffolk (Ashton 1998) |
| Retouched flakes | Multi-activity, although a stronger link with meat processing and butchery activities is evident | Clacton-on-Sea, Golf course, Essex (Keeley 1980) |
| Core tools | Heavy-duty bone or wood processing | Clacton-on-Sea, Golf course, Essex (Keeley 1980) |
| Notches | Most likely wood, but also meat-related activities | Clacton-on-Sea, Golf course, Essex (Keeley 1980) |
| Denticulates | Wood | Clacton-on-Sea, Golf course, Essex (Keeley 1980) |

whether they were geared towards the acquisition of plant- or wood-based resources (dominance of notches, denticulates and flaked flakes), meat or carcass processing (majority of retouched flakes and scrapers) or whether the flake tool signature is mixed.

The results from the artefact analysis serve to identify particular assemblage signatures. A site with a lot of knapping waste, flakes, cores and limited numbers of handaxes or flake tools is identified as having a signature associated with raw material procurement and manufacture. Sites geared towards the acquisition of meat resources display less of a manufacture signature, but contain greater numbers of handaxes, as well as flake tools such as scrapers and retouched flakes. An artefact pattern of this type is categorised as a carcass-processing signature. Conversely, an assemblage containing greater proportions of flaked flakes, denticulates and notches displays a wood- and plant-based signature, and would have been geared towards the exploitation of these resources. The assemblage signatures identified will then be considered in terms of the sites position in the landscape, to determine whether links can be found between the type of landscapes these sites occupy and the activities suggested by the lithic assemblage.

## *Geographical Information Systems (GIS)*

The implementation of GIS (Geographical Information Systems) within archaeological contexts has gained momentum during the last twenty years; however, the use of

GIS as a technique is not without criticism. Concerns have been raised over the emphasis on the physical aspects of the landscape and the potential for environmental determinism to shape interpretations, with limited consideration of cultural constraints, interpretative approaches and the integration of theory (Vermeulen 2001; Llobera 2007). However, most of these are theoretical or even philosophical concerns, and recent research has been focused on addressing these issues, for example the effect of perception on viewsheds (Frieman and Gillings 2007).

Previously GIS has been seen as providing answers to questions (*e.g.* predicting the location of prehistoric sites) drawing a lot of criticism; however, its strength lies in its ability to test hypotheses, and assist in formulating questions to ask of the data (Woodman and Woodward 2002, 22). It is most reliable and powerful when combined within a multi-stranded archaeological analysis, as one component in an array of data to be considered (Williams *et al.* 1990, 269). It is not the purpose of paper to use GIS to create definite answers, but to use it in a way that complements the data from the lithic assemblages to explore ideas of landscape use in areas where our only line of evidence is stone tools. As Fisher notes, provided this is viewed as the investigation of possibilities (1999, 10) rather than certainties, that we remember the models prove nothing, rather give us the freedom to think and test theories (Zimmerman 1978, 28), then GIS techniques are extremely beneficial.

One aspect that has been at the forefront of GIS studies for a number of years is viewshed analysis; however, a number of issues mentioned in the literature (Gillings and Wheatley 2001) need to be covered here. The palaeoenvironment surrounding a site is an important aspect to consider, because the baselayers of most GIS studies are based on modern maps and topography. Normally, dealing with Palaeolithic sites in such a study can be problematic as the majority occur in river valleys, which have been subject to considerable change over time. However, in the case of the upland datasets, the vertical landscape is likely to have changed little for the reasons discussed above. Secondly, hominins could only have accessed the flint clasts from the chalk and sides of the solution features during an open environment with limited vegetation cover (White 1997; Ashton *et al.* 2006), and this is backed up by pollen and geomorphological evidence from the Chilterns suggesting occupation was during a more open, cooler environment, towards the end of an interglacial (Campbell and Hubbard 1978; Catt *et al.* 1978; Sampson 1978c; Avery *et al.* 1982).

Another aspect that has been widely debated is that of 'object-background clarity', which deals with visual recognition and the difference between being able to 'see' something and actually identifying what it is (Gillings and Wheatley 2001). The standard values for the calculation of a viewshed in ArcGIS do not include a constraint over the distance a viewer can see (viewshed will be calculated to infinity). To counteract this aspect a distance of 10 km was specified in the analysis for the viewshed extent to provide an estimation of human vision.

The aim of the visibility analysis in this context is to see whether the location of the site at that particular spot would have had any relevance to the views potentially obtainable from it, and therefore have a bearing on the activities undertaken there, as represented by the assemblage signature. Therefore, the integration of the viewsheds is aimed at seeing whether (in the present time) the sites have good all-round visibility, in which case this could be linked to their assemblage signature (*e.g.* a hunting stand suitable for assessing game movement and planning hunting strategies). Alternatively, if the viewshed is limited, but the site is situated near a good source of raw material, it could be inferred that the activities at a site depended little on the site's situation in the landscape as such. Furthermore, the large (both spatial and temporal) scale of the viewsheds, coupled with the experimental nature of the study (*e.g.* more concerned with the extent of view a site *may* have had, rather than specific lines of sight, or intervisibility between sites) decreases the effects of the traditional problems associated with the use of viewshed data.

GIS analysis was conducted using the ArcGIS 10 software ArcMap and ArcScene. The basemaps were created from DTM (Digital Terrain Model) data (OS land-form profile 1:10,000 DTM) downloaded from Edina (Web 1). ArcScene was used to display the DTM rasters in a three-dimensional format, giving a more visual representation of the landscape and the location of each site within it. The viewsheds were computed using the viewshed function in ArcGIS, and based on the DTM raster data. Hominin height has been estimated (1.5 m) and used as an input in the OBSERVER 'A' field, as has extent of view, using 10 km in the RADIUS2 field to constrain the viewshed calculation, based on the extent of view of the human eye (Garcia 2013).

## Results

### Caddington

The largest of the Chiltern assemblages, Caddington totals 1,431 artefacts (Table 2.2; Figure 2.4).

The assemblage signature is mixed, with all stages of both handaxe and core and flake *chaîne opératoires* present, including nodule decortication, full range of manufacture debris, as well as discard of flake tools and handaxes on site. The flake tools are five times more common than handaxes, which indicates more of a focus on processing activities, compared to butchery tasks associated with handaxes. The tool component also demonstrates a mixed pattern, although this is slanted towards wood-related activities, with notches being most common (35%), as well as a lesser component of denticulates (18%). A smaller proportion of tasks are linked to carcass- or hide-processing with the presence of scrapers (24%) and retouched flakes (14%) (Figure 2.5). The pattern at Caddington fits with what Turq has termed a 'mixed strategy' site (Turq in Mellars 1996), or Price's 'base-camps' (1978), displaying handaxes, flake tools, full range of manufacture debris and evidence of procurement and maintenance activities.

*Table 2.2. Typological composition of the assemblages from Caddington, Gaddesden Row, Westcliffe and Green Lane.*

|  | Caddington |  | Gaddesden Row |  | Westcliffe |  | Green Lane |  |
|---|---|---|---|---|---|---|---|---|
| Typology | n | % | n | % | n | % | n | % |
| Handaxes | 13 | 1 | 45 | 46 | 24 | 2 | 23 | 7 |
| Roughout | 11 | 1 | 3 | 3 | 7 | 1 | 0 | 0 |
| Flakes | 1,249 | 87 | 34 | 35 | 904 | 70 | 199 | 64 |
| Flake tools | 63 | 4 | 11 | 11 | 19 | 1 | 34 | 11 |
| Core tools | 9 | 1 | 0 | 0 | 4 | <1 | 2 | 1 |
| Debitage | 24 | 2 | 1 | 1 | 291 | 22 | 34 | 11 |
| Cores | 4 | <1 | 4 | 4 | 41 | 3 | 12 | 4 |
| Misc | 58 | 4 | 0 | 0 | 4 | <1 | 6 | 2 |
| Total | 1,431 | 100 | 98 | 100 | 1,294 | 100 | 310 | 100 |

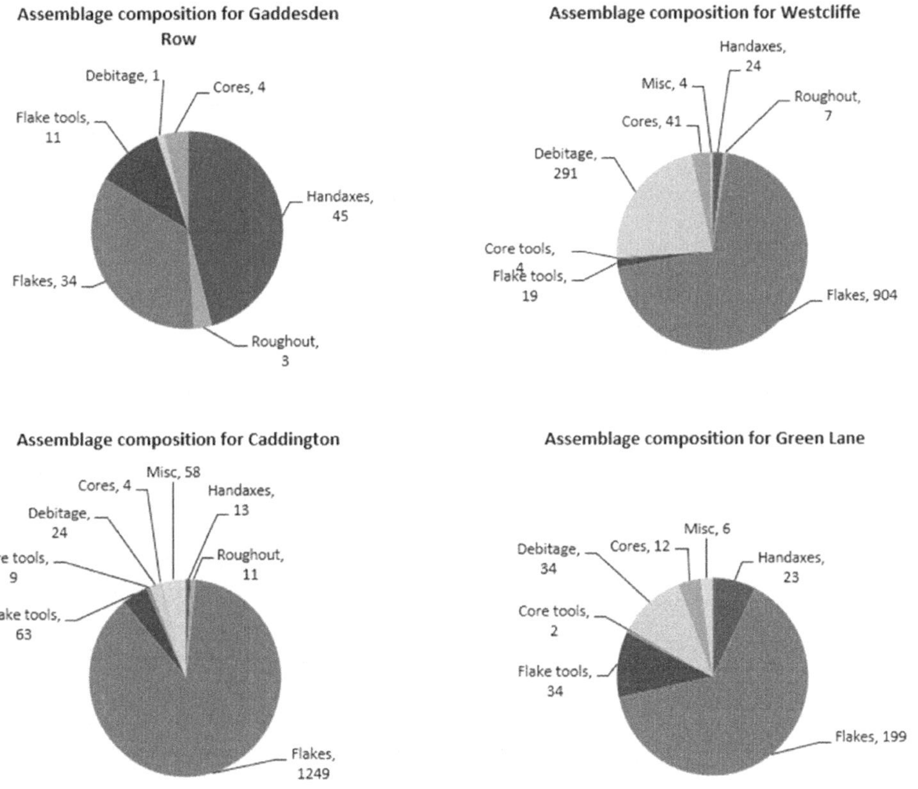

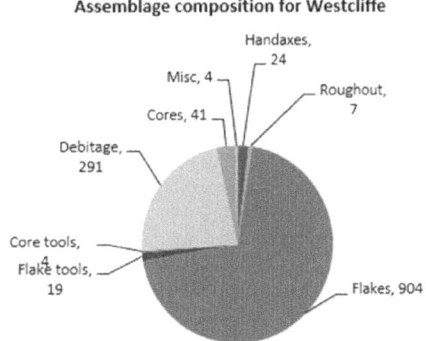

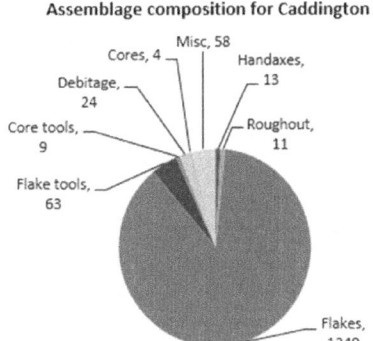

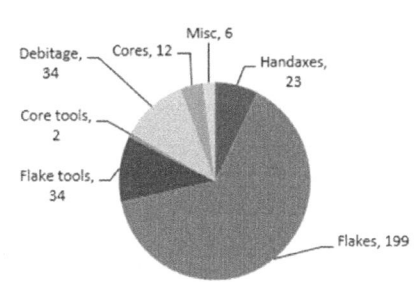

*Figure 2.4. Assemblage composition for the four main Chiltern sites.*

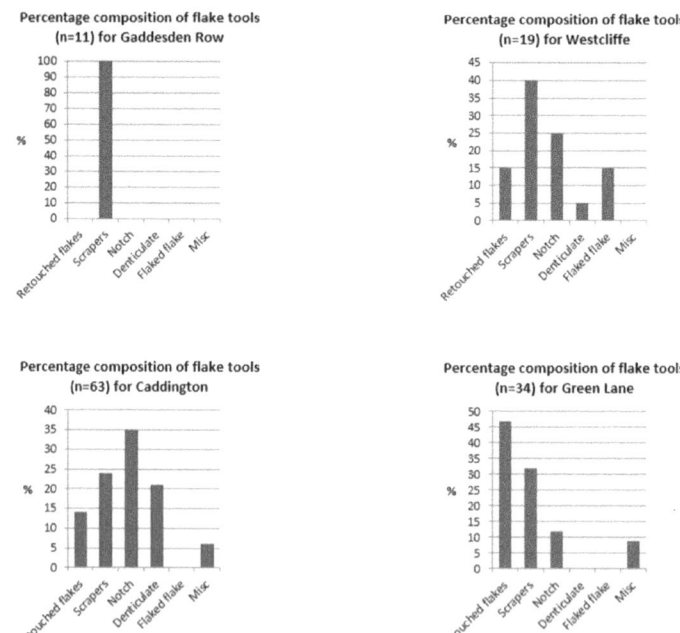

*Figure 2.5. Flake tool composition for the four main Chiltern sites.*

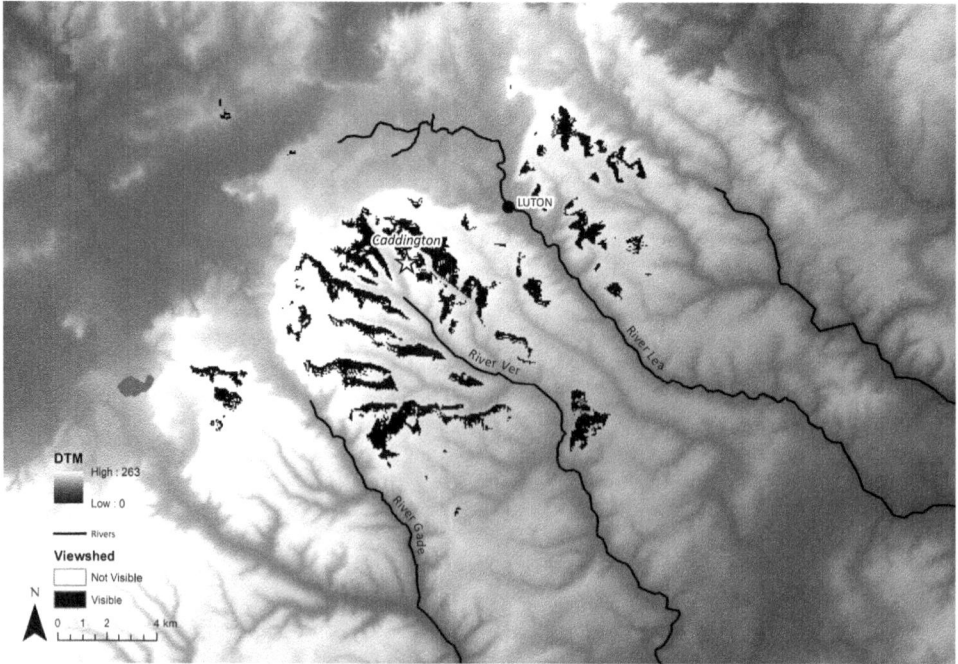

*Figure 2.6. Viewshed as reconstructed from Caddington.*

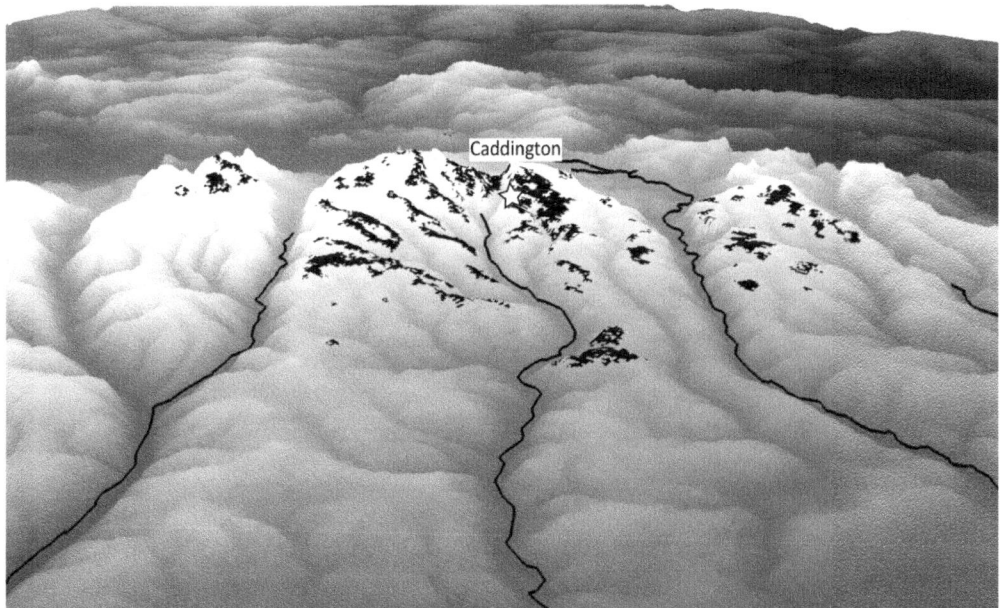

*Figure 2.7. 3D view of the landscape and viewshed for Caddington.*

The large assemblage and mixed nature suggests this spot was one that hominins repeatedly visited. The extensive viewshed from the Cottages site (Figure 2.6) indicates hominins had views over a large part of the Chiltern hills. The slight bias towards flake tools associated with wood procurement could be linked to the site's position on the plateau tops, away from the scarp edge (3 km to the north) (Figure 2.7). The main direction of the viewshed suggests a focus on the surrounding plateaus and the resources they afforded (water-, plant- and wood-based), rather than the lowland plain to the north-west. This ties in with the mixed signature, with manufacture and use of handaxes and flake tools indicates a more 'residential' emphasis with a variety of activities taking place.

## *Gaddesden Row*

Gaddesden Row also demonstrates an extensive viewshed similar to that of Caddington (Figure 2.6); however, the location of the site and assemblage signature provides an interesting contrast. The lithic assemblage is made up of ninety-eight artefacts, and unusually handaxes make up almost half of this amount (46%). This is especially notable if we consider that, in terms of the actual number of handaxes, Gaddesden Row contains nearly four times as many as Caddington, which is a much larger assemblage. This indicates a strong link with carcass and butchery-related activities, with a similar pattern seen in the flake tools. These represent a greater proportion (11%) (Table 2.2; Figure 2.4) than usually seen in upland sites

(Drinkall 2013), and all eleven are scrapers (Figure 2.5), further strengthening the indication that Gaddesden Row was focused on the procurement and processing of meat resources.

Whilst it is true that handaxes were manufactured on site, with a complete *chaîne opératoire* present, they also appear to have been imported. The manufacture of forty-five handaxes on site would have produced a substantial quantity of debitage, which is unlikely to have been missed when the assemblage was originally recovered (Drinkall 2013). It might suggest that the site functioned as a location where carcasses were brought to be processed, with handaxes imported, used then discarded. The assemblage signature exhibited here fits best with Turq's 'episodic' occupation, with low artefact numbers and specialised procurement activities (Turq in Mellars 1996), or with Price's 'extractive' site focused on the procurement of a specific resource (Price 1978).

The unusual composition of the assemblage is matched by the sites position in the landscape. It is situated less than 1 km away from the scarp edge and overlooking the River Gade (Figure 2.8). The viewshed focuses on the plateaus to the north-east and south-west of the site and down the valley of the River Gade. In addition, there is a focus on the higher points across the valley and clustered along the boundary of the scarp, framing the edges overlooking the lowland plain beyond (Figure 2.9). This indicates a focal point along this area, perhaps related to tracking the movement of herds in the northern lowlands. Consequently, a correlation can be seen with the butchery and meat-processing signature, the focus of the viewshed on the scarp edge and down the valley of the Gade, as a way of tracking herds and providing quick access to the lowland hunting grounds. The presence of a raw material source at the site would have provided a way of replenishing tools used in the butchery and processing of the carcass. Gaddesden Row shares similarities in both artefact patterning and landscape setting to Green Lane (below) and suggests it may have been used as a hunting stand, where tools were prepared, prey spotted and carcasses brought back to be processed.

### *Westcliffe St Margaret's*

Westcliffe is the largest of the upland sites in Kent and matches Caddington in size with 1,294 artefacts (Table 2.2; Figure 2.4). The assemblage signature displays a focus on primary manufacture using locally available raw material, with large numbers of cores, flakes and knapping debitage present. The *chaîne opératoire* contains all the stages of both handaxe manufacture and core and flake working; however, the flake cortex results point to a more complex pattern. The number of cortical flakes (n=25) (Table 2.3) is much less than would be expected for the number of cores present (n=41), and certainly does not account for any handaxes that may have been manufactured on site. The careful excavation of the site and recovery of even the smallest chips means this was not the result of excavation biases. It leaves two

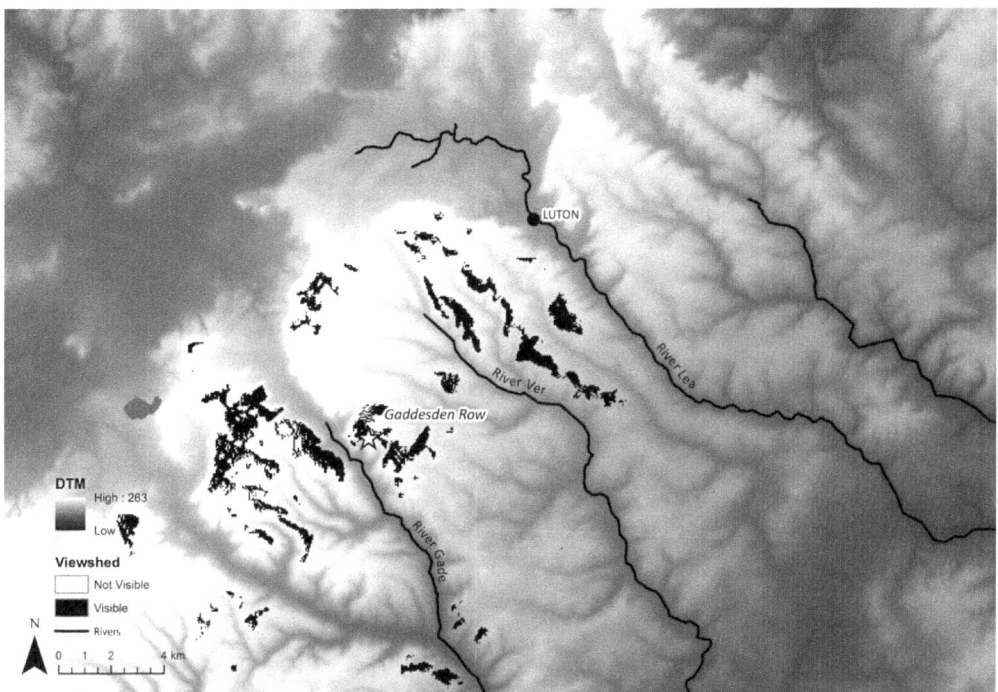

*Figure 2.8. Viewshed as reconstructed from Gaddesden Row.*

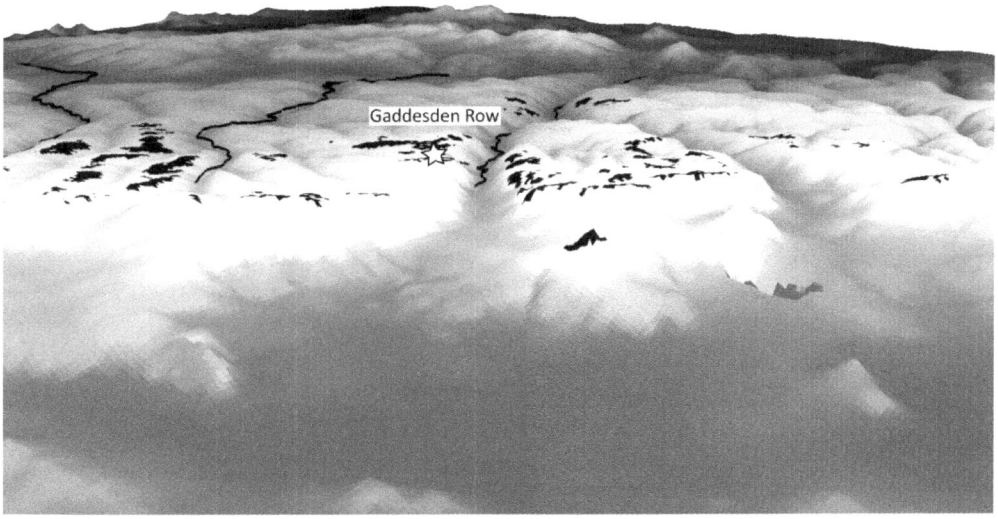

*Figure 2.9. 3D view of the landscape and viewshed for Gaddesden Row.*

Table 2.3. Flake cortex data from Caddington, Gaddesden Row, Westcliffe and Green Lane.

| Flake cortex | Caddington n | Caddington % | Gaddesden Row n | Gaddesden Row % | Westcliffe n | Westcliffe % | Green Lane n | Green Lane % |
|---|---|---|---|---|---|---|---|---|
| None | 95 | 29 | 18 | 53 | 113 | 38 | 51 | 28 |
| < 50% | 158 | 48 | 12 | 35 | 111 | 37 | 85 | 47 |
| > 50% | 45 | 14 | 3 | 9 | 45 | 15 | 33 | 18 |
| Wholly cortical | 29 | 9 | 1 | 3 | 29 | 10 | 11 | 6 |
| Total | 327 | 100 | 34 | 100 | 298 | 100 | 180 | 100 |

possibilities, firstly that cores and handaxes were decorticated off site and brought in partially worked, or, secondly, the larger cortical flakes may have been removed as blanks for other tools.

The flake tools at Westcliffe only represent 1% of the assemblage, which is a comparatively small amount for such an upland site (Drinkall 2013). Caddington, which is a similar-sized lithic assemblage, produced sixty-three compared to Westcliffe's nineteen. This adds support to the interpretation that Westcliffe predominantly functioned as a manufacture site. Similar to the assemblage at Caddington, a diverse range of tool types are present (Figure 2.5), although the comparatively low overall percentage suggests that activities associated with these were of secondary importance. In contrast to the pattern at Caddington, scrapers are the dominant flake tool type at Westcliffe (40%), although the smaller numbers of notches, retouched flakes and flaked flakes indicate a mixed signature equivalent to that from Caddington. The presence of handaxes and scrapers suggests a butchery or carcass-processing component, with smaller proportions of wood- and plant-based activities represented, interpreted as a general spread of subsistence activities. The assemblage signature at Westcliffe can be compared to Turq's 'mixed strategy site' (in Mellars 1996) or Price's 'base camp' (1978), with multiple activities represented, although with a bias towards manufacture.

In contrast to Caddington, the viewshed is restricted, with a focus on the interfluves and the higher plateau to the west and south-west of the site, near the River Dour (Figures 2.10 and 2.11). This pattern indicates that activities conducted at the site were not reliant on extensive views, but more concerned with resources located on the nearby plateaus. Therefore, this location may have been selected for the availability of its raw material resources as opposed to extensive views over the landscape, a pattern that is also seen demonstrated in the assemblage signature.

## Green Lane, Whitfield

The final site, Green Lane, Whitfield is located on the higher plateau close to the valley of the River Dour, and comprises 310 artefacts. The site exhibits unusually high

## 2. A view from the tops

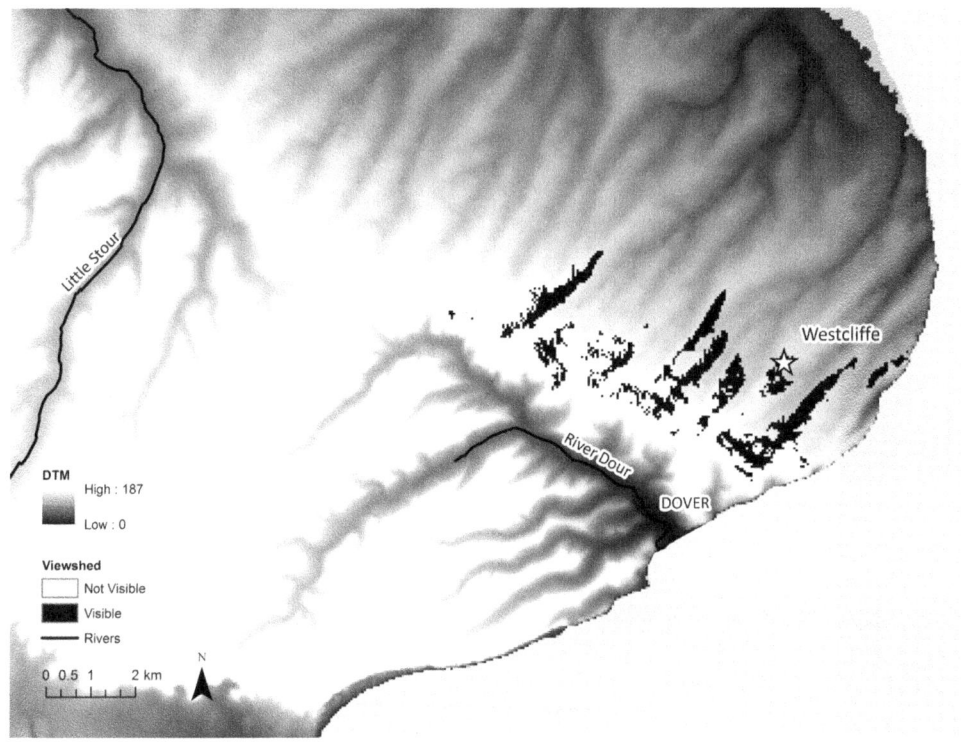

*Figure 2.10. Viewshed as reconstructed from Westcliffe.*

*Figure 2.11. 3D view of the landscape and viewshed for Westcliffe.*

numbers of handaxes and flake tools, with smaller proportions of debitage and flakes (Table 2.2; Figure 2.4) compared to other upland sites (Drinkall 2013). In terms of the *chaîne opératoire*, all stages of core and flake working are represented, as well as some later stage handaxe manufacture (shaping and thinning flakes). However, the number of flakes (n=267), if assumed to come from the handaxes (n=23) and cores (n=12), would give an average of eight flakes per core/handaxe. When we consider that some handaxes can produce over 100 flakes, this indicates that some must have been brought in partially worked. This pattern is also seen in the flake cortex, where there are only eleven wholly cortical flakes (Table 2.3) compared to twelve cores, further indicating that cores were brought in partially worked, with limited decortication occurring on site.

Of the high proportion of flake tools, nearly half of them are retouched flakes (47%), with a further third (32%) represented by scrapers (Figure 2.5). This pattern is strongly biased towards carcass, butchery and hide-processing activities, and ties in with the large proportion of handaxes present. It is also important to note that the majority of handaxes are actually broken, suggesting that usable implements may have been removed for use in the wider landscape.

In a comparable situation to that found at Gaddesden Row, Green Lane likely functioned as a locale to which game was brought back to be processed, with some tool manufacture or repair being carried out. The assemblage signature can be seen as a mix between Turq's 'mixed strategy' and 'episodic' locales, encompassing both manufacture, tool use and processing activities, but skewed towards the procurement of meat-based resources (Turq in Mellars 1996).

The viewshed itself is interesting as there is a limited view of the immediate area of the site, suggesting a specific viewing focus (Figure 2.12 and 2.13). The emphasis, therefore, appears to be on the valley of the Dour and its tributaries, plateaus, interfluves and dry valleys to the south-west. This signifies links with the river valley and potentially the observation of game, with the site likely functioning as a hunting stand. It is curious to note that the site is positioned directly opposite one of the tributaries. Therefore the main valley could have channelled game from the interior of the Downs to the lowland channel plain. The tributaries leading in at right angles would have formed an ideal spot to trap game or drive it along the valley, a valid suggestion given the meat procurement signature observed in the lithic assemblage.

## Discussion

The combination of traditional artefact analysis with a broader GIS-based landscape approach has highlighted some interesting aspects, especially regarding correlations between the assemblage signatures identified and their position in the landscape. It is clear from the results that the function of these sites is different, suggested not only by the assemblage signatures but by the different landscape locations they inhabit.

The two larger sites, which are located on the tops of the plateaus, Caddington and Westcliffe, produced mixed assemblages focused on manufacture, with a large variety

## 2. A view from the tops

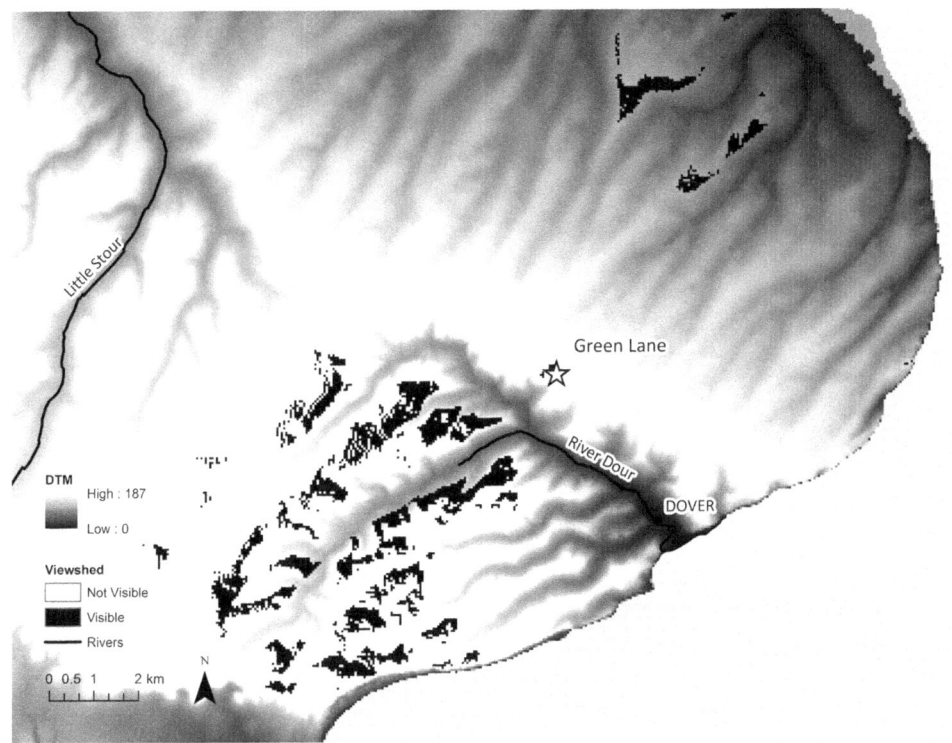

Figure 2.12. Viewshed as reconstructed from Green Lane.

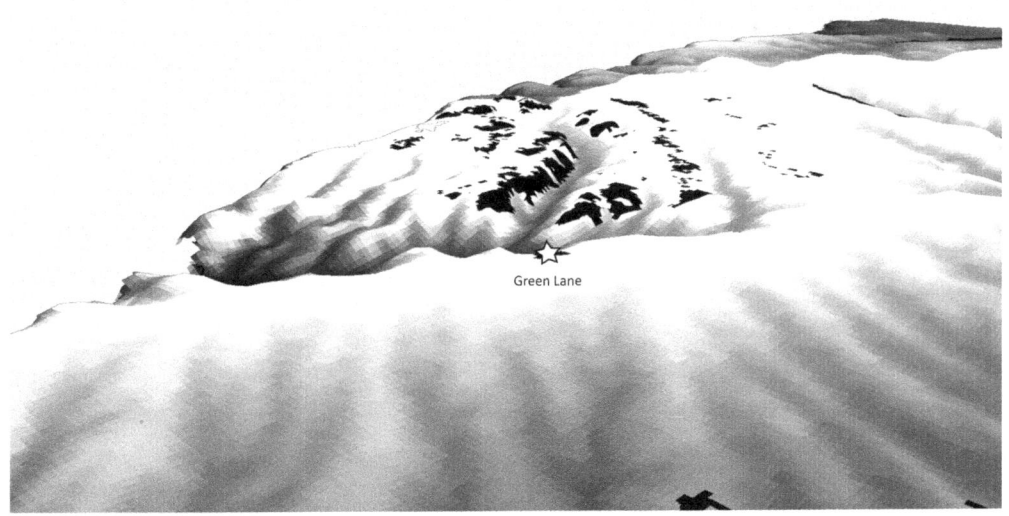

Figure 2.13. 3D view of the landscape and viewshed for Green Lane.

of different tool types present. In contrast, the sites of Green Lane and Gaddesden Row are situated next to river valleys, with easy access out to the plains and lowland hunting grounds beyond, and display a clear hunting and carcass-processing signature. These patterns are most clearly demonstrated by the GIS and viewshed analysis. The results agree with the premise that a site's distance from resources formed a critical aspect of behavioural choices and the activity patterning seen in land-use models in the Lower Palaeolithic (Ashton *et al.* 1998).

Ashton (1998) has suggested that resources are not always tethered to predictable points in the landscape, so a site's function will vary in response to both static and mobile resources. It could be argued that the larger, mixed function sites (Caddington, Westcliffe) are positioned to make use of static rather than mobile resources, a scenario advocated by Boyle (2001) in work on the Middle Palaeolithic. These plateau sites have rapid access to and a focus (suggested by the viewsheds) on the immediate landscape, but directed away from the lowlands, and are geared to exploit nearby water, raw material and plant-based (static) resources.

In Ashton's static versus mobile resource model (1998), mobile resources (prey) are considered to be unpredictable, and would likely be exploited in a more opportunistic fashion compared to other resources. This would have necessitated the occupation of areas with greater views in order to actively intercept prey species and keep abreast of herd movement in the surrounding landscape. The locations of Green Lane and Gaddesden Row, situated next to river valleys that channelled game from the interior of the chalk to the lowland plains, would have been perfect for making the hunting marginally more predictable. These sites were likely geared towards exploiting more 'mobile' animal resources.

The presence of locally available raw material in these upland sites would have made it highly likely that they functioned as places to which carcasses were brought for processing (Foley 1987; Potts 1994), and as 'gearing up' loci, where artefacts were manufactured for transport and use in the wider landscape (Kuhn 1995; Holdaway *et al.* 2010). This would have reduced the energetic costs of transporting tools within the landscape (Potts 1984; Foley 1987), as well as allowing removal of the carcasses from the immediate vicinity of the kill site away from predators. This links in with suggestions made for Boxgrove in Sussex, regarding the movement of tools from the lowland plains to the Downs (Roberts 1999), with Pope (2002) proposing that handaxes were only discarded at locations which hominins repeatedly visited and which contained set resources (water, raw material, plant resources). Therefore, these upland sites, located around solution hollows, may indeed have acted as re-stocking locales, where hominins took carcasses in order to repair or manufacture new tools from the material eroding out of the hollows sides.

The link between artefact signature, landscape context and views can also be seen in examples from Europe. In the Duero Basin, Spain, sites in the uplands, located in similar situations to the British evidence, around solution hollows, displayed comparable assemblage signatures with large numbers of flake tools and a dominance of scrapers. They were interpreted by the authors as viewing places, providing good views and control over the valleys below (Diez-Martin et al. 2008). Interestingly, Ferme de l'Epinette, one of a group of sites in the Somme Valley in France, also contains a high proportion of bifaces. It occupies a higher position above the river valley than the other sites in this area and has been interpreted as a game-viewing station, linked to hominin mobility and resource procurement (Tuffreau et al. 1997; 2008). These examples and the evidence from Green Lane and Gaddesden Row further strengthen observed links between assemblages and landscape, feeding into models of hominin landscape use and behavioural variation.

## Conclusion

The main aim of this paper was to demonstrate how traditional artefact analysis could be combined with a GIS-based approach. The results above show the potential of such an approach to gain a more complete picture of site use and structuring in the Lower Palaeolithic of Britain.

It demonstrates that, despite being located in different areas, similar behavioural choices and artefact patterning was occurring, conditioned by a site's position in the landscape. Artefact signatures related to butchery and the procurement of carcasses are found in close proximity to valleys and lowland hunting grounds, providing ready access to animal resources. In contrast, sites with signatures comparable to what you might expect from a camp site or home base location, geared more towards manufacture and general subsistence, are located on the plateaus, away from the lowland plains and rivers.

The Geographical Information Systems (GIS) approach has proved beneficial in helping to inform site use where other lines of evidence (*e.g.* environmental and faunal) are limited. The upland sites that formed the basis for this paper are extremely important in terms of the information they can offer, their role in hominin behavioural organisation, artefact patterning and settlement systems. The methodological approach, presented here, has proved a powerful technique that has helped further our understanding of that.

For many years the Lower Palaeolithic has often been viewed as a static collection of ubiquitous behaviours, stretching across large temporal and geographic areas, giving an impression of behaviour that is both monotonous and limited in its scope. However, it is clear that when approached from another angle, using different techniques, the evidence displays a fascinating insight into the complexity of hominin landscape use and behavioural choices in this period.

## Bibliography

Ashton, N. (1998) The Spatial Distribution of the Flint Artefacts and Human Behaviour. In: N. Ashton, S.G. Lewis and S. Parfitt (eds) *Excavations at the Lower Palaeolithic Site at East Farm, Barnham, Suffolk 1989-94*, pp. 251–258. British Museum Occasional Paper no. 125. London: British Museum.

Ashton, N., Lewis, S.G. and Parfitt, S. (1998) Summary. In: N. Ashton, S.G. Lewis and S. Parfitt (eds) *Excavations at the Lower Palaeolithic Site at East Farm, Barnham, Suffolk 1989-94*, pp. 259–265. British Museum Occasional Paper no. 125. London: British Museum.

Ashton, N., Lewis, S.G., Parfitt, S. and White, M. (2006) Riparian Landscapes and Human Habitat Preferences During the Hoxnian (MIS 11) Interglacial. *Journal of Quaternary Science* 21, 497–505.

Avery, B.W., Bullock, P., Catt, J.A., Rayner, J.H. and Weir, A.H. (1982) Composition and Origin of Some Brickearths on the Chiltern Hills, England. *Catena* 9, 153–174.

Bailiff, I., Lewis, S., Drinkall, H. and White, M. (2013) Luminescence Dating of Sediments from a Palaeolithic Site Associated with a Solution Feature on the North Downs of Kent, UK. *Quaternary Geochronology* 18, 135–148.

Binford, L.R. (1980) Willow Smoke and Dogs' Tails: Hunter-gatherer settlement systems and archaeological site formation. *American Antiquity* 45, 4–20.

Blumenschine, R.J. (1991) Breakfast at Olorgesailie: The natural history approach to Early Stone Age archaeology. *Journal of Human Evolution* 21, 307–327.

Boyle, K.V. (2001) Middle Palaeolithic Settlement Patterning in Mediterranean France: Human geography and archaeology. In: N.J. Conard (ed.) *Settlement Dynamics in the Middle Palaeolithic and Middle Stone Age* 1, pp. 519–543. Tübingen, Kerns Verlag.

Bridgland, D.R. and Harding, P. (1989) Investigations at Gaddesden Row Brickpit, Hertfordshire. *Quaternary Newsletter* 59, 2–4.

Campbell, J.B. and Hubbard, R.N.L.B. (1978) Biological Investigations of the Rackley Site. In: C.G. Sampson (ed.) *Palaeoecology and Archaeology of an Acheulian Site at Caddington, England*, pp. 47–60. Dallas: Department of Anthropology, Southern Methodist University.

Campbell, J. B. and Sampson, C.G. (1978) The Cottages Site. In: C.G. Sampson (ed.) *Palaeoecology and Archaeology of an Acheulian Site at Caddington, England*, pp. 61–81. Dallas: Department of Anthropology, Southern Methodist University.

Catt, J.A., Hubbard, R.N.L.B. and Sampson, C.G. (1978) Summary and Conclusions. In: C.G. Sampson (ed.) *Palaeoecology and Archaeology of an Acheulian Site at Caddington, England*, pp. 139–149. Dallas: Department of Anthropology, Southern Methodist University.

Clark, J.D. (2001) Ecological and Behavioural Implications of the Siting of Middle Stone Age Rockshelter and Cave Sediments in Africa. In: N.J. Conard (ed.) *Settlement Dynamics of the Middle Palaeolithic and Middle Stone Age* 1, pp. 91–98. Tübingen: Kerns Verlag.

Clarkson, C. (2008) Lithics and Landscape Archaeology. In: B. David and J. Thomas (eds) *Handbook of Landscape Archaeology*, pp. 490–501. Walnut Creek: Left Coast Press.

Diez-Martín, F., Sánchez-Yustos, P., Gómez-González, J.A. and Gómez de la Rúa, D. (2008) Earlier Palaeolithic Settlement Patterns: Landscape archaeology on the River Duero basin plateaus (Castilla y León, Spain). *Journal of World Prehistory* 21, 103–137.

Drinkall, H.C. (2013) Expanding our Horizons: An exploration of hominin landscape use in the Lower Palaeolithic of Britain and the question of upland home bases or lowland living sites. Unpublished PhD thesis, Durham University.

Evans, J. (1908) Some Recent Discoveries of Palaeolithic Implements. *The Quarterly Journal of the Geological Society of London* 64, 1–7.

Fisher, P.F. (1999) Geographical Information Systems: Today and tomorrow? In: M. Gillings, D. Mattingly and J. van Dalen (eds) *Geographical Information Systems and Landscape Archaeology*, pp. 5–12. Oxford: Oxbow Books.

Foley, R. (1987) Hominid Species and Stone-Tool Assemblages: How are they related? *Antiquity* 61, 380–392.

Ford, D. and Williams, P. (1989) *Karst Geomorphology and Hydrology*. London: Chapman and Hall.

Frieman, C. and Gillings, M. (2007) Seeing is Perceiving? *World Archaeology* 39, 4–16.

Garcia, A. (2013) GIS-Based Methodology for Palaeolithic Site Location Preferences Analysis. A case study from Late Palaeolithic Cantabria (Northern Iberian Peninsula). *Journal of Archaeological Science* 40, 217–226.

Gillings, M. and Wheatley, D. W. (2001) Seeing is Not Believing: Unresolved issues in archaeological visibility analysis. In: B. Slapsak (ed.) *On the Good Use of Geographic Information Systems in Ancient Landscape Studies*, pp. 25–36. Brussels, EUR19708.

Halliwell, G. and Parfitt, K. (1993) Non-River Gravel Lower and Middle Palaeolithic Discoveries in East Kent. *Kent Archaeological Review* 114, 80–89.

Harp, P. (2005) Work at the Palaeolithic Site at Rookery Farm, Lower Kingswood 2001–2005. *Surrey Archaeological Collections* 92, 231–244.

Holdaway, S., Wendrich, W. and Phillipps, R. (2010) Identifying Low-Level Food Producers: Detecting mobility from lithics. *Antiquity* 84, 185–194.

Hoskins, R., Halliwell, G. and Parfitt, K. (1998) Lower Palaeolithic Discoveries at Eythorne, Near Dover. *Kent Archaeological Review* 134, 73–80.

Keeley, L.H. (1980) *Experimental Determination of Stone Tool Uses: A microwear analysis*. Chicago: University of Chicago Press.

Kuhn, S.L. (1995) *Mousterian Lithic Technology. An ecological perspective*. Princeton: Princeton University Press.

Lhomme, V. (2007) Tools, Space and Behaviour in the Lower Palaeolithic: Discoveries at Soucy in the Paris basin. *Antiquity* 81, 536–554.

Llobera, M. (2007) Reconstructing Visual Landscapes. *World Archaeology* 39, 51–69.

Loy, T.H. and Hardy, B.L. (1992) Blood Residue Analysis of 90,000-Year-Old Stone Tools from Tabun Cave, Israel. *Antiquity* 66, 24–35.

Mellars, P.M. 1996. *The Neanderthal Legacy*. Princeton: University Press.

Miller, A. and Barton, C.M. (2007) Exploring the Land: A comparison of land-use patterns in the Middle and Upper Palaeolithic of the Western Mediterranean. *Journal of Archaeological Science* 35, 1427–1437.

Mitchell, J.C. (1995) Studying Biface Utilisation at Boxgrove: Roe deer butchery with replica handaxes. *Lithics* 16, 64–69.

Murton, J.B. (1996) Near-Surface Brecciation of Chalk, Isle of Thanet, South-East England: A comparison with ice-rich brecciated bedrocks in Canada and Spitsbergen. *Permafrost and Periglacial Processes* 7, 153–164.

Murton, J.B. and Lautridou, J-P. (2003) Recent Advances in the Understanding of Quaternary Periglacial Features of the English Channel Coastlands. *Journal of Quaternary Science* 18, 301–307.

Parfitt, K. (2002) A Prehistoric Site Off Green Lane, Whitfield, Near Dover. *Archaeologia Cantiana* 122, 373–379.

Parfitt, K. and Halliwell, G. (1996) More Palaeolithic Discoveries in East Kent. *Kent Archaeological Review* 123, 58–64.

Pope, M.I. (2002) The Significance of Biface-Rich Assemblages: An examination of behavioural controls on lithic assemblage formation in the Lower Palaeolithic. Unpublished PhD thesis, University of Southampton.

Potts, R. (1984) Home Bases and Early Hominids: Re-evaluation of the fossil record at Olduvai Gorge suggests that the concentrations of bones and stone tools do not represent fully formed campsites but an antecedent to them. *American Scientist* 72, 338–347.

Potts, R. (1994) Variables Versus Models of Early Pleistocene Hominid Land Use. *Journal of Human Evolution* 27, 7–24.

Price, T.D. (1978) Mesolithic Settlement Systems in the Netherlands. In: P. Mellars (ed.) *The Early Postglacial Settlement of Northern Europe: An ecological perspective*, pp. 81–114. London: Duckworth.

Ramos, J., Bernal, D., Domínguez-Bella, S., Calado, D., Ruiz, B., Gil, M.J., Clemente, I., Durán, J.J., Vijande, E. and Chamorro, S. (2008) The Benzú Rockshelter: A Middle Palaeolithic site on the North African coast. *Quaternary Science Reviews* 27, 2210–2218.

Roberts, M.B. (1999) Concluding Remarks and Discussion. In: M.B. Roberts and S.A. Parfitt (eds) *Boxgrove. A Middle Pleistocene hominid site at Eartham Quarry, Boxgrove, West Sussex*, pp. 422–425. London: English Heritage.

Roebroeks, W. (1984) The Middle Palaeolithic Site Maastricht-Belvédère (Southern-Limburg, The Netherlands). A preliminary report. *Helinium* 24, 3–17.

Rose, J. (1992) High Lodge – Regional context and geological background. In: N.M. Ashton, J. Cook, S.G. Lewis and J. Rose (eds) *High Lodge. Excavations by G. De. G. Sieveking, 1962-8, and J. Cook, 1988*, pp. 13–24. London: British Museum Press.

Sampson, C.G. (ed.) (1978a) *Palaeoecology and Archaeology of an Acheulian Site at Caddington, England*. Dallas: Department of Anthropology, Southern Methodist University.

Sampson, C.G. (1978b) Introduction. In: G.C. Sampson (ed.) *Palaeoecology and Archaeology of an Acheulian Site at Caddington, England*, pp. 3–15. Dallas: Department of Anthropology, Southern Methodist University.

Sampson, C.G. (1978c) Excavation and Stratigraphy of the Rackley Site. In: C.G. Sampson (ed.) *Palaeoecology and Archaeology of an Acheulian Site at Caddington, England*, pp. 29–38. Dallas: Department of Anthropology, Southern Methodist University.

Scott, R. (1999) Hominid Activity on the High Ground: A technological analysis of a flint assemblage from a high level clay-with-flints site at West Cliffe, St Margaret's, Kent. Unpublished Undergraduate dissertation, University of Cambridge.

Scott-Jackson, J.E. (2000) *Lower and Middle Palaeolithic Artefacts from Deposits Mapped as Clay-with-Flints: A new synthesis with significant implications for the earliest occupation for Britain*. Oxford: Oxbow Books.

Scott-Jackson, J.E. and Winton, V.E. (2001) Recent Investigations at Dickett's Field, Yarnhams Farm, Holybourne, Hants. In: S. Milliken and J. Cook (eds) *A Very Remote Period Indeed. Papers on the Palaeolithic presented to Derek Roe*, pp. 214–222. Oxford: Oxbow Books.

Smith, R.A. (1918) Flint Implements from the Palaeolithic 'floor' at Whipsnade, Bedfordshire. *Proceedings of the Society of Antiquarians of London* 31, 39–50.

Smith, W.G. (1894) *Man. The primeval savage. His haunts and relicts from the hill-tops of Bedfordshire to Blackwall*. London: Edward Stanford.

Smith, W.G. (1916) Notes of the Palaeolithic Floor Near Caddington. *Archaeologia* 15–16, 49–74.

Stern, N. (1994) The Implications of Time-Averaging for Reconstructing the Land-Use Patterns of Early Tool-Using Hominids. *Journal of Human Evolution* 27, 89–105.

Stern, N. (2008) Stratigraphy, Depositional Environments and Palaeolandscape Reconstruction in Landscape Archaeology. In: B. David and J. Thomas (eds) *Handbook of Landscape Archaeology*, pp. 365–378. Walnut Creek: Left Coast Press.

Tuffreau, A., Lamotte, A. and Marcy, J.L. (1997) Land-Use and Site Function in Acheulean Complexes in the Somme Valley. *World Archaeology* 29, 225–241.

Tuffreau, A., Lamotte, A. and Goval, E. (2008) Les industries acheuléennes de la France septentrionale. *L'Anthropologie* 112, 104–139.

Turq, A. (1988) Le Paleolithique inférieur et moyen en Haut-Agenais: état des recherches. *Revue de l'Agenais* 115, 83–112.

Turq, A. (1989) Exploitation des matières premières lithiques et occupation du sol: l'exemple du Moustérien entre Dordogne et Lot. In: H. Laville (ed.) *Variations des Paléomiiieux et Peupiement Préhistonique*, pp. 179–204. Paris: Centre National de la Recherche Scientifique.

Van Andel, T.H. and Tzedakis, P.C. (1996) Palaeolithic Landscapes of Europe and Environs, 150,000–25,000 Years Ago: An overview. *Quaternary Science Reviews* 15, 481–500.

Vermeulen, F. (2001) The Potential of GIS in Landscape Archaeology. In: B. Slapsak (ed.) *On the Good Use of Geographic Information Systems in Ancient Landscape Studies (25–36)*, pp. 9–16. Brussels, EUR19708.

Villa, P. (1991) Middle Pleistocene Prehistory in Southwestern Europe: The state of our knowledge and ignorance. *Journal of Anthropological Research* 47, 193–217.

Walls, T. and Cotton, J. (1980) Palaeoliths from the North Downs at Lower Kingswood. *Surrey Archaeological Collections* 72, 15–36.

Wheatley, D. and Gillings, M. (2000) Vision, Perception and GIS: Developing enriched approaches to the study of archaeological visibility. In: G. Lock (ed.) *Beyond the Map. Archaeology and spatial technologies*, pp. 1–27. Oxford: IOS Press.

White, M.J. (1997) The Earlier Palaeolithic Occupation of the Chilterns (Southern England): Re-assessing the sites of Worthington G. Smith. *Antiquity* 71, 912–931.

White, M.J., Lewis, S.G. and McNabb, J. (1999) Excavations at the Lower Palaeolithic Site of Whipsnade, Bedfordshire 1992–94. *Proceedings of the Geological Association* 110, 241–255.

Williams, T., Limp, W.F. and Briuer, F.L. (1990) Using Geographical Information Systems and Exploratory Data Analysis for Archaeological Site Classification and Analysis. In: K.M.S. Allen, S.W. Green and E.B.W. Zubrow (eds) *Interpreting Space: GIS and archaeology*, pp. 239–273. London: Taylor & Francis.

Woodman, R.E. and Woodward, M. (2002) The Use and Abuse of Statistical Methods in Archaeological Site Location Modelling. In: D. Wheatley, G. Earl and S. Poppy (eds) *Contemporary Themes in Archaeological Computing*, pp. 22–27. University of Southampton Department of Archaeology Monograph No. 3. Oxford: Oxbow Books.

Wymer, J.J. (1980) The Excavation of an Acheulian Site at Gaddesden Row. *Bedfordshire Archaeological Journal* 14, 2–4.

Wymer, J.J. (1996) The English Rivers Palaeolithic Survey. In: C. Gamble and A.J. Lawson (eds) *The English Palaeolithic Reviewed*, pp. 7–22. Salisbury: Wessex Archaeology.

Wymer, J. (1999) *The Lower Palaeolithic Occupation of Britain*. Salisbury: Wessex Archaeology and English Heritage.

Zimmerman, L.J. (1978) Simulating Prehistoric Locational Behaviour. In: I. Hodder (ed.) *Simulation Studies in Archaeology*, pp. 27–37. Cambridge: Cambridge University Press.

## Web reference

Web 1– digimap.edina.ac.uk/digimap/home

# Chapter 3

# Clovis and the implications of the peopling of North America

*Alan M. Slade*

### Abstract
*At some time around the end of the last ice age, around 11,500 $^{14}$C yr BP / 13,300 Cal yrs, the first human hunter-gatherer groups entered North America, where they encountered diverse environments and climates. These groups, once separate and exploring these landscapes in a vast continent, were hunting and killing the same megafauna; perhaps for the first time, they would have encountered mammoth, mastodon, giant sloth and camel. Other smaller, more recognisable species were also present and hunted; elk, deer, caribou and bison, for example. The different environments and landscapes encountered by these separate groups may account for the extent of the variability of the fluted projectile points that are characteristic of this period. In my thesis research I suggest that Clovis was not the first stone-tool technology in North America, that fluted projectile points evolved from an earlier technology and that Clovis was a localised fluted form that evolved regionally as these first groups spread out across the continent.*

### Introduction
The purpose of this paper is to provide a general overview of the Late Pleistocene occupation of North America, and in particular the spread of the Clovis culture across an entire continent and its apparent rapid expansion. Ever since the earliest discoveries in the early 1900s of stone tools associated with the remains of extinct mammals, North American archaeologists have been fascinated by the geographic extent, sourcing and procurement strategies, lithic technology, and subsistence practices of the Clovis people and their unique colonising event.

Our current understanding of the peopling of the Americas has advanced greatly over the last few decades through new perspectives on the origins, entry routes and lifeways of the earliest Americans (Meltzer 2003; 2009; Pitblado 2011; Davidson 2013;

Shott 2013; Madsen 2015; Halligan *et al.* 2016; Amick 2017). Studying entry routes, cultural variability and subsistence strategies are critical in understanding how these early peoples moved across a landscape apparently devoid of other humans (Grayson and Meltzer 2002). Some have argued that Clovis represents a culture that spread among an existing population termed as pre-Clovis (Collins *et al.* 2013). However, others have suggested that arguments supporting a pre-Clovis hypothesis are problematic given the lack of secure pre-Clovis evidence (Shott 2013; Haynes 2015). These early hunter-gatherers left behind a sparse material record of their occupation that consists primarily of stone tools and the manufacturing debris associated with their production. The trademark tool of this earliest technology to evolve in North America is a fluted spear point named after its type site, a quarry at Blackwater Draw Locality No. 1, near Clovis, New Mexico (Hester 1972). These artefacts were made by broadly dispersed groups at almost the same time throughout North America. From personal observation, I can attest that the fluted points from Nova Scotia are much the same as those from New Mexico, not identical, but the similarities outweigh the differences. Not only are the fluted points similar across the continent, but other aspects of the Clovis culture appear to be equally similar and widespread (Haynes Jr 1964). Perhaps Clovis cannot be defined accurately because there was no standardised way of producing them, no consistent way of using them and, indeed, no uniform way of life during the late Pleistocene in North America.

No later Palaeoindian or Prehistoric occupation achieved such a wide distribution as these groups. The traditional view had Clovis (Lynch 1983), or descendants of the earliest North American colonisers, in South America, as far south as Tierra del Fuego (Whitley and Dorn 1993), with a distinctively different culture to the Clovis (Dillehay *et al.* 1992; Morrow and Morrow 1999) within a millennium of leaving the ice-free corridor. In less than 500 years Clovis groups had crossed North America during a time of great climatic change, environmental disturbance and massive mammalian extinctions (Martin and Klein 1984), and they seemingly adapted and coped with the challenges with little difficulty.

The original theory of highly mobile, wide-ranging hunter-gatherers arriving in North America coupled with the movements of continental glaciation was a convenient explanation, for a while. But it was difficult to accept an idea that the earliest colonisers, who were completely foreign in this landscape, could spread so swiftly under such diverse climatic and environmental conditions (Beaton 1991). The Clovis and Clovis-like points turned out to be not so uniform as first appeared (*e.g.* Meltzer 1993; Morrow and Morrow 1999; Buchanan *et al.* 2012). Evidence for mammoth hunting, the driving force behind the so-called Clovis 'Blitzkrieg' or rapid overkill hypothesis (Martin and Klein 1984; Martin 1990) proved to be localised and not on a continental wide scale. Further, Clovis hunter-gatherers were not entirely responsible for the extinction of the mammoths and other large Pleistocene megafauna (Grayson and Meltzer 2003). It appeared that they were regularly hunting smaller, less dangerous and slow-moving prey (Johnson 1991; Haynes 2002). Clovis groups could and did occasionally bring down mammoths, but it was not to the exclusion of other smaller and readily available prey (Meltzer 2002).

Despite extensive research investigating Clovis origins, no obvious progenitor exists in Alaska (Bonnichsen 1991; Goebel *et al.* 1991), and more problematic still for the traditional theory, claims of a pre-Clovis presence in North America have grown (*e.g.* Whitley and Dorn 1993; Fiedel 1999; Waters and Stafford 2007).

## Clovis: What is it and who made it?

The Clovis people are best known for their unique, basally fluted lanceolate points (Figure 3.1) produced by bifacial reduction and thinning techniques (Bradley *et al.* 2010). Just as diagnostic, however, is the core-and-blade technology by which most of the utility lithic tools were produced (Collins 1999; Collins and Lohse 2004). Bifaces and flake tools are commonly found in Clovis-aged assemblages, but blades are not present in all regions. Evidence of blade production can be observed along with other components of the Clovis toolkit, and flakes that appear as blades may have been misidentified as being 'true' blades (Sain 2012).

Conical and wedge-shaped cores produced large blades, and discoidal cores were used for flake production. Blades were reduced down to a variety of tools, but sometimes were used without further modification. The core-and-blade technology could have been derived from the Eurasian mid- to late Upper Palaeolithic culture, but its exact origin remains a subject of debate. Clearly, though, Clovis fluted points were a North American innovation. Most of the sites first identified as having Clovis lithics were kill and/or butchery locations and were associated with Pleistocene megafauna such as mammoth, mastodon and extinct bison (Table 3.1).

There are at present as few as fourteen sites that have solid associations of remains of extinct proboscideans with Clovis artefacts, including fluted points (Surovell and Waguespeck 2008). This initially led researchers to put forward various models for colonising North America that included the rapid appearance and spread of Clovis, 'big game' hunters relying on killing large mammals, such as proboscideans, for a large percentage of their diet (*e.g.* Haynes Jr 1969; Kelly and Todd 1988).

Megafauna kill sites are actually quite rare among the total of Clovis sites, and with the discovery of residential campsites (*e.g.* Collins 2002), some Clovis groups appear to have had

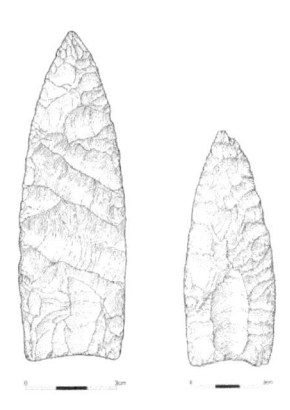

*Figure 3.1. Clovis fluted points from the Clovis type site Blackwater Draw Locality No. 1, New Mexico, found in association with the remains of mammoth in 1964–1965 (on the left), and from the Dent site, Colorado, discovered in association with mammoth bones in 1932 (on the right). Drawn from the author's casts by Craig Williams.*

Table 3.1. Sites that have extinct megafauna remains with definite and probable Clovis association (modified from Grayson and Meltzer 2003; Haynes 2002). * denotes sites were added from Slade (2018).

| Site | Taxa | Clovis association |
| --- | --- | --- |
| Blackwater Draw, NM | Mammoth | Clovis points and other lithics |
| Colby, WY | Mammoth | Clovis point variant |
| Dent, CO | Mammoth | Clovis points |
| Domebo, OK | Mammoth | Clovis points and other lithics |
| Escapule, AZ | Mammoth | Clovis points |
| El Fin del Mundo, Sonora MEX* | Gomphothere | Clovis points and other lithics |
| Heboir, WI | Mammoth | Clovis lithics |
| Jake Bluff, OK* | Bison | Clovis points and other lithics |
| Kimmswick, MO | Mammoth | Clovis points and other lithics |
| Lange-Ferguson, SD | Mammoth | Clovis points and other lithics |
| Lehner, AZ | Mammoth | Clovis points and other lithics |
| Leikem, AZ | Mammoth | Clovis point |
| Lewisville, TX* | Mammoth | Clovis point and other lithics |
| Lubbock Lake, TX | Mammoth | Clovis lithics |
| Miami, TX | Mammoth | Clovis points |
| Murray Springs, AZ | Mammoth/Bison | Clovis points and other lithics |
| Navarette, AZ | Mammoth | Clovis points |
| Naco, AZ | Mammoth | Clovis points |
| Pleasant Lake, MI | Mammoth | Butchered bones |
| Sloth Hole, FL | Mammoth | Clovis points |
| Union Pacific Mammoth, WY* | Mammoth | Un-typed lithics |
| Wally's Beach, Alberta, CAN* | Horse/Camel | Clovis points and other lithics |

a much more varied diet, relying on small game and plants to supplement their food resources. Others differ in their interpretation of the evidence (*e.g.* Cannon and Meltzer 2004). It is certain, however, that large mammals were exploited by the Clovis groups and that they used their fluted points to hunt, kill and butcher them. Many of the fluted points recovered in direct association with the bones of these mammals display impact fractures and scars that were produced on impact with the larger of the bones (Haury *et al.* 1953; 1959; Graham *et al.* 1981; Haynes Jr and Huckell 2007).

In this respect Clovis groups certainly differ from other Paleoindian and later populations in the Americas (Madsen 2015).

In recent years Clovis fluted points and regional variability have been at the centre of considerable research (Morrow and Morrow 1999; Anderson and Faught 2000;

O'Brien *et al.* 2001; 2012; Ellis 2004; Buchanan and Hamilton 2009; Slade 2010; 2018; Prascianus 2011; Buchanan *et al.* 2012; Sholts *et al.* 2012; Smallwood 2012; Gingerich 2013; 2018; Miller *et al.* 2013; Eren *et al.* 2014; 2015). But in spite of the recent attention addressing the issues of Clovis, a few basic questions remain unresolved. At present there are two main theories concerning Clovis fluted point variability on a regional basis. The 'regional environmental adaptation hypothesis' proposes that Clovis-era groups adapted their hunting toolkit to the characteristics of their prey and local habitat, resulting in regional differences within these toolkits, which would have included variation in the Clovis fluted points. This is not an entirely new concept and the origins of this idea can be traced back to the 1950s (Whithoft 1952; 1954).

The hypothesis gained further support more recently during the 1980s and early 1990s (Meltzer 1988; Anderson 1990; Stork and Spiess 1994). The consensus then was that Clovis groups developed different cultural adaptations within diverse environments in eastern North America. An examination of points and bifaces from sites located in Tennessee, South Carolina and Virginia (Smallwood 2012) also identified technological variations among the specimens from these states and concluded they represent regional variation.

In a previous study (Buchanan *et al.* 2011) it was suggested that the particular prey being exploited had an effect on the size and shape of Paleoindian fluted points, in particular Clovis points. Therefore, it might be hypothesised that Clovis fluted point variability may have been associated with different prey that was hunted in the different regions of North America. Zooarchaeological evidence suggests that in eastern North America caribou or deer were the primary prey, whereas in the western, northern and southern plains regions mammoth and bison were the primary prey (Cannon and Meltzer 2004).

The alternative hypothesis suggested that Clovis groups did not alter, or produce specific shapes of their projectile points in relation to local environmental conditions. This 'continent-wide adaptation hypothesis' was also first outlined in the 1950s (see Byers 1954; Willey and Phillips 1958), but it is best recognised by the work done later (Haynes Jr 1964; Kelly and Todd 1988). Recently, two studies have produced results that are consistent with the continent-wide adaptation hypothesis. Buchanan and Hamilton (2009) examined whether Clovis projectile point shape correlated with regional diversity. They found no association between point shape and regional environmental variability, concluding that there had not been enough time elapsed during the Clovis expansion for the development of local variability. Sholts *et al.* (2012) used laser-scanning techniques to examine flake scar patterns on Clovis projectile points from the Great Plains, South-west and Mid-Atlantic regions. They concluded that there were few differences within their sample and argued that it supported widespread standardisation of Clovis technology as well as the notion of one set of behaviours.

More recently, Gingerich (2013; 2018) has published reports of Clovis-like fluted point assemblages from sites located in Massachusetts as well as the sites of Plenge and West Athens Hill, both in New Jersey. These sites have been in the archaeological record for some time but have recently been attributed to Clovis and belong to the

Eastern Fluted Point Tradition (Miller and Gingerich 2013). Concurrently, Eren *et al.* (2014) discuss Clovis regional variation with regards to the effects of raw material shape, size and quality. Their analysis also looked at flake scar patterns on projectile points and confirmed that production techniques were similar across the sample, but they did find that differences in shape correlated highly with the toolstone selected.

According to Mason (1962), the south-east region of North America has the greatest Paleoindian point diversity. By 'diversity', Mason refers specifically to 'richness' as defined as the number of types in an assemblage (Anderson and Faught 2000; 1998; Broster *et al.* 2013). With a greater point richness, the south-east was assumed to be the 'homeland' of the Clovis culture, whose tools represented the earliest widespread and currently recognisable remains of hunter-gatherers (Anderson 1990). However, greater point richness in the south-east (or in parts of the region) could be a result of cultural, environmental and colonisation factors or a combination of all or some of the above. A recent study (Eren *et al.* 2016) addressing Mason's original model has agreed that the south-east, as defined by Anderson (1990), does indeed exhibit greater point diversity than neighbouring regions, but is cautious in agreeing that this indicates a Clovis origin in the south-east.

For my analysis on the distribution of Clovis and Clovis-like points in North America (Slade 2018) I identified seven regions that were selected and defined more by modern political boundaries rather than distinctions in geography, climate or archaeological bias (Figure 3.2). I chose and adapted the seven regions for my thesis research based on a literature review of Clovis sites and locations, which have been previously defined (Buchanan *et al.* 2012; Haynes 2002; Miller *et al.* 2013). The Clovis point types or forms I identified are ones that have previously been classified in the literature. The traditionally recognised Clovis form (Figure 3.1) is sometimes referred to as 'true' or 'classic' Clovis in the old literature, and more recently western Clovis (Morrow 2005a; 2005b). For my study, I refer to this form as Clovis fluted, and to avoid confusion with the points from the South-west and North-west regions I dropped the term 'western'. The other variants I redefined included the Eastern Fluted Tradition Clovis-like points from the North-east, other Clovis-like points such as the Debert/Colby form (a deep concaved base rounded eared point) of the North-east and in some other regions, the waisted Clovis of the Middle Atlantic and South-east regions, Ross County Clovis and St Louis Clovis variants from the Midcontinent and Great Lakes region, and the Clovis fluted forms from the South-west and North-west regions. There are probably more variants than these, as the literature mentions more point forms (Justice 1987; Willig 1991).

The majority of sites that have Clovis lithic technology are more closely distributed in the south-eastern quadrant of North America (Anderson *et al.* 2015; but see also Prascianus 2011; Buchanan *et al.* 2012; Miller *et al.* 2013) but become more thinly spread on the margins of this area. The earliest dated sites occur in the south-western part of the region, whilst later sites are found in the eastern woodlands of the north-eastern region and north-western North America (Beck and Jones 2010; Collins 2014).

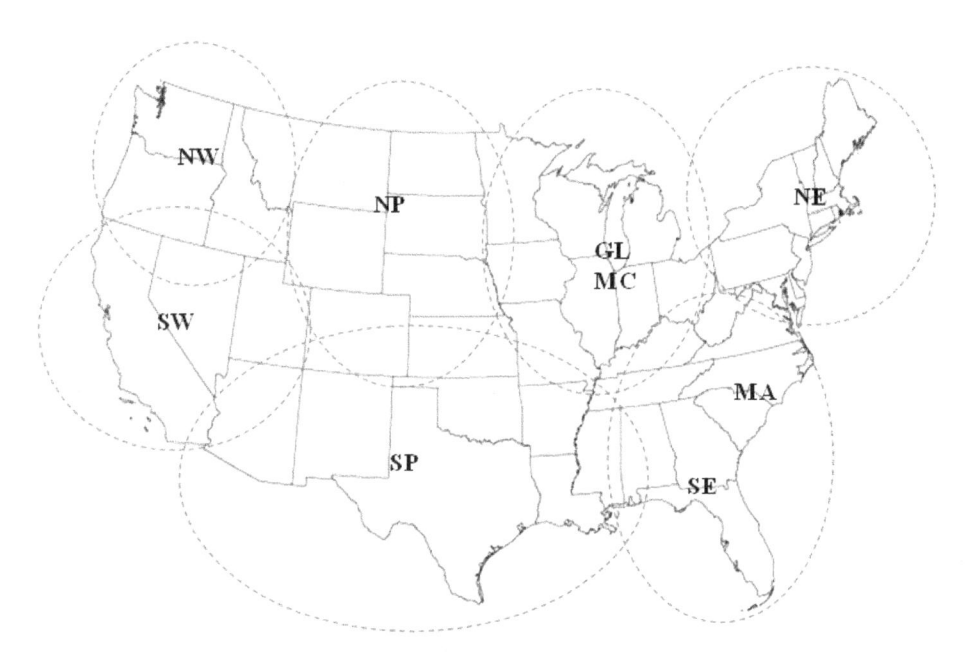

*Figure 3.2. Map of North America highlighting the seven regions that I identified (NE = North-east; MA = Middle Atlantic; SE = South-east; GL / MC = Great Lakes and Midcontinent; NP = Northern Plains; SP = Southern Plains; NW = North-west; SW = South-west and Great Basin (after Slade 2018).*

Whether this represents an actual movement of people as opposed to movement of resources for trade purposes remains open for debate (Madsen 2015; Amick 2017).

## When did they get there and where did they come from?

Identifying when Clovis first appears as well as the duration of the culture are crucial in explaining the colonisation of the Americas, determining the role of humans on the Pleistocene megafaunal extinction and assessing whether humans inhabited the Americas before Clovis. It was held that a period of ~600 years, from 11,500 to 10,900 $^{14}$C yr BP was how long the Clovis lasted (Haynes Jr 2005). More recently, a shorter chronology was offered (Waters and Stafford 2007), suggesting the Clovis period lasted 250 years from 10,800–11,050 $^{14}$C yr BP. This chronology was determined by analysing existing Clovis $^{14}$C dates and more recent high-precision accelerator mass spectrometry (AMS) $^{14}$C dates from previously dated Clovis sites (Waters and Stafford 2007). The samples were from culturally specific organics: bone, ivory, and seeds that AMS can date accurately (Stafford *et al.* 1991) to within ± 30 years at 11,000 $^{14}$C yr BP. Not everybody, however, agreed with the date range (Haynes *et al.* 2007), for there were several Clovis sites that were thought to be older than this time frame that were not redated using the same protocol as on the other sites, such as the Aubrey (Ferring 2001) and Wilson-Leonard (Collins 1998) sites in Texas. More recently, the El Fin del Mundo site in the Sonoran

Desert in northern Mexico (Sanchez *et al.* 2014) has a probable date older than this date range offered by Waters and Stafford (Waters and Stafford 2007).

One implication for this shorter Clovis time frame is that it provides little time for the rapid spread of peoples across such a large area as North America. Therefore it suggests that the dispersal of the Clovis technology was a product of interaction across existing pre-Clovis groups (Bradley and Collins 2013). However, the same criticism is not often levelled against the older 600-year chronology. Rather, the newer date range perpetuates the argument over a 'long' vs. a 'short' Clovis chronology. The gomphothere Clovis kill site in northern Mexico (Sanchez *et al.* 2014) has a single date of ~11,600 $^{14}$C yr BP, lending support to the 'long' period model and puts it among the oldest Clovis sites in North America (Table 3.2). With the suggestion that other early Clovis sites are located in the southern Great Plains, the south-western United States and northern Mexico, Clovis could have had its origins much further south than previously thought (Meltzer 2014), suggesting a development *in situ* by pre-Clovis hunter-gatherer/forager populations. In the same way, others suggest that the earliest Clovis groups in the south-western and south-eastern North America may have come from groups that spread along the Pacific Coast before moving inland (Hamilton and Buchanan 2007; Anderson 2013; Waters and Stafford 2013).

There are a handful of sites in North and South America that provide a credible case for pre-Clovis occupation. All have strong geological contexts, are well dated and have humanly worked artefacts. Some of these sites have unfluted points. All of these sites are at least 1,000 or 2,000 years older than Clovis. Monte Verde II in southern Chile is probably the best known and most important of these early sites (Dillehay 1989; 1997). With the acceptance of Monte Verde, at 1,200 to 1,400 years older than Clovis, comes the reality that there must be earlier pre-Clovis sites in North America. Most recently, reinvestigation at the Page-Ladson site in Florida suggests that there was a pre-Clovis presence, ~12,495 $^{14}$C yr BP (Halligan *et al.* 2016). It has also been suggested (Madsen 2015) that the Americas were colonised earlier than 16,000 $^{14}$C yr BP, before the Last Glacial Maximum (LGM), with site candidates from both North and South America (see Adovasio and Pedler 2004; 2013; Meltzer 2009; Collins *et al.* 2013). The credibility of the evidence from each site largely depends on how far one is willing to accept the data. The evidence from these sites, albeit intriguing, and suggestive of an even older human presence in the Americas, will require much more study. What we do now know is that around 11,500 $^{14}$C yr BP or about 13,300 Cal yrs BP Clovis technology appeared abruptly on the landscape and within a relatively short period spread across North America. Whilst many questions remain, it is evident that Clovis does not represent the first evidence of human occupation in the Americas.

If there were groups in the Americas by 16,000 $^{14}$C yr BP, and as widespread as the evidence suggests, how did they get there? There are several theories that address this question, but after more than a century of extensive studies we are no closer to knowing the answer. Three routes are considered the most

Table 3.2. *Clovis sites with accepted, credible, and problematic radiocarbon dates (modified from Slade 2018).*

| Site | Date ¹⁴C yr B.P. | Calibrated BP date Min | Max |
|---|---|---|---|
| *Clovis sites with accepted dates and diagnostic artefacts* | | | |
| Lange-Ferguson, SD | 11,080 ± 40 | 12,942 | 13,046 |
| Sloth Hole, FL | 11,050 ± 50 | 12,912 | 13,026 |
| Anzick, MT | 11,040 ± 35 | 12,902 | 12,994 |
| Dent, CO | 10,990 ± 25 | 12,888 | 12,933 |
| Paleo Crossing, OH | 10,980 ± 75 | 12,857 | 12,968 |
| Domebo, OK | 10,960 ± 30 | 12,873 | 12,917 |
| Lehner, AZ | 10,950 ± 40 | 12,866 | 12,916 |
| Shawnee-Minisink, PA | 10,935 ± 15 | 12,867 | 12,899 |
| Murray Springs, AZ | 10,885 ± 50 | 12,838 | 12,887 |
| Colby, WY | 10,870 ± 20 | 12,841 | 12,870 |
| Jake Bluff, OK | 10,765 ± 25 | 12,802 | 12,833 |
| *Clovis sites with diagnostic artefacts but lack precise dates and are uncalibrated* | | | |
| Sheriden Cave, OH | 10,600 ± 30 (above artefacts) | | |
| | 10,920 ± 50 (below artefacts) | | |
| Blackwater Draw, NM | 11,300 ± 235 | | |
| Cactus Hill, VA | 10,920 ± 250 | | |
| Union Pacific, WY | 11,280 ± 350 | | |
| Aubrey, TX | 11,570 ± 70 | | |
| Sheaman, WY | 10,305 ± 15 | | |
| *Clovis sites indirectly dated with diagnostic artefacts* | | | |
| Casper, WY | 11,190 ± 50 | 13,169 | 13,403 |
| East Wenatchee, WA | 11,125 ± 130 | 12,920 | 13,130 |
| *Clovis sites indirectly dated with diagnostic artefacts* | | | |
| Indian Creek, MT | 10,980 ± 110 | 12,850 | 13,000 |
| Lubbock Lake, TX | 11,100 ± 60 | 12,949 | 13,071 |
| Bonneville Estates, NV | 11,010 ± 40 | 12,886 | 12,959 |
| Kanorado, KS | 10,980 ± 40 | 12,878 | 12,935 |
| Arlington Springs, CA | 10,960 ± 80 | 12,848 | 12,955 |
| *Clovis-age sites with credible dates with Clovis and Clovis-like artefacts* | | | |
| Vail, ME | 10,710 ± 50 | 12,735 | 12,823 |
| Debert, Nova Scotia, CAN | 10,590 ± 50 | 12,413 | 12,445 |
| Hedden, ME | 10,550 ± 40 | 12,401 | 12,471 |
| Hiscock, NJ | 10,795 ± 40 | 12,809 | 12,848 |
| Big Eddy, MO | 10,830 ± 60 | 12,814 | 12,869 |
| El Fin del Mundo, Sonora, MEX* | ~11,550 ± 60 | Avg. 13,384 | |

* Some dates were obtained from the site's publications and have not been reliably confirmed

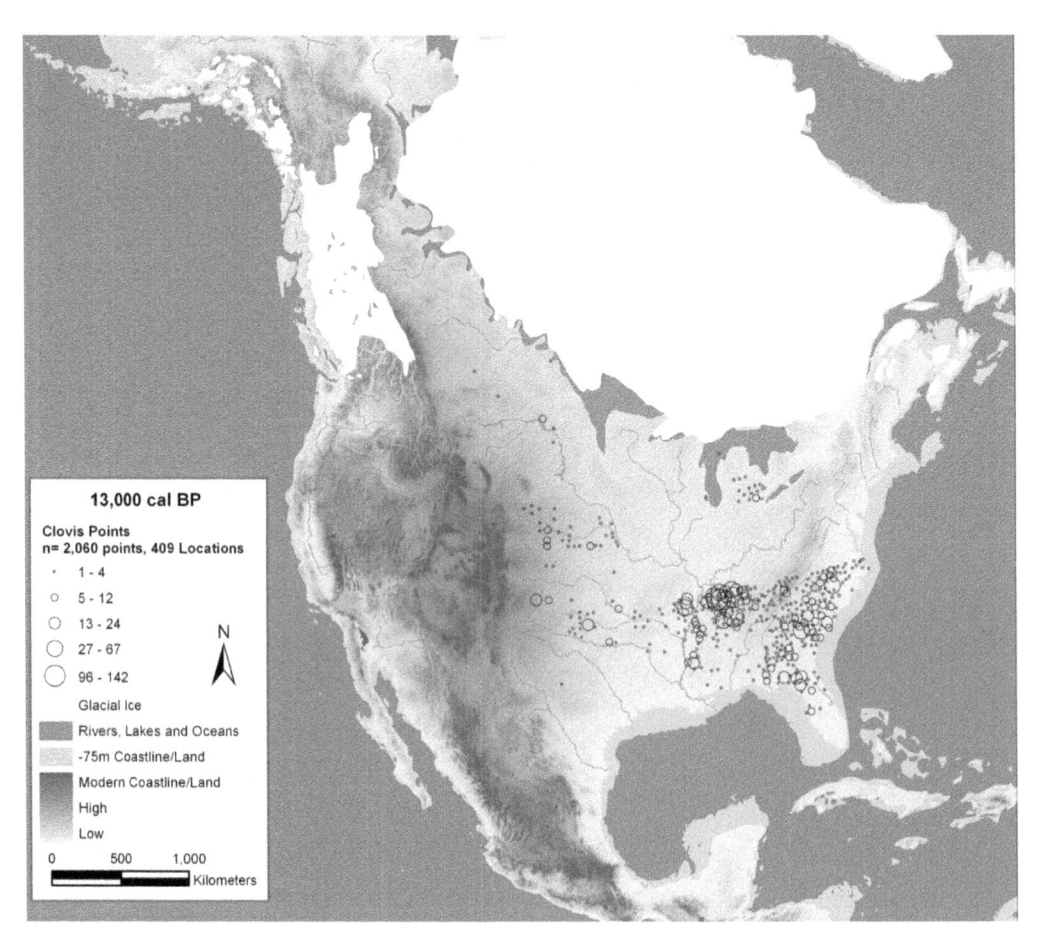

*Figure 3.3. Map of North America at the time of Clovis showing the extent of the Cordilleran and Laurentide ice sheets (after Anderson et al. 2005).*

reasonable (*e.g.* Dixon 2013). The first is the traditional model of Pleistocene hunter-gatherers entering North America via the Bering land bridge and ice-free corridor between the Cordilleran and Laurentide ice sheets (Figure 3.3), entering sometime after the LGM, spreading rapidly through North America, hunting mammoths and other megafauna, developing the distinctive Clovis fluted point, spreading into the northern and southern high plains and south-eastern North America (Figure 3.4) and causing Pleistocene megafauna extinctions as they went (Martin 1973). The second model is a Pacific coastal route proposed many years ago (Fladmark 1979) and has had a recent revival (Dixon 1999; Erlandson 2002).

It suggests that groups of foragers having the use of boats exploited marine and estuarine coastal marsh resources and navigated the margins of the north Pacific, entering the coastline of North America at some point during the LGM and spreading rapidly south to Central and South America. The Pacific coast model has not altered

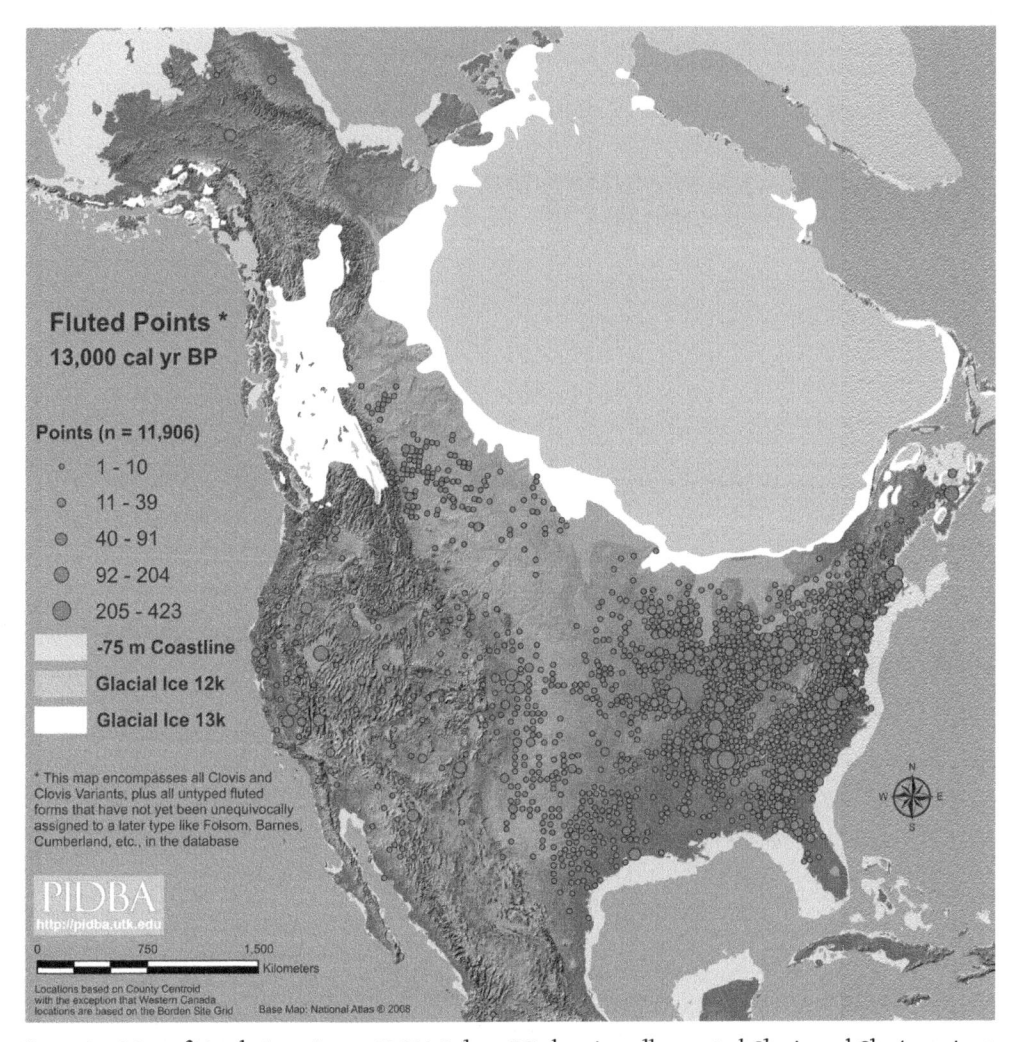

*Figure 3.4. Map of North America at 13,000 Cal yrs BP showing all reported Clovis and Clovis variants, plus points designated as being 'fluted' and of Clovis age (after Anderson et al. 2005).*

much since first suggested, just modifications to the dating of North and South American material. However, recent research into the Channel Islands off the coast of California suggests that the Western Stemmed points and a diagnostic crescent, or lunate tool type (Beck and Jones 2010; Erlandson et al. 2011), are not only contemporaneous, but could be older than Clovis (Bryan 1980; Beck and Jones 2012; Fiedel and Morrow 2012). The crescent biface tools have been found along the Californian coast and in cave sites (Jertberg 1986), and stemmed points have been recovered from buried stratified sites in the Great Basin (Jenkins et al. 2012), the Columbia Plateau rivers (Davis et al. 2014) and as far north as south-eastern Alaska (Dixon 2007). The third, and most intriguing, model is the so-called 'Solutrean' hypothesis (Stanford and Bradley 2012).

It suggests that Upper Palaeolithic European hunter-gatherers took to the Atlantic and exploited the coastal resources of the now-submerged Atlantic shelf of north-western Europe and north-eastern North America (Anderson *et al.* 2005; O'Brien *et al.* 2014; Stanford and Bradley 2014), hunting maritime and deep-water marine wildlife along the North Atlantic ice margins, and eventually reaching and colonising North America sometime during the LGM. The hypothesis is largely based on similarities between the Solutrean and Clovis lithic technology and relies to some extent on whether these Pleistocene seafarers had developed subsistence strategies capable of hunting sea mammals, surviving along the North Atlantic ice shelf margins. I will not thoroughly go into the three proposed migration routes further, as they are not the main focus of this paper, but they are relevant in showing how Clovis progenitors may have reached North America (Goebel 2004; Meltzer 2009; Madsen 2015; Amick 2017).

## Summary and concluding remarks

So, what do we know? All North American prehistoric human remains, of what little survives, are anatomically modern humans, AMH (*Homo sapiens*). AMH did not colonise central and north-east Asia until ~30,000 to 40,000 years ago (Goebel *et al.* 2008, but see Liu *et al.* 2015) so this puts a realistic baseline date on the earliest arrival of people in the Americas. The traditional model has the ancestors of Native Americans diverging from the Asian gene pool through genetic isolation somewhere in greater Beringia some 30,000 years ago (Kitchen *et al.* 2008). Whilst it is unlikely that the first groups came over all at once, it has been argued that small bands from the first wave made their way to the Americas over a number of years (Auerbach 2012).

As for the 'Clovis-First' paradigm, this can now be firmly dismissed. There is good evidence that both North and South America was occupied at ~11,500 $^{14}$C yr BP/13,300 Cal yr BP. North America has Clovis, with its distinctive technology, and in South America the sites of this age have generalised toolkits with flake tools and bifaces. Although Fishtail points have technological and morphological similarities to Clovis (Flegenheimer *et al.* 2013), they and stemmed points are generally accepted as being later than Clovis. There are several sites that have credible dates before Clovis. These sites have biface, blade and bone tool technologies that date to at least 12,500 $^{14}$C yr BP, and are found in both North and South America.

It also now appears clear that Clovis developed south of the ice sheets from a previous technology, possibly in south-eastern North America, from groups already there. If the Aubrey dates are correct (Table 3.2), it could represent a transitional Clovis event. This would make the Aubrey site, in Texas, a key location. The lithic assemblage from Aubrey is very similar to that of the Friedkin site. Small expedient tools made on flakes, blades and bladelets are present. By adding the El Fin del Mundo site into the argument, it raises the possibility that Clovis originated in the south; if it did not, then Clovis is even older than the ~11,500 $^{14}$C yr BP that has been suggested.

Clovis colonisation of North America was unique in its speed and range. Most of the evidence is demonstrated through Clovis lithic technology, and in the case of Clovis as 'material culture has the potential to carry information' (Gamble 1982). It is the lithic artefacts that have revealed substantial amounts of information related to the behaviour of these people. Paleoindians were unique in many ways (Davidson 2013). It is unlikely that all of these groups were specialised big-game hunters, but evidence suggests a general reliance on hunting, which would have played a part in driving several declining megafauna species to extinction around 11,200 $^{14}$C yr BP (Surovell *et al.* 2016; Martin 1984). If these groups of early hunter-gatherers passed through an arctic environment, which is at present the most likely explanation, then we can assume rapid group mobility, some experience in watercraft, dog domestication, sewing and needlecraft, and even high reproductive behaviour.

In conclusion, the overview of the initial occupation of North America presented here is just an overview, but I hope contributes to the peopling of the Americas research. The understanding of when, how and where the first groups entered must be based on hard evidence and archaeological derived data (Anderson and Miller 2017). As the data is accumulated in the period from around ~15,000 Cal yr BP and later, our understanding of the First Americans will be better understood.

## Acknowledgements

Special thanks for the organisers of a conference at the University of Durham in 2014 and for the session that led to my presentation and a previous version of this paper being accepted for inclusion in a proceedings volume due for future publication. This paper has been possible through generous and thoughtful contributions from Dr John McNabb, Prof. Clive Gamble and Prof. Nicholas Ashton. The illustrations of the Clovis points were produced by an admired colleague and close friend, Craig Williams. Special thanks to Prof. Dennis Stanford for his generous support and tireless encouragement. Two anonymous reviewers provided constructive comments in previous drafts of this paper, and I appreciate their thoughtful and specific comments. I thank the aforementioned Prof. Nick Ashton for providing feedback from proofreading previous drafts. Ultimately, however, I remain responsible for this work, and the inevitable inadequacies remain my own. This paper is dedicated to the memory of Robert Patten and Dennis Stanford.

## Bibliography

Adovasio, J.M. and Pedler, D.R. (2004) Pre-Clovis Sites and their Implications for Human Occupation Before the Last Glacial Maximum. In: D.B. Madsen (ed.) *Entering America: Northeast Asia and Beringia before the Last Glacial Maximum*, pp. 139–158. Salt Lake City: University of Utah Press.

Adovasio, J.M. and Pedler, D.R. (2013) The Ones that Still Won't Go Away: More biased thoughts on the pre-Clovis peopling of the Americas. In: K.E. Graf, C.V. Ketron and M.R. Waters (eds) *Paleoamerican Odyssey*, pp. 511–520. College Station, Texas: Center for the Study of the First Americans, Texas A&M University.

Amick, D.S. (2017) Evolving Views on the Pleistocene Colonization of North America. *Quaternary International* 431, 125–151.

Anderson, D.G. (1990) The Paleoindian Colonization of Eastern North America. In: K.B. Tankersley and B.L. Isaac (eds) *Early Paleoindian Economies of Eastern North America*, pp. 163–216. Greenwich: JAI Press.

Anderson, D.G. (2013) Paleoindian Archaeology in Eastern North America: Current approaches and future directions. In: J.A.M. Gingerich (ed.) *The Eastern Fluted Point Tradition*, pp. 371–403. Salt Lake City: University of Utah Press.

Anderson, D.G. and Faught, M.K. (1998) The Distribution of Fluted Paleoindian Projectile Points: Update 1998. *Archaeology of Eastern North America* 26, 163–187.

Anderson, D.G. and Faught, M.K. (2000) Paleoindian Artefact Distributions, Evidence and Implications. *Antiquity* 75, 507–513.

Anderson, D.G. and Miller, S.D. (2017) PIDBA (Paleoindian Database of the Americas): Call for data. *PaleoAmerica* 3, 1–5.

Anderson, D.G., Miller, S.D., Yerka, S. J., Gillam, C.J. and Faught, M.K. (2005) Paleoindian Artefact Distributions in the Southeast and Beyond. Paper presented at 'Clovis in the Southeast' Conference, October 2005, Columbia, South Carolina.

Anderson, D.G., Smallwood, A.M. and Miller, S.D. (2015) Pleistocene Human Settlement in the Southeastern United States: Current evidence and future directions. *PaleoAmerica* 1, 3–45.

Auerbach, B.M. (2012) Skeletal Variation Among Early Holocene North American Humans: Implications for origins and diversity in the Americas. *American Journal of Physical Anthropology* 149, 525–536.

Beaton, J. (1991) Colonizing Continents: Some problems from Australia and the Americas. In: T.D. Dillehay and D.J. Meltzer (eds) *The First Americans: Search and research*, pp. 209–230. Baton Rouge: CRC Press.

Beck, C. and Jones, G.T. (2010) Clovis and Western Stemmed: Population migration and the meeting of two technologies in the intermountain West. *American Antiquity* 75, 81–116.

Beck, C. and Jones, G.T. (2012) Clovis and Western Stemmed Again: Reply to Fiedel and Morrow. *American Antiquity* 77, 386–397.

Bonnichsen, R. (1991) Clovis Origins. In: R. Bonnichsen and K.L. Turnmire (eds) *Clovis: Origins and Adaptations*, pp. 309–329. Corvallis, Oregon: Center for the Study of the First Americans.

Bradley, B.A., Collins, M.B. and Hemmings, A. (2010) *Clovis Technology*. International Monographs in Prehistory 17. Ann Arbor: University of Michigan.

Bradley, B.A. and Collins, M.B. (2013) Imagining Clovis as a Cultural Revitalization Movement. In: K.E. Graf, C.V. Ketron and M.B. Waters (eds) *Paleoamerican Odyssey*, pp. 247–256. College Station, Texas: Center for the Study of the First Americans, Texas A&M University.

Broster, J.B., Norton, M., Miller, D.S., Tune, J.W. and Baker, J.D. (2013) Tennessee Paleoindian Record: The Cumberland and Lower Tennessee River watersheds. In: J.A.M. Gingerich (ed.) *In the Eastern Fluted Point Tradition*, vol.1, pp. 299–314. Salt Lake City: University of Utah Press.

Bryan, A.L. (1980) The Stemmed Point Tradition: An early technological tradition in western North America. In: L.B. Harten, C.N. Warren and D.R. Tuohy (eds) *Anthropological Papers in Memory of Earl H. Swanson*, pp. 77–107. Pocatello: Idaho State Museum of Natural History.

Buchanan, B. and Collard, M. (2007) Investigating the Peopling of North America Through Cladistic Analyses of Early Paleoindian Projectile Points. *Journal of Anthropological Archaeology* 26, 366–393.

Buchanan, B. and Collard, M. (2010) A Geometric Morphometrics-Based Assessment of Blade Shape Differences Among Paleoindian Projectile Point Types from Western North America. *Journal Archaeological Science* 37, 350–359.

Buchanan, B., Collard, M., Hamilton, M.J. and O'Brien, M.J. (2011) Points and Prey: An evaluation of the hypothesis that prey size predicts early Paleoindian projectile point form. *Journal of Archaeological Science* 38, 852–864.

Buchanan, B. and Hamilton, M.J. (2009) A Formal Test of the Origins of Variation in North American Early Paleoindian Projectile Points. *American Antiquity* 74, 279–298.

Buchanan, B., Kilby, J.D., Huckell, B.B., O'Brien, M.J. and Collard, M. (2012) A Morphometric Assessment of the Intended Function of Cached Clovis Points. *PLoS ONE* 7, 1–13.

Byers, D.S. (1954) Bull Brook – A fluted point site in Ipswich, Massachusetts. *American Antiquity* 19(4): 343–351.

Cannon, M.D. and D.J. Meltzer (2004) Early Paleoindian Foraging: Examining the faunal evidence for large mammal specialization and regional variability in prey choice. *Quaternary Science Review* 23, 1955–1987.

Collins, M.B. (1998) *Wilson-Leonard: Special studies.* Texas Archaeological Research Laboratory 10. Austin, Texas: University of Texas.

Collins, M.B. (1999) *Clovis Blade Technology.* Austin, Texas: University of Texas.

Collins, M.B. (2002) The Gault Site, Texas, and Clovis Research. *Athena Review* 3, 31–42.

Collins, M.B. (2007) Discerning Clovis Subsistence from Stone Artifacts and Site Distributions on the Southern Plains Periphery. In: R. Beauchamp Walker and B.N. Driskell (eds) *Foragers of the Terminal Pleistocene in North America Foragers of the Terminal Pleistocene in North America*, pp. 59–87. Lincoln, Nebraska: University of Nebraska Press.

Collins, M.B. (2014) Initial Peopling of the American Continent, Findings and Issues. In: C. Renfrew and P. Bahn (eds) *The Cambridge World Prehistory*, pp. 907–922. Cambridge: Cambridge University Press.

Collins, M.B. and Lohse, J.C. (2004) The Nature of Clovis Blades and Blade Cores. In: D.B. Madsen (ed.) *Entering America: Northeast Asia and Beringia before the Last Glacial Maximum*, pp. 159–186. Salt Lake City: University of Utah Press.

Collins, M.D., Stanford, D.J., Lowery, D.L. and Bradley, B.A. (2013) North America Before Clovis: Variance in temporal/spatial cultural patterns, 27,000–13,000 Cal yr BP. In: K.E. Graf, C.V. Ketron and M.B. Waters (eds) *Paleoamerican Odyssey*, pp. 521–539. College Station, Texas: Texas A&M University Press.

Davidson, L. (2013) Peopling the Last New Worlds: The first colonisation of Sahul and the Americas. *Quaternary International* 285, 1–29.

Davis, L.G., Nyers, A.J. and Willis, S.C. (2014) Context, Provenance and Technology of a Western Stemmed Tradition from the Coopers Ferry Site, Idaho. *American Antiquity* 79, 596–632.

Dillehay, T.D. (1989) *Monte Verde: A Late Pleistocene settlement in Chile. Vol. 1. Paleoenvironment and site context.* Washington DC: Smithsonian Institution Press.

Dillehay, T.D. (1997) *Monte Verde: A Late Pleistocene settlement in Chile. Vol. 2. The archaeological context and interpretation.* Washington DC: Smithsonian Institution Press.

Dillehay, T.D., Calderon, G., Politis, G. and Beltrao, M. (1992) Earliest Hunters and Gatherers of South America. *Journal of World Prehistory* 6, 145–204.

Dixon, E.J. (1999) *Bones, Boats, and Bison.* Albuquerque: University of New Mexico Press.

Dixon, E.J. (2007) Bifaces from On Your Knees Cave, Southeast Alaska. In: R.L. Carlson and M.P.R. Magne (eds) *Projectile Point Sequences in Northwestern North America*, pp. 11–18. Burnaby: Archaeology Press, Simon Fraser University.

Dixon, E.J. (2013) Late Pleistocene Colonization of North America from Northeast Asia: New insights from large scale paleogeographic reconstructions. *Quaternary International* 285, 57–67.

Ellis, C.J. (2004) Understanding 'Clovis' Fluted Point Variability in the Northeast: A perspective from the Debert site, Nova Scotia. *Canadian Journal of Archaeology* 28, 205–253.

Eren, M.I., Buchanan, B. and O'Brien, M.J. (2015) Social Learning and Technological Evolution during the Clovis Colonization of the New World. *Journal of Human Evolution* 80, 159–170.

Eren, M.I., Chao, A., Chun-Huo, C., Colwell, R.K., Buchanan, B., Boulanger, M.T., Darwent, J. and O'Brien, M.J. (2016) Statistical Analysis of Paradigmatic Class Richness Supports Greater Paleoindian Projectile-Point Diversity in the Southeast. *American Antiquity* 81, 174–192.

Eren, M.I., Roos, C.I., Story, B.A., von Cramon-Taubadel, N. and Lycett, S.J. (2014) The Role of Raw Material Differences in Stone Tool Shape Variation: An experimental assessment. *Journal of Archaeological Science* 49, 472–487.

Erlandson, J.M. (2002) Anatomically Modern Humans, Maritime Voyaging, and the Pleistocene Colonization of the Americas. In: N.G. Jablonski (ed.) *First Americans: The Pleistocene colonization of the New World*, pp. 59–92. Memoirs of the California Academy of Science 27. Berkeley: California Academy of Science Press.

Erlandson, J.M., Rick, T.C., Braje, T.J., Casperson, M., Culleton, B., Fulfrost, B., Garcia, T., Guthrie, D.A., Jew, N., Kennett, N.J., Moss, M.L., Reeder, L., Skinner, C., Watts, J. and Willis, L. (2011) Paleoindian Seafaring, Maritime Technologies, and Coastal Foraging on California's Channel Islands. *Science* 331, 1181–1185.

Ferring, C.R. (2001) *The Archaeology and Paleoecology of the Aubrey Clovis Site (41DN479) Denton County, Texas*. Denton, Texas: Center for Environmental Archaeology, Department of Geography, University of North Texas.

Fiedel, S.J. (1999) Older Than We Thought: Implications for corrected dates for Paleoindians. *American Antiquity* 64, 95–115.

Fiedel, S.J. and Morrow, J.E. (2012) Comment on 'Clovis and Western Stemmed: Population migration and the meeting of two technologies in the intermountain west' by Charlotte Beck and George T. Jones. *American Antiquity* 77, 376–385.

Fladmark, K.R. (1979) Routes: Alternate migration corridors for early man in North America. *American Antiquity* 44, 59–69.

Flegenheimer, N., Miotti, L. and Mazzia, N. (2013) Rethinking Early Objects and Landscapes in the Southern Cone: Fishtailed-Point concentrations in the Pampas and northern Patagonia. In: K.E. Graf, C.V. Ketron and M.R. Waters (eds) *Paleoamerican Odyssey*, pp. 359–376. College Station, Texas: Center for the Study of the First Americans, Texas A&M University.

Gamble, C. (1982) Interaction and Allegiance in Paleolithic Society. *Man* 17, 92–107.

Gingerich, J.A.M. (ed.) (2013) *In the Eastern Fluted Point Tradition, Volume 1*. Salt Lake City: University of Utah Press.

Gingerich, J.A.M. (ed.) (2018) *In the Eastern Fluted Point Tradition, Volume 2*. Salt Lake City: University of Utah Press.

Goebel, T. (2004) The Search for a Clovis Progenitor in Subarctic Siberia. In: D.B. Madsen (ed.) *Entering America: Northeast Asia and Beringia before the Last Glacial Maximum*, pp. 311–356. Salt Lake City: University of Utah Press.

Goebel, T., Powers, R. and Bigelow, N. (1991) The Nenana Complex of Alaska and Clovis Origins. In: R. Bonnichsen and K. L. Turnmire (eds) *Clovis: Origins and Adaptations*, pp. 40–79. Corvallis, Oregon: Center for the Study of the First Americans.

Goebel, T., Waters, M.R. and O'Rourke, D.H. (2008) The Late Pleistocene Dispersal of Modern Humans in the Americas. *Science* 319, 1497–1502.

Graham, R.W., Haynes. Jr, C.V., Johnson, D.L. and Kay, M. (1981) Kimmswick: A Clovis–Mastodon association in eastern Missouri. *Science* 213, 1115–1117.

Grayson, D.K. and Meltzer, D.J. (2002) Clovis Hunting and Large Mammal Extinctions: A critical review of the evidence. *Journal of World Prehistory* 15, 313–359.

Grayson, D.K. and Meltzer, D.J. (2003) A Requiem for North American Overkill. *Journal of Archaeological Science* 30, 585–593.

Halligan, J.J., Waters, M.R., Perotti, A., Owens, I.J., Feinburg, J.M., Bourne, M.D., Fenerty, B., Winsborough, B., Carlson, D., Fisher, D.C., Stafford Jr, T.W. and Dunbar, J.S. (2016) Pre-Clovis Occupation 14,550 Years Ago at the Page-Ladson Site, Florida, and the Peopling of the Americas. *Science Advances* 2, 1–8.

Hamilton, M.J. and Buchanan. B. (2007) Spatial Gradients in Clovis-Age Radiocarbon Dates Across North America Suggest Rapid Colonisation from the North. *Proceedings of the National Academy of Sciences* 104, 15625–15630.

Haynes, Jr, C.V. (1964) Fluted Points: Their age and dispersal. *Science* 145, 1408–1413.

Haynes, Jr, C.V. (1969) The Earliest Americans. *Science* 166, 709–715.
Haynes Jr, C.V. (2005) Clovis, Pre-Clovis, Climate Change, and Extinction. In: R. Bonnichsen., B.T. Lepper, D.J. Stanford and M.R. Waters (eds) *Paleoamerican Origins: Beyond Clovis*, pp. 113–132. College Station, Texas: Center for the Study of the First Americans, Texas A&M University Press.
Haynes, Jr, C.V. and Huckell, B.B. (eds) (2007) *Murray Springs: A Clovis site with multiple activity areas in the San Pedro Valley, Arizona*. Anthropological Papers of the University of Arizona 71. Tucson: University of Arizona Press.
Haynes, G. (2002) *The Early Settlement of North America: The Clovis era*. New York: Cambridge University Press.
Haynes, G., Anderson, G., Ferring, C.R., Fiedel, S.J., Grayson, D.K., Haynes Jr, C.V., Holliday, V.T., Huckell, B.B., Kornfeld, M., Meltzer, D.J., Morrow, J.E., Surovell, T.A., Waguespack, N.M., Wigand, P. and Yohe II, R.M. (2007) Comment on Redefining the Age of Clovis: Implications for the peopling of the Americas. *Science* 317, 320.
Haynes, G. (2015) The Millennium Before Clovis. *PaleoAmerica* 2, 137–162.
Haury, E.W., Antevs, E. and Lance, J. (1953) Artefacts with Mammoth Remains, Naco, Arizona. *American Antiquity* 19, 1–24.
Haury, E.W., Sayles, E.B. and Wasley, W.W. (1959) The Lehner Mammoth Site, Southeastern Arizona. *American Antiquity* 25, 2–30.
Hester, J.J. (1972) *Blackwater Draw Locality No. 1*. Rancho de Taos: Fort Burgwin Research Center, SMU.
Jenkins, D.L., Davis, L.G., Stafford, T.W., Campos, P.F., Hockett, B., Jones, G.T., Cummings, L.S., Yost, C., Connolly, T.J., Yohe II, R.M., Gibbons, S.C., Raghavan, M., Rasmussen, M., Paijmans, J.L.A., Hofreiter, M., Kemp, B.M., Barta, J.L., Monroe, C., Thomas, M., Gilbert, P. and Willerslev, E. (2012) Clovis Age Western Stemmed Projectile Points and Human Coprolites from the Paisley Caves. *Science* 337, 223–228.
Jertberg, P.M. (1986) The Eccentric Crescent: Summary analysis. *Pacific Coast Archaeological Quarterly* 22, 35–64.
Johnson, E.A. (1991) Late Pleistocene Cultural Occupation on the Southern Plains. In: R. Bonnichsen and K.L. Turnmire (eds) *Clovis: Origins and Adaptations*, pp. 215–236. Corvallis, Oregon: Center for the Study of the First Americans.
Justice, N.D. (1987) *Stone Age Spear and Arrow Points of the Midcontinent and Eastern United States*. Bloomington: Indiana University Press.
Kelly, R.L. and Todd, L. (1988) Coming into the Country: Early Paleoindian hunting and mobility. *American Antiquity* 53, 231–244.
Kitchen, A., Miyamoto, M.M. and Mulligan, C.J. (2008) A Three-Stage Colonization Model for the Peopling of the Americas. *PLoS ONE* 3, 1–7.
Liu, W., Martinón-Torres, M., Cai, Y., Xing, S., Tong, H., Pei, S., Sier, M.J., Wu, X., Edwards, R.L., Cheng, H., Li, Y., Yang, X., Bermúdez de Castro, J.M. and Wu, X. (2015) The Earliest Unequivocally Modern Humans in Southern China. *Nature* 526, 696–699.
Lynch, T. (1983) The Paleo-Indians. In: J.D.W.H. Jennings (ed.) *Ancient South Americans*, pp. 87–137. New York: Freeman.
Madsen, D.B. (2015) A Framework for the Initial Occupation of the Americas. *PaleoAmerica* 1, 217–250.
Martin, P.S. (1973) The Discovery of America. *Science* 179, 969–974.
Martin, P.S. (1984) Prehistoric Overkill: The global model. In: P.S. Martin and R.G. Klein (eds) *Quaternary Extinctions: A prehistoric revolution*, pp. 354–403. Tucson: University of Arizona Press.
Martin, P.S. and Klein, R.G. (eds) (1984) *Quaternary Extinctions: A prehistoric revolution*. Tucson: University of Arizona Press.
Martin, P.S. (1990) Who or What Destroyed the Mammoths? In: L.D. Agenbroad, J. Mead and L.W. Nelson (eds) *Megafauna and Man: Discovery of America's heartland*, pp. 109–117. Scientific Papers Vol. 1. South Dakota: The Mammoth Site of Hot Springs.

Mason, R.J. (1962) The Paleo-Indian Tradition in Eastern North America. *Current Anthropology* 3, 227–283.
Meltzer, D.J. (1988) Late Pleistocene Human Adaptations in Eastern North America. *Journal of World Prehistory* 2, 1–52.
Meltzer, D.J. (1993) Is There a Clovis Adaptation? In: O. Soffer and N. Praslov (eds) *Kostenki to Clovis: Upper Palaeolithic-Paleo-Indian Adaptations*, pp. 293–310. New York: Plenum Press.
Meltzer, D.J. (2002) What Do You Do When No One's Been There Before? Thoughts on the exploitation and colonization of new lands. In: N.G. Jablonski (ed.) *The First Americans: The Pleistocene colonization of the New World*, vol. 27, pp. 27–58. San Francisco: Memoirs of the California Academy of Sciences.
Meltzer, D.J. (2003) Peopling of North America. In: A.R. Gillespie, S.C. Porter and B.J. Atwater (eds) *The Quaternary Period in the United States, Developments in Quaternary Sciences*, vol. 1, pp. 539–563. Amsterdam: Elsevier.
Meltzer, D.J. (2009) *First Peoples in a New World: Colonizing Ice Age America*. Berkeley: University of California Press.
Meltzer, D.J. (2014) Clovis at the End of the World. *Proceedings of National Academy of Sciences* 111, 12276–12277.
Miller, D.S. and Gingerich, J.A.M. (2013) Paleoindian Chronology and the Eastern Fluted Point Tradition. In: J.A.M. Gingerich (ed.) *In the Eastern Fluted Point Tradition*, vol. 1, pp. 9–21. Salt Lake City: University of Utah Press.
Miller, D.S., Holliday, V.T. and Bright, J. (2013) Clovis Across the Continent. In: M.R. Waters, T. Goebel and K.E. Graf (eds) *The Paleoamerican Odyssey*. College Station, Texas: Texas A&M University Press.
Morrow, J.E. and Morrow, T. (1999) Geographic Variation in Fluted Points: A hemispheric perspective. *American Antiquity* 64, 215–231.
Morrow, J.E. (2005a) The Myth of Clovis: East v west. Pt 1. *Central States Archaeological Journal* 52, 51–54.
Morrow, J.E. (2005b) The Evolution of Paleoindian Projectile Point Styles. Pt 2. *Central States Archaeological Journal* 52, 79–82.
O'Brien, M.J., Darwent, J. and Lyman, R.L. (2001) Cladistics is Useful for Reconstructing Archaeological Phylogenies: Paleoindian points from the southeastern United States. *Journal Archaeological Science* 28, 1115–1136.
O'Brien, M.J., Buchanan, B., Collard, M. and Boulanger, M.T. (2012) Cultural Cladistics and the Early Prehistory of North America. In: P. Pontarotti (ed.) *Evolutionary Biology: Mechanisms and trends*, pp. 23–42. Berlin: Springer-Verlag.
O'Brien, M.J., Boulanger, M.T., Collard, M., Buchanan, B., Tarle, L., Straus, L.G. and Eren, M.I. (2014) The Origins of the First Settlers in the Americas. *Antiquity* 88, 606–613.
Pitblado, B.L. (2011) A Tale of Two Migrations: Reconciling recent biological and archaeological evidence in the Pleistocene peopling of the Americas. *Journal of Archaeological Research* 19, 327–375.
Prascianus, M.M. (2011) Mapping Clovis: Projectile points, behaviour, and bias. *American Antiquity* 76, 107–126.
Sain, D.A. (2012) *Clovis Blade Technology at the Topper Site (38AL23): Assessing lithic attribute variation and regional patterns of technological organization*. Southeastern Paleoamerican Survey Occasional Papers No. 2. Columbia, South Carolina: South Carolina Institute of Archaeology and Anthropology, University of South Carolina.
Sanchez, G., Holliday, V.T., Gaines, E.P., Arroyo-Cabrales, J., Martinez-Tagüeň, N., Kowler, A., Lange, T., Hodgins, G.W.L., Mentzer, S. M. and Sanchez-Morales, I. (2014) Human (Clovis) - Gomphothere (*Cuvierronious* sp) association ~13,390 calibrated yr B.P. in Sonora, Mexico. *Proceedings of the National Academy of Sciences* 111, 10972–10977.
Slade, A.M. (2010) Clovis: What's the point? Unpublished Master's dissertation, University of Southampton.

Slade, A.M. (2018) Is There a Regional Variability Within Clovis Fluted Points Influenced by Raw Material Selection? An analysis of basal concavity shape. Unpublished MPhil thesis, University of Southampton.

Sholts, S.B., Stanford, D.J., Flores, L.M. and Wämländer, S.K.T.S. (2012) Flake Scar Patterns of Clovis Points Analyzed with a New Digital Morphometrics Approach: Evidence for direct transmission of technological knowledge across early North America. *Journal Archaeological Science* 39, 3018–3026.

Shott, M.J. (2013) Human Colonization and Late Pleistocene Lithic Industries of the Americas. *Quaternary International* 285, 150–160.

Smallwood, A.M. (2012) Clovis Technology and Settlement in the American Southeast: Using biface analysis to evaluate dispersal models. *American Antiquity* 77(4): 689–713.

Speth, J.D. (2013) Paleoindian Big-Game Hunters in North America: Are we misreading the evidence? *Quaternary International* 285, 197–198.

Stafford, T.W., Hare, P.E., Currie, L., Jull, A.J.T. and Donahue, D.J. (1991) Accelerator Radiocarbon Dating at the Molecular Level. *Journal of Archaeological Science* 18, 35–72.

Stanford, D.J. and Bradley, B.A. (2012) *Across Atlantic Ice: The origins of America's Clovis culture*. Berkeley: University of California Press.

Stanford, D.J. and Bradley, B.A. (2014) Reply to O'Brien et al. *Antiquity* 88, 614–621.

Stork, P.L. and Spiess, A.E. (1994) The Significance of new Faunal Identification Attributed to an Early Paleoindian (Gainey Complex) Occupation at the Udora Site, Ontario. *American Antiquity* 59, 121–142.

Surovell, T.A. and Waguespack, N.M. (2008) How Many Elephant Kills are 14? Clovis mammoth and mastodon kills in context. *Quaternary International* 191, 82–97.

Surovell, T.A., Pelton, S.R., Anderson-Sprecher, R. and Myers, A.D. (2016) Test of Martin's Overkill Hypothesis Using Radiocarbon Dates on Extinct Megafauna. *Proceedings of the National Academy of Sciences* 113, 886–891.

Waters, M.R. and Stafford, T.W. (2007) Redefining the Age of Clovis: Implications for the peopling of the Americas. *Science* 315, 1122–1126.

Waters, M.R. and Stafford, T.W. (2013) The First Americans: A review of the evidence for the Late-Pleistocene peopling of the Americas. In: K.E. Graf, C.V. Ketron and M.B. Waters (eds) *Paleoamerican Odyssey*, pp. 541–560. College Station, Texas: Center for the Study of the First Americans, Texas A&M University.

Whithoft, J. (1952) A Paleo-Indian Site in Eastern Pennsylvania: An early hunting culture. *Proceedings of the American Philosophical Society* 96, 464–495.

Whithoft, J. (1954) A Note on Fluted Point Relationships. *American Antiquity* 19, 271–273.

Whitley, D.S. and Dorn, R. (1993) New Perspectives on the Clovis vs. Pre-Clovis Controversy. *American Antiquity* 58, 626–647.

Willey, G.B. and Phillips, P. (1958) *Method and Theory in American Archaeology*. Chicago: University of Chicago Press.

Willig, J.A. (1991) Clovis Technology and Adaptation in the Far Western North America: Regional pattern and environmental context. In: R. Bonnichsen and K.L. Turnmire (eds) *Clovis: Origins and Adaptations*, pp. 91–118. Corvallis, Oregon: Center for the Study of the First Americans.

# Chapter 4

# Experimental magnetic susceptibility signatures for identifying hearths in the Mesolithic period in North East England, UK

*Lisa Snape and Mike J. Church*

## Abstract

*Evidence for Mesolithic activity in North East England mainly occurs as distinct concentrations of artefact scatters. Evidence for small-scale hearths is limited and is restricted to sites with evidence for repeated occupation. The application of magnetic susceptibility signatures and macrocharcoal remains to identify single or multi-use hearths typical of the Mesolithic has not been addressed to date. To assess the archaeological visibility of these types of hearths, a series of experiments was undertaken to retrieve charcoal and magnetic susceptibility data to identify different scales of burning on small replica hearths. Results have shown that magnetic enhancement occurs during single and multiple burning events and that the size of the charcoal assemblage is not indicative of the duration and intensity of hearth use, due to re-ignition of debris and taphonomic biases when exposed for short periods. However, for hearth features to survive in the archaeological record, they would have to undergo rapid sedimentation in order to be detected using geophysical techniques.*

## Introduction

Prehistoric pyrotechnology was an important feature of human society and was a major tool for cooking, lighting, heating, smoking of food, processing raw materials and for protection against predators (Aldeias *et al.* 2012; Barfield 1991; Berna and Goldberg 2007; Goldberg *et al.* 2012; Roebroeks and Villa 2011). The use of fire has been well documented for the Mesolithic of Britain, with clear evidence for large-scale fires from pollen and charcoal records, suggested to be anthropogenic in origin (Balaam *et al.* 1987; Simmons and Innes 1987; 1996; Bush 1988; Bennett *et al.* 1990; Edwards 1990; 1998; Simmons 1996; Blackford 2000). Hearths are also prominent features of the archaeological record of this period, allowing small-scale fires to be controlled and contained, resulting in the build-up of hearth deposits when repeatedly used. Theoretical models based on ethnographic studies have shown that mobile hunter-gatherers migrated around the landscape to exploit resources available on a seasonal basis, resulting in the establishment of multiple campsites beyond the home-base (Binford 1980; Keeley 1988; Kelly 1983; Rowley-Conwy 2001). The hearths produced due to this activity are likely to be ephemeral archaeologically, due to the limited amount of time for hearth debris to accumulate.

The definition of hearths can vary between sites of different periods in terms of function, structure, size and its relation to other features. Prehistoric hearths are often characterised in the field as features composed of burnt bone (Théry-Parisot 2002; Villa *et al.* 2002; Schiegl *et al.* 2003), burnt flint (Sergant *et al.* 2005), hazelnuts (Mithen *et al.* 2001), charcoal (Poole *et al.* 2002) and areas of discoloured sediment (Canti and Linford 2000). However, there are biases in the archaeological record towards hearths that have been used over sustained periods of time, such as the features at the site of Howick in Northumberland, where distinct pits have been found filled with charcoal and other hearth debris (Waddington 2007; Waddington and Pedersen 2007). In different situations, the construction of stone-lined hearths and pits more resistant to post-depositional processes and are likely to survive in the archaeological record (Gose 2000; Backhouse *et al.* 2005; Backhouse and Johnson 2007).

A range of methods and techniques have been used to characterise combustion features and debris, including phytoliths (Albert and Cabanes 2007; Cabanes *et al.* 2010; Lancelotti and Madella 2012), soil micromorphology (Matthews 2005; Mallol *et al.* 2007; 2013a; 2013b; Huisman *et al.* 2012), geochemistry (Berna and Goldberg 2007) and mineral magnetic measurements of archaeological samples containing ash (Peters *et al.* 2000; 2001; Church and Peters 2004; Church *et al.* 2007; Herries and Fisher 2010; Powell *et al.* 2012). This paper will mainly focus on the identification of magnetic susceptibility signatures from a series of experimental hearths, as this is a relatively rapid and cost-effective technique that can be undertaken in the field. In combination with this, an assessment of the macrocharcoal remains recovered from each experimental hearth was undertaken in order to understand the preservation potential of charcoal remains within hearth features from Mesolithic contexts in North East England. This experimental study does not necessarily have to be tied to Mesolithic contexts, but can be used as a reference for detecting small ephemeral 'firespots' or hearths in both the field and laboratory for any archaeological time period.

## Mesolithic evidence: North East England

The regional and chronological focus of this paper is the Mesolithic of North East England, as there is a significant amount of information for Mesolithic activity and landscape utilisation, from lowland, upland and coastal settings with evidence for fire activity. The majority of evidence occurs between the Tyne and Tweed rivers (Clack and Gosling 1976), an area that has undergone repeated phases of archaeological investigation (examples of investigations by date – Trechmann 1905; Buckley 1922; Raistrick 1933; Raistrick *et al.* 1936; Jacobi 1978; Weyman 1984; Haselgrove and Healey 1992). This has created investigative biases, as most known sites are located within naturally eroding coastal sections and exposed river sections, or have been identified as lithic scatters through fieldwalking (Young 2007). Furthermore, due to the inundation of the coastline during the onset of the Holocene (Boomer *et al.* 2007; Shennan *et al.* 2000), there is only a partial picture of the early Mesolithic coastline (Young 2007). However, more recently, excavations at Howick (Waddington 2007) and Lower Hauxley in Northumberland have added a wealth of new information to our understanding of Mesolithic settlement patterns and landscape utilisation in North East England.

Beyond this, the only compelling evidence for individual, ephemeral Mesolithic hearths or 'firespots' found in North East England include March Hill Carr (Spikins *et al.* 2002), March Hill Top (Manzi and Spikins 2008), Dunford bridge A and B (Radley *et al.* 1974) and Highcliff Nab, Guisborough, in Teesside (Harbord 1996; Waughman 2006; see Figure 4.1), and Goldsborough in North Yorkshire (Waugmann 2006). Many of these examples were found in association with extensive flint scatters exposed after a period of peat erosion in upland areas, with the peat protecting the archaeological hearths over the millennia. However, no evidence for similar features has been identified to date in lowland areas, making it difficult to understand the wider settlement system of Mesolithic hunter-gatherers in the region.

Geophysical prospection is now key for targeting excavation of firespots, hearths and midden deposits, particularly for Prehistoric contexts. These features are often too small and ephemeral to be detected in large-scale geophysical survey as features are likely to be missed or misinterpreted. Detailed closely spaced geophysical survey has been successfully used for targeted excavation of Mesolithic features, both at Hawkcombe Head, Somerset (Gardiner 2007) and in Goldsborough, North Yorkshire (Waugmann 2006). Results from these surveys enabled the identification, location and size of features to be detected on the surface, but a detailed understanding of their duration and scale of use remains unclear without complete excavation and sampling. To understand the use of ephemeral hearths during Prehistory, particularly during the Mesolithic, experimental hearths used over different durations can offer new insights as to how we can detect and interpret different types of fire activity in the past.

*Figure 4.1. Location of the Mesolithic sites mentioned in text, and the Botanic Garden of Durham University where the experiments were conducted.*

## Research aims

The focus of this experiment will explore magnetic susceptibility signatures and macrocharcoal remains recovered from single repeatedly used hearths within open-air settings, and how this data can inform our identification of isolated hearths, 'firespots' and charcoal horizons in the archaeological record.

The following hypotheses will be tested:

1. The magnetic susceptibility signatures of the underlying sediment following use of the hearths will increase.
2. Multiple burnings episodes representing sustained hearth use will produce a stronger magnetic susceptibility signature.
3. Hearths representing multiple burning events will produce a larger charcoal assemblage.
4. The resulting charcoal (fuel) assemblage will match the size profile of the wood burnt.

## Methodology

### Experimental hearths

The setting of this experiment was based at the Botanic Garden of Durham University and was undertaken on five 1 × 1 m² plots, which were deturfed to expose the subsoil in order to construct the hearths (Figure 4.2a). The surface soil (A horizon) was greyish brown (Munsell soil colour 10YR5/2) in colour with a silty clay texture and was 10 cm deep, and the subsoil (B horizon) was light yellowish brown (Munsell soil colour 10YR6/4) with a clay texture and was recorded between 10–15 cm and continued beyond the limit of excavation. The experiment involved the collection, cutting and drying of locally available kindling and branchwood of willow (*Salix* sp.), birch (*Betula* sp.) and hazel (*Corylus* sp.). These species were present in early to mid-Holocene deciduous woodlands in North East England (Huntley and Birks 1983; Simmons *et al.* 1993). The wood was sourced from young trees and shrubs grown in Houghall, a farm adjacent to the Botanic Garden. The wood for each hearth firing

*Figure 4.2. Photographs taken at various stages of the experiment: A) plots taken prior to experiment; B) arrangement of smaller twigs and branches during early stages of ignition; C) two days after the first burning event of Hearth 1, and D) Hearth 3, three months after the experiment.*

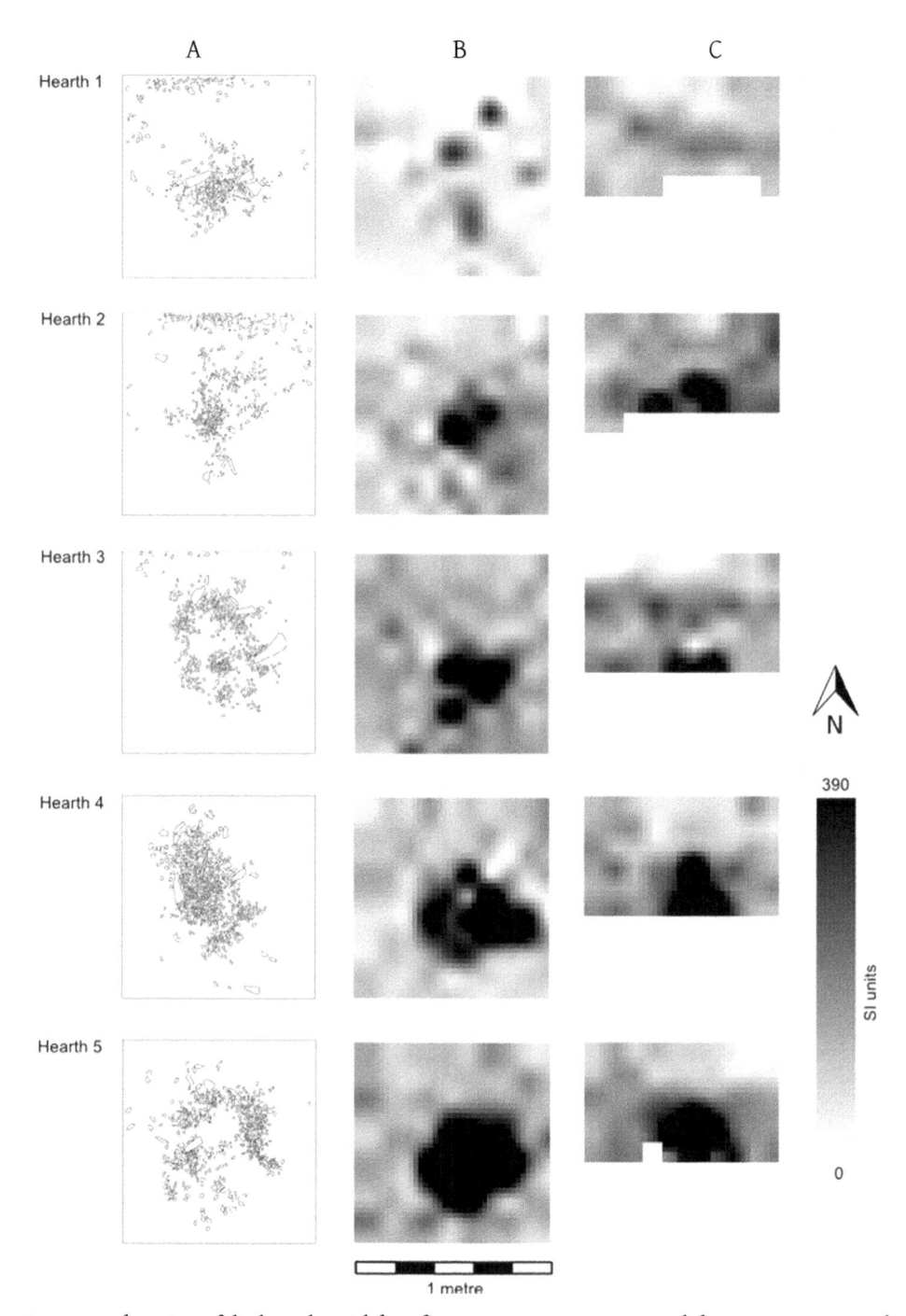

Figure 4.3. Plan view of the hearths with low-frequency magnetic susceptibility measurements shown: A) plan of hearths prior to excavation; B) magnetic susceptibility readings from three months after experiment and C) magnetic susceptibility readings of hearths six months after experiment and excavation.

was a mix of these three species in varying proportions. Each burning event utilised 100 pieces of wood seasoned for three weeks and the diameter and length of each piece was measured. Prior to ignition, five control soil samples for magnetic susceptibility were taken from the surface of each plot.

The experimental fires took place within the duration of a week during dry conditions for a period of 3–4 hours in the summer of June 2010. The hearths were constructed by first adding the kindling, then the smaller pieces of wood, and gradually adding the remaining larger pieces. From Hearth 1 through to 5, the number of burning events was increased each time. One burning event was undertaken on Hearth 1, two burning events on Hearth 2, three burning events on Hearth 3, four burning events on Hearth 4 and five burning events on Hearth 5. All five plots were left exposed for three months in order to observe short-term taphonomic alterations to the soil and charcoal assemblages. After three months (Phase 1) the charcoal and burnt soil/ash was planned *in situ* (Figure 4.3, column A) and bulk sampled. After 6 months (Phase 2) the second half of each hearth was sampled and excavated in the same way.

A second experiment was carried out shortly after the initial experiment had taken place, to assess the variability in temperature within one of these open-air hearths. The size and species of fuel and duration of the hearth firing was the same as the first experiment. Temperatures were measured using a thermocouple every 10 minutes from the centre of the hearth during 1 hour of ignition.

## *Magnetic susceptibility*

The theory and application of magnetic susceptibility applied to sediments exposed to elevated temperatures in archaeological contexts have been discussed in detail elsewhere (see Bellomo 1993; Dockrill and Simpson 1994; Peters *et al.* 2000; 2001; 2002; Crowther 2003; Maki 2005; Church *et al.* 2007; Powell *et al.* 2012). Prior to the experiment, five samples were taken from the surface of each plot to determine the background magnetic susceptibility signature of the soil before igniting the hearths; these were taken from the centre, top, bottom, right and left areas of each plot, to avoid disturbing the area prior to undertaking the experiment. Three months after the initial experiment (Phase 1), the plots were gridded (10 × 10 cm) and then surveyed at every 10 cm intervals using an MS2 Bartington Susceptibility meter attached with an MS2B sensor and probe (Dearing 1994). This enabled the initial low-frequency susceptibility of the soil to be measured in the field. This data was processed using Geoplot 3.0 (Geoscan Research, n/d) using SI units to produce colour shade plots (Figure 4.3, columns B and C).

After three months (Phase 1), each hearth was then half-sectioned, planned and photographed. Bulk samples of the surface charcoal (BS1) and the underlying burnt soil and charcoal fragments (BS2) were taken. Sections through each hearth were recorded to indicate the extent of burnt soil and charcoal/ash deposits. Samples were taken at every 1 cm interval from this section for accurate magnetic susceptibility measurements to be recorded under controlled laboratory conditions. A series of

Table 4.1. Bulk samples taken from each hearth.

| | | | | |
|---|---|---|---|---|
| 1 | 1 | 1 | 0.51 | 0.24 |
| | 2 | 1 | 1.66 | 0.26 |
| | 3 | 2 | 1.54 | 0.19 |
| | 4 | 2 | 2.93 | 0.28 |
| | **Total** | | **6.64** | **0.97** |
| 2 | 5 | 1 | 0.14 | 0.11 |
| | 6 | 1 | 2.82 | 0.28 |
| | 7 | 2 | 1.03 | 0.29 |
| | 8 | 2 | 1.29 | 0.15 |
| | **Total** | | **5.28** | **0.83** |
| 3 | 9 | 1 | 0.11 | 0.12 |
| | 10 | 1 | 2.40 | 0.19 |
| | 11 | 2 | 1.43 | 0.18 |
| | 12 | 2 | 1.34 | 0.20 |
| | **Total** | | **5.28** | **0.69** |
| 4 | 13 | 1 | 0.14 | 0.10 |
| | 14 | 1 | 1.90 | 0.17 |
| | 15 | 2 | 0.18 | 0.11 |
| | 16 | 2 | 1.50 | 0.15 |
| | **Total** | | **3.72** | **0.53** |
| 5 | 17 | 1 | 0.08 | 0.10 |
| | 18 | 1 | 2.78 | 0.28 |
| | 19 | 2 | 0.90 | 0.14 |
| | 20 | 2 | 1.23 | 0.22 |
| | **Total** | | **4.99** | **0.74** |

controls were obtained from spits extended from Hearths 2 and 4. The soil samples were dried at room temperature and then ground to a fine powder and sieved using a 2 mm mesh to remove large particles to avoid influencing the magnetic properties of the sample (Dearing 1994). Cylindrical pots (10 ml by volume) were weighed before and after the soil samples were added, and the nature and concentration of magnetic grains were measured under low (0.47 kHz) and high (4.7 kHz) frequencies using a Bartington MS2B susceptibility bridge producing a 0.1 mT alternating magnetic field. Mass specific susceptibility ($\chi^{in}$) and frequency dependent susceptibility ($\kappa^{fd}\%$) values were calculated following Dearing (1994).

# 4. Experimental magnetic susceptibility signatures for identifying hearths

*Table 4.2. Charcoal and wood counts.*

| Hearth | Wood/quantifiable charcoal | A | B | C | D | E | F | G | H | I | Total |
|---|---|---|---|---|---|---|---|---|---|---|---|
| **Hearth 1** | Wood added to hearth | 3 | 76 | 12 | 3 | 3 | 2 | 1 | | | 100 |
| | Charcoal (PB/OR >2 mm) quantified | 33 | 215 | 28 | 12 | 8 | 1 | 6 | | | 303 |
| **Hearth 2** | Wood added to hearth | 22 | 138 | 27 | 6 | 3 | 1 | 2 | 1 | | 200 |
| | Charcoal (PB/OR >2 mm) quantified | 36 | 163 | 42 | 8 | 8 | 1 | 2 | 4 | | 264 |
| **Hearth 3** | Wood added to hearth | 14 | 222 | 33 | 6 | 12 | 11 | 1 | | 1 | 300 |
| | Charcoal (PB/OR >2 mm) quantified | 22 | 157 | 50 | 18 | 13 | 1 | 1 | | 2 | 264 |
| **Hearth 4** | Wood added to hearth | 18 | 298 | 32 | 22 | 17 | 8 | 5 | | | 400 |
| | Charcoal (PB/OR >2 mm) quantified | 13 | 143 | 37 | 20 | 17 | 5 | 2 | | | 237 |
| **Hearth 5** | Wood added to hearth | 16 | 383 | 50 | 17 | 16 | 16 | 1 | | 1 | 500 |
| | Charcoal (PB/OR >2 mm) quantified | 12 | 126 | 58 | 30 | 15 | 5 | 8 | 3 | 1 | 258 |

## Macrocharcoal quantification

Bulk samples were obtained in two stages; after three months (Phase 1) and after six months (Phase 2). The volume and weight of each sample was measured and recorded (Table 4.1). The bulk samples were wet-sieved through a 4, 2 and 0.5 mm sieve stack. Each fraction was dried at 40° C and systematically sampled using a riffle box (van der Veen and Feiller 1982). In addition to the 4 mm charcoal assemblage, all charcoal fragments from the 2 mm flots with pith-to-bark (PB) or outer-ring (OR) intact were quantified in order to obtain a statistically robust sample for the charcoal diameter calculations (Table 4.2). The diameter of the charcoal was measured using a ring diameter chart (Table 4.3). An assessment of the amount of shrinkage and other deformation structures were not recorded as part of this experiment. Charcoal counts were used to assess the level of fragmentation between hearths.

*Table 4.3. Charcoal and wood diameter size classes used (following Ludemann 2002; 2006).*

| Size range | Diameter category |
|---|---|
| 0–0.9 cm | A |
| 1–1.9 cm | B |
| 2–2.9 cm | C |
| 3–3.9 cm | D |
| 4–4.9 cm | E |
| 5–5.9 cm | F |
| 6–6.9 cm | G |
| 7–7.9 cm | H |
| 8–8.9 cm | I |
| 9–9.9 cm | J |
| 10–10.9 cm | K |

## Statistical analysis

In order to test whether the size profiles of the charcoal remains correlated with the wood added to each hearth, a Student T-test was applied to the two populations (Table 4.4). The test was run on all charcoal (Phases 1 and 2) >2 mm in size retrieved from bulk samples of the surface charcoal and burnt soil and charcoal fragments from each hearth. This population was tested against the 100 pieces of wood used for each burning event combined.

## Results

### General observations of experimentation

A thin layer of approximately 1 cm thick grey/white ash was observed after each burning event. After a short period of exposure to wind and rain, all visible ash had disappeared, exposing a thin layer of charcoal and underlying burnt sediment (Figure 4.2c). The wood fuel produced a strong flame and burnt very rapidly; each hearth had to be constantly refuelled. After two hours all of the fuel had been consumed during a single burning episode. Each hearth went through a smouldering phase when the hearths were hottest and all fuel had turned to ash and charcoal. The hearths completely burnt out after 4–4.5 hours after ignition. The temperatures within the hearth of experiment 2 ranged from 380–780º C during firing (see Table 4.5), which reached a peak of 780º C after 30 minutes of ignition.

### Surface charcoal patterns

Surface charcoal produced from the experiments was recorded *in situ* to show the spread of charcoal over the plots after a three-month period (Figure 4.3, column A). Post-depositional processes such as water, wind and animal trampling could be seen after a short time of exposure. The influence of these processes resulted in smaller fragments of charcoal moving from the original position of the hearth while large partially charred pieces of wood remained *in situ*.

### Surface magnetic susceptibility controls

The five surface samples taken from the surface of each plot prior to the building and ignition of each hearth revealed that the magnetic susceptibility values were very low which represented the overall background signals of the sediment (Table 4.6).

### Low-frequency magnetic susceptibility signatures

The first phase of low-frequency magnetic susceptibility measurements recorded in the field clearly illustrated enhancement and become more pronounced with

Table 4.4. Results from the charcoal analysis and Student T-test.

| Hearth | Wood/quantifiable charcoal | Number of quantifiable fragments | Average diameter (cm) | Standard deviation | t value | p value |
|---|---|---|---|---|---|---|
| **Hearth 1** | Wood added to hearth | 100 | 1.81 | 0.99 | 3.69 | <0.001 |
| | Charcoal (PB/OR >2 mm) quantified | 303 | 1.39 | 1.00 | | |
| **Hearth 2** | Wood added to hearth | 100 | 1.57 | 0.98 | 1.13 | 0.26 |
| | Charcoal (PB/OR >2 mm) quantified | 264 | 1.46 | 1.13 | | |
| **Hearth 3** | Wood added to hearth | 300 | 1.78 | 1.13 | 1.98 | 0.04 |
| | Charcoal (PB/OR >2 mm) quantified | 264 | 1.59 | 1.09 | | |
| **Hearth 4** | Wood added to hearth | 400 | 1.77 | 1.09 | 0.71 | 0.48 |
| | Charcoal (PB/OR >2 mm) quantified | 237 | 1.70 | 1.13 | | |
| **Hearth 5** | Wood added to hearth | 500 | 1.75 | 1.05 | 2.38 | 0.018 |
| | Charcoal (PB/OR >2 mm) quantified | 258 | 1.99 | 1.43 | | |

increasing burning events (Figure 4.3, column B). Hearth 1 produced very low values, ranging between 82–175 SI units, and does not clearly show the position of the hearth. However, two small patches of magnetic enhancement occurred towards the centre and to the southeast of the plot ranging between 200–365 SI units. Hearth 2 shows more of a defined area of burning in the centre of the plot. Low values ranging between 80 and 180 SI units occurred in the east and south of the plot with high values in the north-west up to 250 SI units. The area of enhancement appears to get bigger in Hearth 3. There were also some patches of enhancement surrounding the hearth, which reached up to 290 SI units. After four burning cycles, Hearth 4 produced a much larger area of magnetic enhancement, peaking at 390 SI units in the centre, surrounded by areas of low enhancement. Finally, Hearth 5 shows a clearly defined area of significant enhancement in the centre of the plot, with values ranging between 360 and 390 SI units.

Table 4.5. Temperature measurements from experiment 2.

| Time (minutes) | Temperature °C |
|---|---|
| 0 | 380 |
| 10 | 560 |
| 20 | 550 |
| 30 | 780 |
| 40 | 740 |
| 50 | 630 |
| 60 | 570 |

Table 4.6. Mass specific magnetic susceptibility measurements of samples obtained from the surface of the plots prior to firing.

| Hearth number | Sample number | Location within plot | Mass specific magnetic susceptibility ($\chi^{in}$ - $\mu m^3 kg^{-1}$) |
|---|---|---|---|
| 1 | 1 | Centre | 1.95 |
|   | 2 | Left | 1.84 |
|   | 3 | Top | 2.27 |
|   | 4 | Right | 1.63 |
|   | 5 | Bottom | 1.91 |
| 2 | 6 | Centre | 2.39 |
|   | 7 | Left | 2.77 |
|   | 8 | Top | 2.88 |
|   | 9 | Right | 2.73 |
|   | 10 | Bottom | 2.77 |
| 3 | 11 | Centre | 2.75 |
|   | 12 | Left | 2.53 |
|   | 13 | Top | 2.63 |
|   | 14 | Right | 2.49 |
|   | 15 | Bottom | 2.67 |
| 4 | 16 | Centre | 2.10 |
|   | 17 | Left | 1.92 |
|   | 18 | Top | 2.02 |
|   | 19 | Right | 1.98 |
|   | 20 | Bottom | 1.82 |
| 5 | 21 | Centre | 2.51 |
|   | 22 | Left | 2.43 |
|   | 23 | Top | 2.68 |
|   | 24 | Right | 2.40 |
|   | 25 | Bottom | 2.71 |

The second phase of low-frequency magnetic susceptibility measurements after six months revealed that, in most plots, the magnetic enhancement had become more dispersed from the original position of the hearth (Figure 4.3, column C). Hearth 1 showed peaks up to 286 SI units but low values of 76 SI units still occurring in the north. Hearth 2 showed that the magnetic enhancement had spread out from the centre of the plot. Enhancement also spread to the north and north-east between 260 and 312 SI units. The position of Hearth 3 can still be clearly seen in the centre of the plot. However, considerable changes had taken place, with high and lower levels of magnetic enhancement occurring in the north, compared to those recorded after three months. The area of highest enhancement from below Hearth 4 was reduced as it spread across the plot, where enhancement was recorded between 233 and 310 SI units. Hearth 5 showed little change in enhancement, with peaks remaining in the centre of the plot, along with the surrounding areas being enhanced slightly from 183 to 260 SI units. To the north-east of the plot, a small area of low enhancement was identified in the first phase. However, by the second phase this had reduced to 79 SI units and spread over the area.

## Frequency dependent and mass specific susceptibility measurements

This experiment showed a significant increase in frequency dependent susceptibility ($\kappa^{fd}\%$) from Hearths 1 to 5. This indicates the formation of fine-grained ferromagnetic minerals (*e.g.* Peters and Thompson 1999; Herries and Fisher 2010), presumably as a result of an increase in superparamagnetic grains. The top layer 0–1 cm with depth through each hearth showed a clear increase from direct heat from the hearth. $\kappa^{fd}\%$ through the profile of each hearth revealed that, at the top of the profile, values were fairly low and increased with frequency of burning events; 4.9% (Hearth 1), 5.3% (Hearth 2), 7.8% (Hearth 3), 8.3% (Hearth 4) and 8.5% (Hearth 5). $\kappa^{fd}\%$ fluctuates with depth through the profile.

Figure 4.4 displays the variation in mass specific susceptibility ($\chi^{in}$) measurements taken through the hearths and underlying deposits. Hearths 3 to 5 showed an obvious enhancement of the top 3 cm of each plot, however, Hearths 1 and 2 showed little change compared to the two controls taken adjacent to Hearths 2 and 4. In Hearth 1, at 1 cm through the profile, $\chi^{in}$ measurements started at 1.88 µm³kg⁻¹ and measurements continued to show an increase in $\chi^{in}$ on the surface of each hearth when repeatedly ignited; 2.87 µm³kg⁻¹ (Hearth 2), 4.49 µm³kg⁻¹ (Hearth 3), 5.89 µm³kg⁻¹ (Hearth 4), 7.37 µm³kg⁻¹ (Hearth 5). Mass specific susceptibility signatures showed a general decrease through the profile from 3 to 14 cm with slight peaks around 10 cm, and then a rapid decrease to <1 µm³kg⁻¹ from 14 to 25 cm.

## Domain states

Domain states enable detection of fine-grained superparamagnetic particles of hematite and magnetite in soils and sediments, which significantly enhance magnetic susceptibility signatures. By comparing $\kappa^{fd}\%$ and $\chi^{in}$ signatures in each profile, domain states were plotted to determine whether fine-magnetic particles influenced the results (Figure 4.5). The signatures revealed a weak negative correlation between the two variables, with most points concentrating within the middle range of $\kappa^{fd}\%$ and the lower range of $\chi^{in}$. There appear to be no distinct populations within the dataset, other than Hearth 2, which showed no enhancement of fine-grained magnetic particles. This is not surprising, considering the wood fuel was the same for each hearth. All other samples from the top of the profile showed an increase in fine-magnetic particles due to elevated temperatures. Therefore, domain states cannot be used to identify multiple burning events.

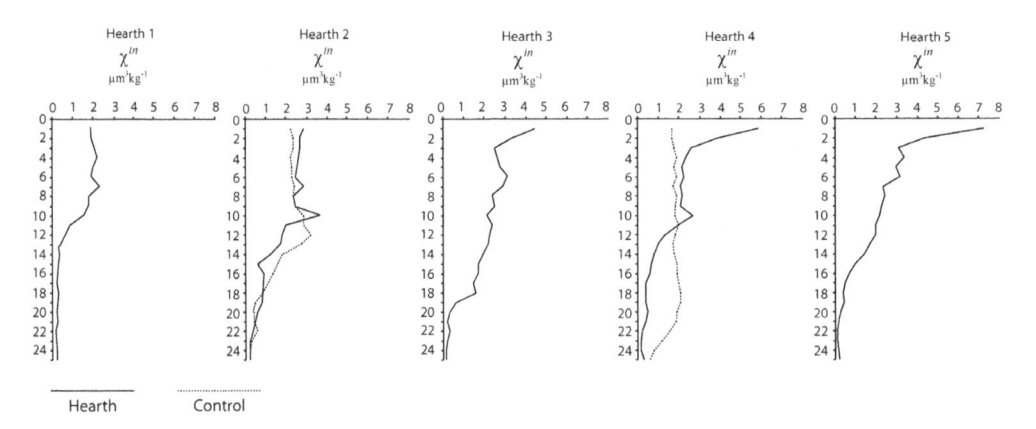

*Figure 4.4. Mass specific susceptibility ($\chi^{in}$) of hearths and two controls from spits extended from Hearths 2 and 4.*

## Macrocharcoal and Student T-test

The bulk sample mass and volumes are presented in Table 4.1. Charcoal and wood counts for the bulk samples and for each burning cycle are presented in Table 4.5, with the results of the Student T. Figure 4.6 shows the percentage of measurable wood and charcoal in each diameter size category. There is no systematic increase in the mass/volume of the remaining charcoal and ash after repeated burning cycles, and there is also no increase in the number of quantifiable/measurable charcoal after repeated burning cycles. The average diameter for the quantifiable/measurable charcoal compared to the wood added to each hearth shows that a slight size reduction occurred for Hearths 1 to 4 and Hearth 5 saw a slight average size increase. On initial visual inspection of Figure 4.6, there is no dramatic size transformation in the wood to charcoal size proportions for each of the hearths, though the Student T-test has indicated a statistical difference between the wood and charcoal assemblages for Hearths 1, 3 and 5.

## Discussion

Each of the hypotheses outlined in the research questions will be addressed individually below.

## The magnetic susceptibility signatures of the underlying sediment following use of the hearths will increase

As discussed previously, fire and exothermal heat leads to magnetic enhancement of the soil (Le Borgne 1960; Bellomo 1993; McClean and Kean 1993; Canti and Linford 2000).

## 4. Experimental magnetic susceptibility signatures for identifying hearths

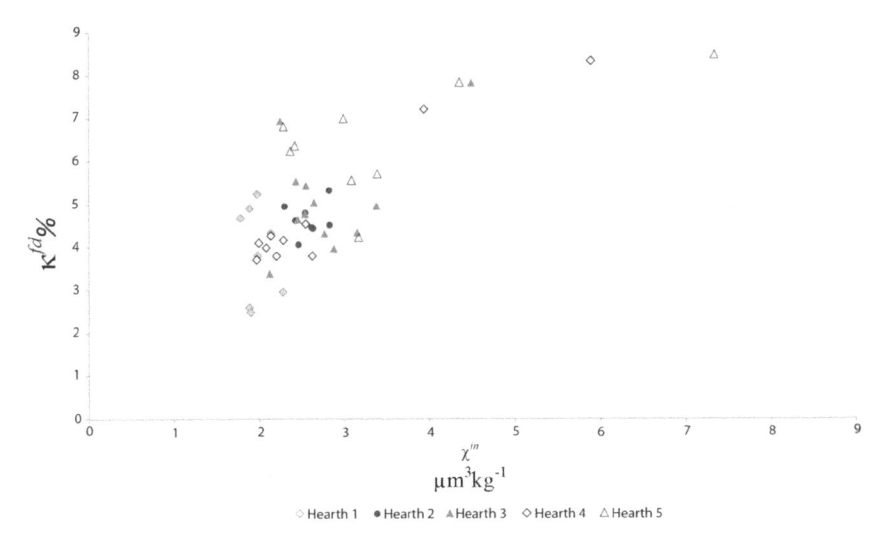

*Figure 4.5. Scatter plot of mass specific susceptibility ($\chi^{in}$) and frequency dependent susceptibility ($\kappa^{fd}\%$) values of samples obtained from the top 7 cm through each hearth.*

However, this research has shown, through the comparative analysis of both hearth and control samples, that enhancement can be used to identify small-scale surface hearths and different intensities of hearth use (single or multiple burning events). This demonstrates that small-scale hearths can be identified in the archaeological record, not only by the presence of charcoal, burnt flint, fire-cracked rocks and areas of discoloured sediment, but also from the magnetic susceptibility signature left behind on the surface. Figure 4.4 shows that, at 10 cm, there is a sudden increase in mass specific susceptibility, particularly in Hearths 2 and 4. This is likely to reflect the transition from topsoil to subsoil, containing a slightly higher concentration of ferromagnetic minerals. This is also evident in the low-frequency measurements, which are more difficult to interpret, as signatures fluctuated through the profile suggesting an accumulation of fine magnetic minerals at the base of soil horizons (Dearing *et al.* 1996). Further investigation into various fuel types and heat applied to different types of sediment underlying hearths should be investigated to see if these signatures identified in this experiment occur in different situations.

### *Multiple burnings episodes representing sustained hearth use will produce a stronger magnetic susceptibility signature*

The hearths that represent multiple burning events (*i.e.* repeated use within a day or over a week) displayed lateral and vertical enhancement, retaining their signature over the 6-month experimental period. Hearths that went through repeated burnings had burnt material and ash spread over the plots, resulting in the mixing of magnetically enhanced sediment with surrounding sediment, and led to a dispersal of magnetic

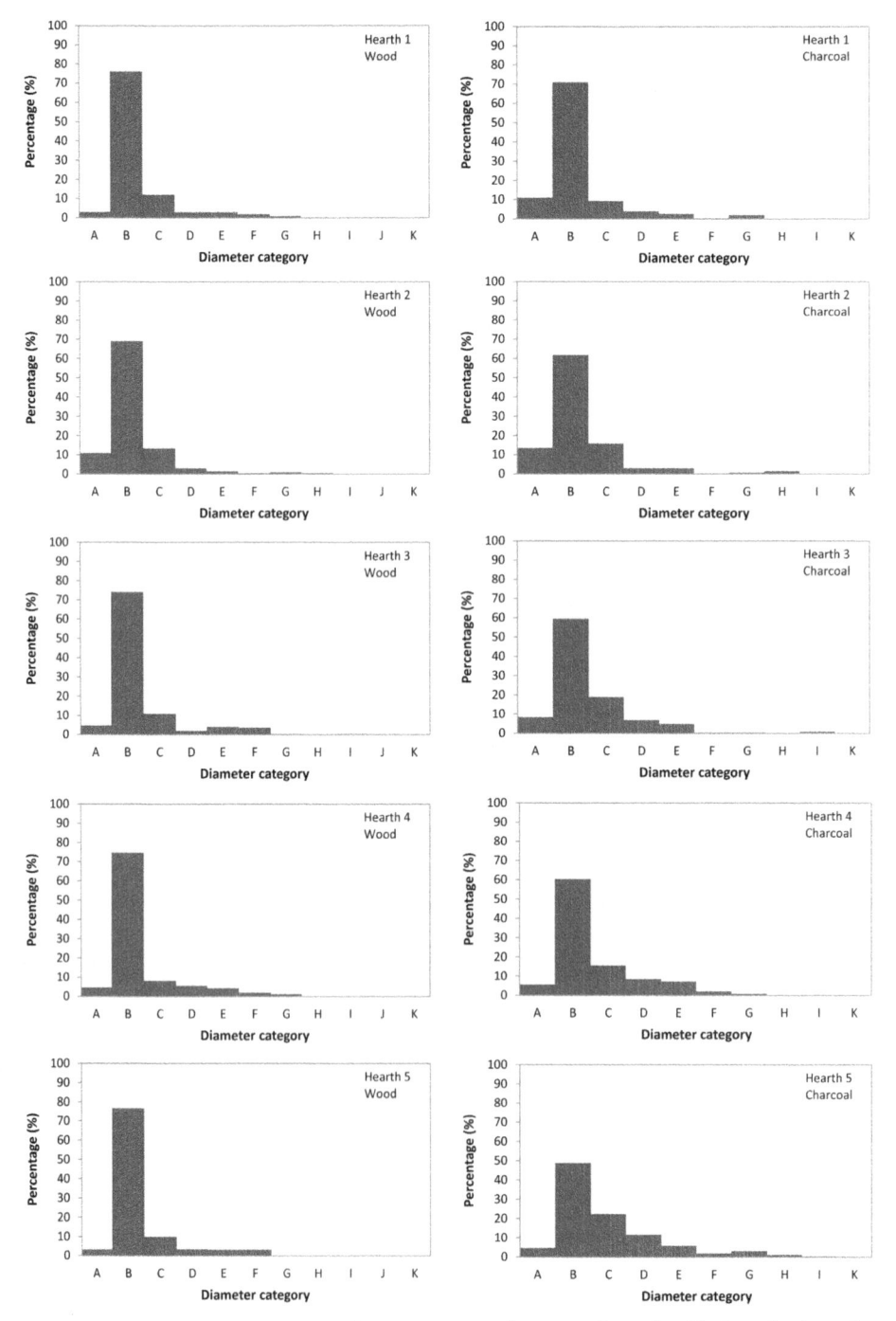

Figure 4.6. Histogram percentage graphs to compare the size of wood added to the hearths and measurable charcoal recovered.

susceptibility from the centre of the hearths. Hearth 5 revealed marked low-frequency magnetic susceptibility signatures as multiple layers of wood ash and charcoal became concentrated in the centre of each plot. This signature remained unchanged after six months and could be easily identified as a hearth based on prospection alone due to the shape, intensity and concentration of enhancement within the plot. By comparing this to hearths that went through fewer burning events, the signatures of the latter were weaker and surface enhancement would be more challenging to interpret if encountered in the field. Furthermore, areas of low enhancement may be due to the presence of organic matter such as moss, weeds and leaves that had accumulated over the course of three months, which enhanced the reduction of iron oxides (Le Borgne 1960; Raison 1979).

This experiment has enabled short-term post-depositional alterations of hearth debris to be seen, as it is evident that material can be modified and transported from its original position by a variety of climatic and faunal taphonomic processes. Due to their small scale, the hearths revealed that enhancement only penetrated the top 3 cm; this becomes more pronounced through Hearths 3, 4 and 5. For the magnetic signature to be recorded at deeper depths, the hearth would need to be heated to >500º C for the signature to be non-reversible (Raison 1979).

## Hearths representing multiple burning events will produce a larger charcoal assemblage

It has been demonstrated that repeated burning events does not produce larger assemblages of charcoal, as the residual charcoal is re-ignited in the next event and then turned to ash. The concentration of charcoal obtained from the first series of bulk samples from each hearth was much larger than the second phase of sampling. This demonstrated that, within a short period of exposure, small-scale taphonomic changes took place (animal trampling, wind and rain), causing a reduction of measurable charcoal and a spread of material. Experimental burning of archaeobotanical remains has demonstrated that plant material will be totally destroyed by fires hotter than 700°C (Boardman and Jones 1990; Boardman 1995). This is likely to be the cause of the small charcoal assemblages produced in this experiment, as the hearth (experiment 2) reached peak temperatures of 780°C. Therefore, we can confirm that 100% recovery of all macrocharcoal remains, both from the surface and directly below the hearth, revealed that the frequency, fragmentation and preservation of charcoal did not reflect the duration of use within hearths. Many other variables are at play in the archaeobotanical record, particularly variations between species, age, size and pre-treatment of wood and how they are preserved within a hearth would also vary.

Single-use open-air hearths found in North East England mainly survive as heat-affected stones and charcoal fragments. Taphonomic processes observed over a short period of time caused a considerable reduction of measurable charcoal.

Large charcoal fragments found in hearths that are left exposed for a long period of time are likely to be removed from the archaeological record and finer charcoal particles may not be recorded during initial fieldwork. Micromorphology and bulk sampling of such contexts would help to identify the presence of microcharcoal and burnt sediment that may not be easily spotted and recovered during excavation. This would also confirm if hearths are *in situ*, as it is generally difficult to determine based on the arrangement of heat-affected stone, flint artefacts and occasional charcoal fragments alone.

## *The resulting charcoal assemblage will match the size profile of the wood burnt*

Charcoal size profiles are used in archaeobotany to assess possible wood selection and woodland management strategies in the wider landscape, and this is an important research topic in human/environment research in the Mesolithic of north-west Europe (cf. Bishop *et al.* 2015). For the experimentation undertaken, the resulting charcoal assemblage did, in general terms, match the size profile of the wood burnt. This suggests that size-profile histograms of archaeological charcoal assemblages can provide insights into wood fuel procurement strategies, especially if a restricted range of roundwood/branchwood is burnt. However, some alterations did occur. For example, Hearths 1, 2 and 3 produced an increase in charcoal frequency in the smallest size category A, compared to that measured for wood from each hearth, but little change occurred in 4 and 5. However, with increasing burning events and the addition of more fuel, the assemblages have indicated that more charcoal fragments occur at the higher end of the diameter-size scale. It is likely that a single log can produce abundant charcoal fragments, which can skew results and make interpretation problematic, especially for woodland reconstruction and evidence for management. Overall, with hearths that undergo multiple burning events, a charcoal histogram is likely to depict one produced for the assemblage from Hearth 5, which shows a gradual spread of data, compared to the pattern produced by Hearth 1.

## *Archaeological visibility of small-scale hearths in the Mesolithic*

Site taphonomy is a major influence on the visibility of hearths. This factor can be dictated by a combination of processes, *i.e.* how many times the hearth was used, differential preservation of remains and post-depositional processes, such as bioturbation, pedogenesis, wind exposure and rain/frost weathering (Braadbaart *et al.* 2009; Théry-Parisot *et al.* 2010). Long-term occupation enables debris to build up, making them more visible in the archaeological record (Schiffer 1972). Charcoal-rich deposits in the Mesolithic usually occur in association with other burnt or unburnt material, which accumulates over time in the form of thick midden deposits, occupation layers and fire pits. These tend to be more visible in the archaeological record, especially sites located near coastal areas, which have been exposed by coastal erosion. Sites found in coastal settings such as at Northton, on the Isle of Harris, Western Isles (Gregory *et al.* 2005) and Howick, Northumberland (Waddington 2007), has triggered more extensive survey and excavation. These are particularly interesting and unique sites, which have been preserved by large volumes of sediment deposited by anthropogenic and natural processes.

Sustained occupation of Mesolithic sites such as Howick, Northumberland (Waddington 2007), East Barns, East Lothian (Gooder 2007), Star Carr, Yorkshire (Mellars and Dark 1988) and Mount Sandel, Ireland (Woodman 1985), have complex Simple structures have shown to create areas of task-related assemblages, such as flint, bone and plant macrofossils, associated with activities, *e.g.* cooking and tool production (Weiss *et al.* 2008). Furthermore, in single-use hearths or different site-types such as open-air campsites undergo further post-depositional alteration if not rapidly covered, resulting in the removal of ephemeral remains that typically comprise a small-scale hearth (*e.g.* Sergant *et al.* 2005). In this experiment, a short period of exposure (6 months) of the hearths revealed that small-scale single-occupation camps are likely to go undetected. This is due to the small areas of magnetically enhanced sediments dispersed over the area, whereas repeatedly occupied camps produce a more permanent magnetic signature. This finding has important implications for comparing site-formation processes between short-term and long-term occupations. Anthropogenic processes acting on long-term sites are more complex and the identification of phases of occupation from hearths may be problematic due to the removal of material through maintenance. The build-up of hearth debris within a dwelling would require constant maintenance (such as brushing, scooping and discarding ashes and charcoal), leaving behind little trace of burning events and activities carried out (Mallol *et al.* 2007; 2013b). Alternatively, open-air single use campsites may not have been maintained in the same way and were simply abandoned after use.

Charcoal taphonomy is a key factor to consider when quantifying archaeobotanical data obtained from the experimental hearths. The charcoal (fuel) assemblage produced from this experiment showed that a significant proportion of the assemblage becomes too fragmented to be included in the quantification. Post-depositional processes can mechanically (Ascough *et al.* 2010; 2011) and chemically (Poole *et al.* 2002; Braadbaart and Poole 2008) fragment charcoal. The findings from this study suggest that microcharcoal needs to be considered, especially in Prehistoric contexts and exposed open-air sites (*e.g.* Marquer *et al.* 2012; Mentzer 2012; Mallol *et al.* 2013b). Furthermore, anthropogenic factors can also influence the survival of charcoal. Woodland management (Asouti 2003), species selection, wood condition (dead, green, drift or dry wood – Théry-Parisot *et al.* 2010; Théry-Parisot and Henry 2012) and pre-treatment of the wood (gathering, storing, bark removal) are some of the anthropogenic factors influencing charcoal assemblages. Macrocharcoal is best preserved in structured fireplaces, stone-lined hearths or pits (Ludemann 2002; 2008;

Théry-Parisot *et al.* 2010), unlike open-air simple surface hearths or wildfires which undergo post-depositional alterations resulting in taphonomic biases (position, size and quantity) in the charcoal assemblage, as observed in this experiment.

Considering the density of artefactual evidence for Mesolithic activity in North East England, the number of sites containing hearths does not reflect the size, density and concentration of hunter-gatherer populations that lived in this region. Only a limited number of well-excavated sites with a detailed chronological framework have yielded evidence for *in-situ* hearths. These sites have undergone investigation as they are easily accessible and have become naturally exposed over-time. However, the results of this study show that small-scale temporary hearths can only be identified if systematic, small-scale geophysical surveys are undertaken in between known Mesolithic sites. An appreciation of the local geomorphic systems is also required, as these hearths and their associated magnetic signatures would only survive in the archaeological record if rapidly covered over and protected by overlying sediments.

## Conclusions

Rapid low-frequency magnetic susceptibility enabled small-scale surface hearths to be determined in the field. Hearths that are repeatedly ignited produce anomalies that undergo little change during a short period of exposure. In order to determine the full extent of a small-scale Mesolithic campsite based on initial field observations and flint/artefact scatters, this technique enables the visible evidence to be differentiated and enable a classification of sites (*i.e.* flint scatter, campsite, semi-permanent dwellings) in the field.

High-frequency magnetic susceptibility measured through each hearth section revealed obvious enhancement of 2 $\mu m^3$ $kg^{-1}$ after each burning event; however, only the top 3 cm of the underlying sediment was altered. Open-air prehistoric sites are often heavily bioturbated, and the survival of a thin layer of magnetically enhanced sediment is unlikely. Long-term experiments need to be conducted to determine how long these deposits are able to survive for.

The volume of the charcoal assemblage does not reflect the intensity of hearth use, as hearth debris left behind by the previous event becomes reignited when re-fired. Diameter of fuel pre- and post-burning shows that fuel wood procurement and selection strategies can be indicated from archaeological remains and that short-term taphonomic processes can cause fragmentation of surface charcoal.

The application of magnetic susceptibility combined with archaeobotanical remains should be used routinely in the field to detect the presence of hearths to further our understanding of Mesolithic settlement patterns and landscape utilisation in the region. In this research, the application of simple low-frequency and mass-specific/frequency-dependent susceptibility signatures enabled subtle differences between burning cycles and intensity of hearth use to be identified. Further research into the application of other magnetic parameters in the study of sediments and soils associated with Mesolithic sites will enable a detailed understand of the fuel types and sedimentary environments to be determined.

## Acknowledgements

The authors would like to thank Mike Hughes (Head Gardener, Botanic Garden of Durham University) for his assistance in the sourcing and cutting of the wood and for allowing this experiment to take place within the grounds of the Botanic Garden. Thanks to Duncan Hale, Durham University Archaeological Services, for his help and support with Geoplot software.

## Bibliography

Albert, R.S. and Cabanes, D. (2007) Fire in Prehistory: An experimental approach to combustion processes and phytolith remains. *Israel Journal of Earth Sciences* 56, 175–189.

Aldeias, V., Goldberg, P., Sandgathe, D., Berna, F., Dibble, H.L., McPherron, S.P., Turq, A. and Rezek, Z. (2012) Evidence for Neanderthal Use of Fire at Roc de Marsal (France). *Journal of Archaeological Science* 39, 2414–2423.

Ascough, P.L., Bird, M.I., Francis, S.M. and Lebl, T. (2011) Alkali Extraction of Archaeological and Geological Charcoal: Evidence for diagenetic degradation and formation of humic acids. *Journal of Archaeological Science* 38, 69–78.

Ascough, P.L., Bird, M.I., Scott, A.E., Collinson, M.E., Cohen-Ofri, I., Snape, C.E. and le Manquais, K. (2010) Charcoal Reflectance Measurements: Implications for structural characterization and assessment of diagenetic alteration. *Journal of Archaeological Science* 37, 1590–1599.

Asouti, E. (2003) Woodland Vegetation and Fuel Exploitation at the Prehistoric Campsite of Pınarbaşı, South-Central Anatolia, Turkey: The evidence from the wood charcoal macro-remains. *Journal of Archaeological Science* 30, 1185–1201.

Backhouse, P.N. and Johnson, E. (2007) Where Were the Hearths? An experimental investigation of the archaeological signature of prehistoric fire technology in the alluvial gravels of the Southern Plains. *Journal of Archaeological Science* 34, 1367–1378.

Backhouse, P.N., Johnson, E., Brackenreed-Johnston, A. and Buchanan, B. (2005) Experimental Hearths and the Thermal Alteration of Caliche on the Southern High Plains. *Geoarchaeology* 20, 695–716.

Balaam, N.D., Bell, M.G., David, A.E.U., Levitan, D.B., Macphail, R.I., Robinson, M. and Scaife, R.G. (1987) Prehistoric and Romano-British Sites at Westwards Ho!, Devon: Archaeological and palaeoenvironmental surveys 1983 and 1984. In: N.D. Balaam, B. Levitan and V. Straker (eds) *Studies in Palaeoeconomy and Environment in Southwest England*, pp. 163–264. British Archaeological Reports, British Series 181. Oxford: Archaeopress.

Barfield, L.H. (1991) French Research on Prehistoric Hearths: A review of conference proceedings. In: M.A. Hodder and L.H. Barfield (eds) *Burnt Mounds Hot Stone Technology*, pp. 109–111. Sandwell: Sandwell Metropolitan Borough Council.

Bellomo, R.V. (1993) A Methodological Approach for Identifying Archaeological Evidence of Fire Resulting from Human Activities. *Journal of Archaeological Science* 20, 525–553.

Bennett, K.D., Simonson, W.D. and Peglar, S.M. (1990) Fire and Man in Post-Glacial Woodlands. *Journal of Archaeological Science* 17, 635–642.

Berna, F. and Goldberg, P. (2007) Assessing Palaeolithic Pyrotechnology and Associated Hominin Behaviour in Israel. *Israel Journal of Earth Sciences* 56, 107–121.

Binford, L.R. (1980) Willow Smoke and Dogs' Tails: Hunter-gatherer settlement system and archaeological site formation. *American Antiquity* 45, 4–20.

Bishop, R.R., Church, M.J. and Rowley-Conwy, P.A. (2015) Firewood, Food and Niche Construction: The potential role of Mesolithic hunter-gatherers in actively structuring Scotland's woodlands. *Quaternary Science Reviews* 108, 51–75.

Blackford, J.J. (2000) Charcoal Fragments in Surface Samples Following a Fire and the Implications for Interpretation of Subfossil Charcoal Data. *Palaeogeography Palaeoclimatology Palaeoecology* 164, 33–42.

Boardman, S.J. (1995) Charcoal and Charred Macrofossils. In: K. Branigan and P. Foster (eds) *Barra: Archaeological research on Ben Tangaval*, pp. 149–157. Sheffield: Sheffield Academic Press.

Boardman, S.J. and Jones, G.E.M. (1990) Experiments on the Effects of Charring on Cereal Plant Components. *Journal of Archaeological Science* 17, 1–11.

Boomer, I., Waddington, C., Stevenson, C. and Hamilton, T.D. (2007) Holocene Coastal Change and Geoarchaeology at Howick, Northumberland, UK. *The Holocene* 17, 89–104.

Braadbaart, F. and Poole, I. (2008) Morphological, Chemical and Physical Changes During Charcoalification of Wood and its Relevance to Archaeological Contexts. *Journal of Archaeological Science* 35, 2434–2445.

Braadbaart F., Poole I. and van Brussel, A.A.N. (2009) Preservation Potential of Charcoal in Alkaline Environments: An experimental approach and implications for the archaeological record. *Journal of Archaeological Science* 36, 1672–1679.

Buckley, F. (1922) A Pygmy Industry on the Northumberland Coast. *Antiquaries Journal* 11, 376.

Bush, M.B. (1988) Early Mesolithic Disturbance: A force on the landscape. *Journal of Archaeological Science* 15, 452–462.

Cabanes, D., Mallol, C., Expósito, I. and Baena, J. (2010) Phytolith Evidence for Hearths and Beds in the Late Mousterian Occupations of Esquilleu Cave (Cantabria, Spain). *Journal of Archaeological Science* 37, 2947–2957.

Canti, M.G. and Linford, N. (2000) The Effects of Fire on Archaeological Soils and Sediments: Temperature and colour relationships. *Proceedings of the Prehistoric Society* 66, 385–395.

Church, M.J., Peters, C. and Batt, C.M. (2007) Sourcing Fire Ash on Archaeological Sites in the Western and Northern Isles of Scotland, Using Mineral Magnetism. *Geoarchaeology* 22, 747–774.

Church, M.J. and Peters, C. (2004) Application of Mineral Magnetism in Atlantic Scotland Archaeology 2: Magnetic susceptibility and archaeobotanical taphonomy in West Lewis, Scotland. In: R.A. Housley and G.M. Coles (eds) *Atlantic Connections and Adaptations: Economies, Environments and Subsistence in Lands Bordering the North Atlantic*, pp. 99–115. Oxford: Oxbow Books.

Clack, P.G. and Gosling, P.F. (1976) *Archaeology in the North: Report of the Northern Archaeological Survey*. Durham: University of Durham.

Crowther, J. (2003) Potential Magnetic Susceptibility and Fractional Conversion Studies of Archaeological Soils and Sediments. *Archaeometry* 45, 685–701.

Dearing, J.A. (1994) *Environmental Magnetic Susceptibility: Using the Bartington MS2 system*. Kenilworth: Chi Publishing.

Dearing, J.A., Hay, K.L., Baban, S.M.J., Huddleston, A.S., Wellington, E.M.H. and Loveland, P.J. (1996) Magnetic Susceptibility of Soil: An evaluation of conflicting theories using a national data set. *Geophysical Journal International* 127, 728–734.

Dockrill S.J. and Simpson, I. (1994) The Identification of Prehistoric Anthropogenic Soils in the Northern Isles Using an Integrated Sampling Methodology. *Archaeological Prospection* 1, 75–92.

Edwards, K.J. (1990) Fire and the Scottish Mesolithic: Evidence from microscopic charcoal. In: P.M. Vermeersch and P. van Peer (eds) *Contributions to the Mesolithic in Europe*, pp. 71–79. Leuven: Leuven University Press.

Edwards, K.J. (1998) Detection of Human Impact on the Natural Environment: Palynological views. In: J. Bayley (ed.) *Science in Archaeology: An agenda for the future*, pp. 69–88. London: English Heritage.

Gardiner, P. (2007) Mesolithic Activity at Hawcombe Head, Somerset: An interim report on the 2002-3 excavations. In: C. Waddington and K. Pedersen (eds) *Mesolithic Studies in the North Sea Basin and Beyond*, pp. 81–95. Oxford: Oxbow Books.

Goldberg, P., Dibble, H., Berna, F., Sandgathe, D., McPherron, S.J.P. and Turq, A. (2012) New Evidence on Neanderthal Use of Fire: Examples from Roc de Marsal and Pech de l'Azé IV. *Quaternary International* 247, 325–340.

Gooder, J. (2007) Excavation of a Mesolithic House at East Barns, East Lothian, Scotland: An interim view. In: C. Waddington and K. Pedersen (eds) *Mesolithic Studies in the North Sea Basin and Beyond: Proceedings of a conference held at Newcastle in 2003*, pp. 49–59. Oxford: Oxbow Books.

Gose, W.A. (2000) Palaeomagnetic Studies of Burned Rocks. *Journal of Archaeological Science* 27, 409–421.

Gregory, R.A., Murphy, E.M., Church, M.J., Edwards, K.J., Guttmann, E.B. and Simpson, D.D.A. (2005) Archaeological Evidence for the First Mesolithic Occupation of the Western Isles of Scotland. *The Holocene* 15, 944–950.

Harbord, N.H. (1996) A North Yorkshire Moors Mesolithic Marginal Site on Highcliff Nab, Guisborough. *Durham Archaeological Journal* 12, 17–26.

Haselgrove, C.C. and Healey, E. (1992) The Prehistory of the Tyne-Tees Lowlands: Some recent flint finds. *Durham Archaeological Journal* 8, 1–24.

Herries, A.I. and Fisher, E.C. (2010) Multidimensional GIS Modelling of Magnetic Mineralogy as a Proxy for Fire Use and Spatial Patterning: Evidence from the Middle Stone Age bearing sea cave of Pinnacle Point 13B (Western Cape, South Africa). *Journal of Human Evolution* 59, 306–320.

Huisman, D.J., Braadbaart, F., van Wijk, I.M. and van Os, B.J.H. (2012) Ashes to Ashes, Charcoal to Dust: Micromorphological evidence for ash induced disintegration of charcoal in Early Neolithic (LBK) soil features in Elsloo (The Netherlands). *Journal of Archaeological Science* 39, 994–1004.

Huntley, B. and Birks, H.J.B. (1983) *An Atlas of Past and Present Pollen Maps of Europe 0–13000 Years Ago*. Cambridge: Cambridge University Press.

Jacobi, R.M. (1978) Northern England in the Eighth Millennium BC: An essay. In: P. Mellars (ed.) *The Early Post-Glacial Settlement of Northern Europe*, pp. 295–332. London: Duckworth.

Keeley, L.H. (1988) Hunter-Gatherer Economic Complexity and 'Population Pressure': A cross-cultural analysis. *Journal of Anthropological Archaeology* 7, 373–411.

Kelly, R. (1983) Hunter-Gatherer Mobility Strategies. *Journal of Anthropological Research* 39, 277–306.

Lancelotti, C. and Madella, M. (2012) The Invisible Product: Developing markers for identifying dung in archaeological contexts. *Journal of Archaeological Science* 39, 953–963.

Le Borgne, E. (1960) Influence du feu sur les proprietes magnetique du sol et sur celles du schiste et du granite. *Annals of Geophysics* 16, 159–195.

Ludemann, T. (2002) Anthracology and Forest Sites – the contribution of charcoal analysis to our knowledge of natural forest vegetation in south-west Germany. In: S. Thiébault (ed.) *Charcoal Analysis. Methodological Approaches, Palaeoecological Results and Wood Uses*, pp. 209–217. British Archaeological Reports, vol. 1063. Oxford: Archaeopress.

Ludemann, T. (2006) Anthracological Analysis of Recent Charcoal-Burning in the Black Forest. Southwest Germany. In: A. Dufraisse (ed.) *Charcoal Analysis: New analytical tools and methods for archaeology*, pp. 61–70. British Archaeological Reports, vol. 1483. Oxford: Archaeopress.

Ludemann, T. (2008) Experimental Charcoal Burning with Special Regard to Anthracological Wood Diameter Analysis. In: G. Fiorentino and D. Magri (eds) *Charcoals from the Past: Cultural and palaeoenvironmental implications*, pp. 147–158. British Archaeological Reports, vol. 1807. Oxford: Archaeopress.

Maki, D. (2005) Lightning Strikes and Prehistoric Ovens: Determining the source of magnetic anomalies using techniques of environmental magnetism. *Geoarchaeology* 20, 449–459.

Mallol, C., Marlowe, F., Porter, C., Wood, B. and Bar-Yosef, O. (2007) Earth, Wind and Fire: Ethnoarchaeological signals of Hadza fires. *Journal of Archaeological Science* 34, 2035-2052.

Mallol, C., Hernández, C.M., Cabanes, D., Sistiaga, A., Machado, J., Rodríguez, A., Pérez, L. and Galván, B. (2013a) The Black Layer of Middle Palaeolithic Combustion Structures. Interpretation and archaeostratigraphic implications. *Journal of Archaeological Science* 40, 2515-2537.

Mallol, C., Hernández, C.M., Cabanes, D., Machado, J., Sistiaga, A., Pérez, L. and Galván, B. (2013b) Human Actions Performed on Simple Combustion Structures: An experimental approach to the study of Middle Palaeolithic fire. *Quaternary International* 315, 3-15.

Manzi, L. and Spikins, P.A. (2008) El fuego en las altas latitudes: Los Selk'nam de Tierra del Fuego como referente etnográfico para el Mesolítico europeo. *Complutum* 19, 79-96.

Marquer, V.L., Otto, T., Valladas, H., Haesaerts, P., Messager, E., Nuzhnyi, D. and Péan, S. (2012) Charcoal Scarcity in Epigravettian Settlements with Mammoth Bone Dwellings: The taphonomic evidence from Mezhyrich (Ukraine). *Journal of Archaeological Science* 39, 109-120.

Matthews, W. (2005) Micromorphological and Microstratigraphic Traces of Uses and Concepts of Space. In: I. Hodder (ed.) *Inhabiting Çatalhöyük: Reports from the 1995-1999 seasons*, pp. 355-399. London: McDonald Institute for Archaeological Research/BIAA.

McClean, R. and Kean, W. (1993) Contributions of Wood Ash Magnetism to Archaeomagnetic Properties of Fire Pits and Hearths. *Earth and Planetary Science Letters* 119, 387-394.

Mellars, P. and Dark, P. (1988) *Star Carr in Context*. Cambridge: McDonald Institute for Archaeological Research.

Mentzer, S.M. (2014) Microarchaeological Approaches to the Identification and Interpretation of Combustion Features in Prehistoric Archaeological Sites. *Journal of Archaeological Method and Theory* 21, 616-668.

Mithen, S., Finlay, N., Carruthers, W., Carter, S. and Ashmore, P. (2001) Plant Use in the Mesolithic: Evidence from Staosnaig, Isle of Colonsay, Scotland. *Journal of Archaeological Science* 28, 223-234.

Peters, C., Church, M.J. and Coles, G. (2000) Mineral Magnetism and Archaeology at Galson on the Isle of Lewis, Scotland. *Physics and Chemistry of the Earth* 25, 455-460.

Peters, C., Church, M.J. and Mitchell, C. (2001) Investigation of Domestic Fuel Sources on Lewis Using Mineral Magnetism. *Archaeological Prospection* 8, 227-237.

Peters C. and Thompson R. (1999) Super Magnetic Enhancement, Superparamagnetism and Archaeological Soils. *Geoarchaeology* 14, 401-413.

Peters, C., Thompson, R., Harrison, A. and Church, M. J. (2002) Low Temperature Magnetic Characterisation of Fire Ash Residues. *Physics and Chemistry of the Earth* 27, 1355-1361.

Poole, I., Braadbaart, F., Boon, J.J. and van Bergen, P.P.F. (2002) Stable Carbon Isotope Changes During Artificial Charring of Propagules. *Organic Geochemistry* 33, 1675-1681.

Powell, A.J., Wheeler, J. and Batt, C.M. (2012) Identifying Archaeological Wood Stack Charcoal Production Sites Using Geophysical Prospection: Magnetic characteristics from a modern wood stack charcoal burn site. *Journal of Archaeological Science* 39, 1197-1204.

Radley, J., Switsur, V.R. and Tallis, J.H. (1974) The Excavation of Three 'Narrow Blade' Mesolithic Sites in the Southern Pennines, England. *Proceedings of the Prehistoric Society* 40, 1-19.

Raison, R.J. (1979) Modification of the Soil Environment by Vegetation Fires, with Particular Reference to Nitrogen Transformation: A review. *Plant and Soil* 51, 73-108.

Raistrick, A. (1933) The Distribution of Mesolithic Sites in the North of England. *Yorkshire Archaeological Journal* 31, 141-152.

Raistrick, A., Coupland, F. and Coupland, G. (1936) A Mesolithic Site on the South-East Durham Coast. *Transactions of the Northern Naturalist Union* 1, 207-216.

Roebroeks, W. and Villa, P. (2011) On the Earliest Evidence for Habitual Use of Fire in Europe. *Proceedings of the National Academy of Sciences* 108, 5209-5214.

Rowley-Conwy, P. (2001) Time, Change and the Archaeology of Hunter-Gatherers: How original is the 'Original Affluent Society'? In: C. Panter-Brick, R.H. Layton and P. Rowley-Conwy (eds) *Hunter-Gatherers: An interdisciplinary perspective*, pp. 39–72. Cambridge: Cambridge University Press.

Schiegl, S., Goldberg, P., Pfretzschner, H.-U. and Conard, N.J. (2003) Palaeolithic Burnt Bone Horizons from the Swabian Jura: Distinguishing between *in situ* fireplaces and dumping areas. *Geoarchaeology* 18, 541–565.

Schiffer, M.B. (1972) Archaeological Context and Systemic Context. *American Antiquity* 37, 156–165.

Sergant, J., Crombe, P. and Perdaen, Y. (2005) The 'Invisible' Hearths: A contribution to the discernment of Mesolithic non-structured surface hearths. *Journal of Archaeological Science* 33, 999–1007.

Shennan, I., Lambreck, K., Flather, R., Horton, B., McArthur, J., Innes, J., Lloyd, J., Rutherford, M. and Wingfield, R. (2000) Modelling Western North Sea Palaeogeographies and Tidal Changes during the Holocene. In: I. Shennan, and J.E. Andrews (eds) *Holocene Land-Ocean Interactions and Environmental Change around the North Sea*, pp. 299–319. London: Geological Society.

Simmons, I.G. (1996) *The Environmental Impact of Later Mesolithic Cultures*. Edinburgh: Edinburgh University Press.

Simmons, I.G., Atherden, M.A., Cloutman, E.W., Cundill, P.R., Innes, J.B. and Jones, R.L. (1993) Prehistoric Environments. In: D.A. Spratt (ed.) *Prehistoric and Roman Archaeology of North East Yorkshire*, pp. 15–50. Council for British Archaeology Research Report 87. London: CBA.

Simmons, I.G. and Innes, J.G. (1987) Mid-Holocene Adaptations and Later Mesolithic Forest Disturbance in Northern England. *Journal of Archaeological Science* 14, 385–394.

Simmons, I.G. and Innes, J.G. (1996) Prehistoric Charcoal in Peat Profiles at North Gill, North Yorkshire Moors, England. *Journal of Archaeological Science* 23, 193–197.

Spikins, P.A., Conneller, C.J., Ayestaran, H. and Scaife, B. (2002) GIS Based Interpolation Applied to Distinguishing Occupation Phases of Hunter-Gatherer Sites. *Journal of Archaeological Science* 29, 1235–1245.

Théry-Parisot, I. (2002) Fuel Management (Bone and Wood) During the Lower Aurignacian in the Pataud Rock Shelter (Lower Palaeolithic, Les Eyzies de Tayac, Dordogne, France): Contribution of experimentation. *Journal of Archaeological Science* 29, 1415–1421.

Théry-Parisot, I., Chabal, L. and Chrzavzez, J. (2010) Anthracology and Taphonomy, from Wood Gathering to Charcoal Analysis. A review of the taphonomic processes modifying charcoal assemblages in archaeological contexts. *Palaeogeography, Palaeoclimatology, Palaeoecology* 291, 142–153.

Théry-Parisot, I. and Henry, A. (2012) Seasoned or Green? Radial cracks analysis as a method for identifying the use of green wood as fuel in archaeological charcoal. *Journal of Archaeological Science* 39, 381–388.

Trechmann, C.T. (1905) Neolithic Remains on the Durham Coast. *The Naturalist* 587, 361–363.

Van der Veen, M. and Feiller, N. (1982) Sampling Seeds. *Journal of Archaeological Science* 9, 287–98.

Villa, P., Bon, F. and Castel, J.B. (2002) Fuel, Fire and Fireplaces in the Palaeolithic of Western Europe. *The Review of Archaeology* 23, 33–42.

Waddington, C. (2007) Rethinking Mesolithic Settlement and a Case Study from Howick. In: C. Waddington and K. Pedersen (eds) *Mesolithic Studies in the North Sea Basin and Beyond*, pp. 101–113. Oxford: Oxbow Books.

Waddington, C. and Pedersen, K. (eds) (2007) *Mesolithic Studies in the North Sea Basin and Beyond*. Oxford: Oxbow Books.

Waughman, M. (2006) North East Yorkshire Mesolithic: Phase 1 report. Unpublished Tees Archaeology Report TA/06/11 for English Heritage.

Weiss, E., Kislev, E.M., Simchoni, O., Nadel, D. and Tschaune, H. (2008) Plant-Food Preparation Area on an Upper Palaeolithic Brush Hut Floor at Ohalo II, Israel. *Journal of Archaeological Science* 35, 2400–2414.

Weyman, J. (1984) The Mesolithic in North-East England. In: R. Miket and C.B. Burgess (eds) *Between and Beyond the Walls: Essays on the prehistory and history of northern Britain in honour of George Jobey*, pp. 38–73. Edinburgh: John Donald.

Woodman, P.C. (1985) *Excavations at Mount Sandel 1973-77, County Londonderry*. Belfast, Northern Ireland, Archaeological Monographs Number 2, HMSO.

Young, R. (2007) 'I must go down to the sea again …' A review of early research on the 'coastal' Mesolithic of North-East England. In: C. Waddington and K. Pedersen (eds) *Mesolithic Studies in the North Sea Basin and Beyond*, pp. 16–24. Oxford: Oxbow Books.

# Chapter 5

# In the fringes, at the twilight: Encountering deer in the British Mesolithic

*Ben Elliott*

**Abstract**

*The relationship between people and deer has been a persistent theme within British Mesolithic Studies since the early twentieth century, and has been approached from a range of economic, ontological, cultural and chronological perspectives. Yet our understanding of the ways in which deer and people interacted has been undermined by a failure to recognise the plasticity of deer behaviour in different environments, and the variability of social contexts in which they might be encountered. This paper will seek to address this by considering the current body of knowledge concerning the ecology and behaviour of* Cervus elaphus *(Red deer),* Capreolus capreolus *(Roe deer) and* Alces alces *(Elk), and model the actions of these species within a range of different British Mesolithic environments. In doing so, it will create a platform for new discussions of the relationship between people and deer, in a way that affords the actions of the animals themselves an unprecedented level of agency.*

## Introduction

Historically, cervids have played a central role in the study of the British Mesolithic (Finlay 2000; Elliott 2015). Early analyses of fauna recovered from cave sequences often relied on the distinction between *Rangifer tarandus* (Reindeer) and *Cervus elaphus* (Red deer) as a key biostratigraphic marker for the transition from the Pleistocene to the Holocene (Burkitt 1926), and the role of red deer antler within the technological repertoires of Britain's Mesolithic inhabitants has also been noted from an early stage in the conceptualisation of the period (Munro 1908: Bishop 1914; Burkitt 1926; Clark 1932). The initial excavation of Star Carr (Clark 1954) and the subsequent use of this assemblage to pursue a bio-economic approach to the study of the British Mesolithic (Clark 1972) placed further emphasis on the role of red deer within the dietary and material economies of Britain's Mesolithic inhabitants. Since then, the exploitation of deer – and in particular red deer – have become central to interpretations of transhumance mobility and settlement patterns, variation in lithic assemblages (Mellars 1976a), macro-scale shifts in hunting technologies (Myers 1987), intentional burning of forested areas (Mellars 1976b), the collection and storage of plant resources (Simmons and Dimbleby 1974) and the movement of people and materials across land- and seascapes (Grigson and Mellars 1987; Mithen and Finlayson 1991; Finlayson 1995). More recently, the social and ritual significance of red deer within Mesolithic societies has been highlighted, and the structured deposition of red deer remains at Star Carr has been suggested (Bevan 2003; Chatterton 2003; Conneller 2004).

## Problems with the 'special relationship'

The dominance of red deer within the British Mesolithic has been critiqued by Finlay (2000), who notes the heavily gendered nature of these hunting-based narratives, and the apparent attention that this 'special relationship' receives. The dominance of the 'boys and arrows' imagery within Mesolithic literature is identified as the process responsible for the marginalisation of women and children within these discourses. Finlay's work raises a key issue for British Mesolithic studies, which needs addressing if the field is to progress. Whilst there is no inherent gender bias in studying the relationship between people and red deer, the material evidence that archaeologists refer to when analysing this relationship inevitably leads to a focus on hunting activities. The recovery of red deer skeletal remains, often showing signs of hunting traumas and butchery, is direct evidence for the practice of hunting. Simultaneously, the use of un-shed antler to produce material culture also infers the hunting of deer, and embeds this firmly within *chaîne opératoire* narratives of antler technology.

The problem can be tackled from a number of angles. Bevan (2003) stresses the importance of ethnographic accounts which demonstrate the role of women and children in hunting activities, thus implicitly raising the profile of women at Star Carr, and more generally within these established narratives of human and deer interaction. Alternatively, Cobb (2005) highlights the ways in which contemporary Western attitudes towards sexuality underpin all concepts of gender roles in our narratives of the British Mesolithic – and thus challenges modern assumptions concerning women and the hunting.

Beyond these gender-biases, previous approaches to people and deer in the British Mesolithic have also been critiqued from a series of ontological perspectives. Conneller (2004; 2011) cites the work of the anthropologist Viveros de Castro (1998) on perspectivist ontologies as new ways of exploring the fragmentation and reassembly of red deer bodies at Star Carr. She uses this non-Western approach to personhood to explore how materials derived from animal remains might be used to actively define human and animal identities at the site. Overton and Hamilakis (2013) note that analyses of animal remains focused on subsistence and the exploitation of animals as economic resources are inherently anthropocentric; and are underpinned by Cartesian distinctions between culture and nature, which are unlikely to have relevance within prehistoric societies. Following these critiques, several authors (Conneller 2011; Elliott 2013; Brittain and Overton 2013; Overton and Hamilakas 2013; Overton 2016) have pursued more detailed descriptions of animal ecology and behaviour as a means to afford the actions of animals themselves a higher degree of agency within zooarchaeological and material-culture based discourses.

The current interest in animal behaviour and the gender-biases of hunting-based narratives creates an opportunity to address the relationship between people and deer from a new angle. Whilst material evidence doubtlessly demonstrates that deer were hunted at various times in the Mesolithic, little consideration has been given to the ways in which people and deer may have interacted in non-hunting contexts. The archaeological record attests that humans and cervids lived alongside each other within a series of varied environments for millennia during the Mesolithic, and it seems implausible to suggest that every encounter between these species would have resulted in hunting, killing and butchery of an animal. Through the consideration of the ecology and behaviour of red deer, roe deer and elk within Mesolithic environment types, a concerted attempt can be made to develop archaeological narratives that go beyond hunting. How often did people encounter deer when not actively hunting, and were these encounters more likely in specific environments or locations within a landscape? Does the behaviour of deer allow their presence to be determined without a direct sighting, and how does this vary seasonally and between species? This approach affords the animals themselves a substantial degree of agency and also has the potential to break free of the heavily gendered imagery of the traditional 'boys-and arrows' motifs that characterise much of the extant literature, and leave other forms of gender neglected and marginalised.

## Red deer, roe deer and elk in the British Mesolithic

The recovery of skeletal remains from a limited number of archaeological sites attests to the presence of red deer, roe deer and elk during the period. Radiocarbon dating has established that both red and roe deer were continuously present throughout the Mesolithic. The evidence for elk is more contested, with older models noting the lack of elk remains from archaeological sites that post-date the Early Mesolithic. Traditional interpretations ascribed this disappearance of elk to a combination of over-hunting, ameliorating climatic conditions, a loss of habitat and genetic isolation from mainland Europe due to the rising sea levels and the submersion of Doggerland (Clutton-Brock 1991). However, recent AMS dating of material recovered from non-archaeological contexts (Kitchener and Bonsall 1997) now suggest that elk persisted in refugia populations throughout the period – presumably in the more northern latitudes and high altitudes, which produce favourably cool environments (Yalden

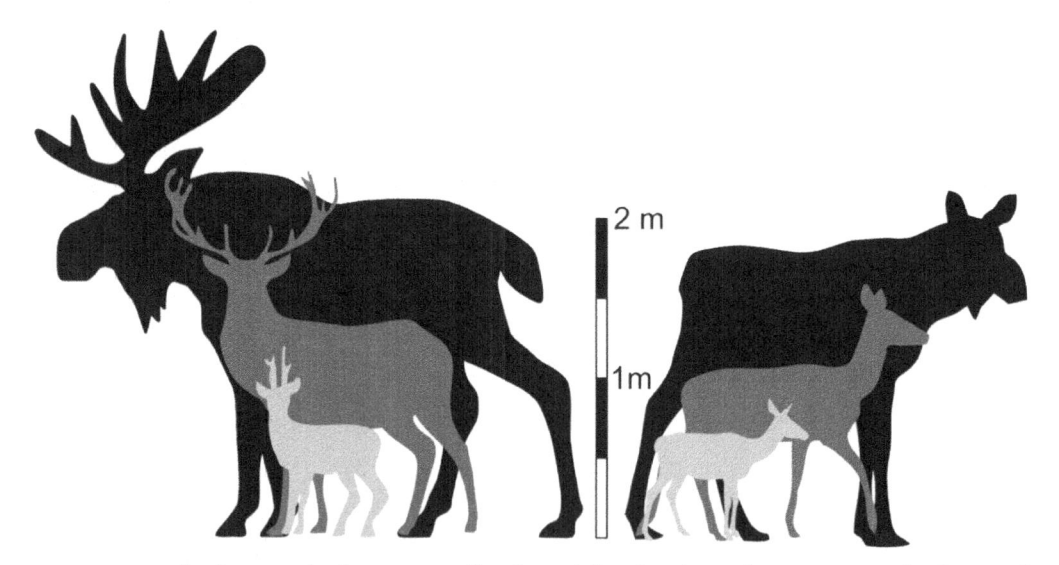

*Figure 5.1. Body shape and relative size of male and female* Alces alces, Cervus elpahus *and* Capreolus capreolus.

1999; Kitchener 2010). Coarse-scale ecological models (Maroo and Yalden 2000) suggest that, even when isolated from Europe, Britain would have been capable of supporting a population of *c.* 64,617 elk, *c.* 832,793 roe deer and *c.* 1,253,613 red deer during the Mesolithic.

The physiology of red deer varies between sexes and throughout an individual's life-cycle, but the basic body shape is shown in Figure 5.1. Modern British red deer males (stags) grow to a shoulder height of 107–137 cm, whilst females (does) are slightly shorter at 107–122 cm (The Deer Initiative 2008a). Body mass is known to vary in different contexts. In twentieth-century Britain, red deer stags are known to grow to a maximum live-weight value of around 150 kg, with equally large hinds being roughly one-third lighter (Carne 2000, 11). Roe deer are notably smaller, with a shoulder height of 60–75 cm (Carne 2000, 13), and an average live weight of 25 kg for males (bucks) and 23 kg for females (does). Roe deer physiology displays much less environmental plasticity in comparison to red deer – even animals living in controlled, optimal conditions rarely obtain a live weight of 30 kg (Geist 1998, 306). Elk are the largest member of the cervid family, reaching shoulder heights of 2–2.3 m (Whitehead 1993, 244) with an unusual physiology in relation to other species. Through the study of North American populations, mean live weights of around 530 kg have been calculated for mature adults, but individuals can obtain weights of up to 700 kg (Geist 1998, 254).

In terms of diet, red deer favour flowering plants, foliage and browse, and tend to focus feeding at a height of 1.6 m above ground, producing a characteristic pattern of damage on browsed foliage (The Deer Initiative 2008b). Gerbert and Verheyden-Tixier's (2001) review of primary studies into red deer stomach contents demonstrates a wide-ranging diet, generally dominated by four principal groups. These include grasses and sedges, Calluna (Heather) and Vaccinium (Berries), leaves of deciduous trees, and shrubs and conifers (Gebert and Verheyden-Tixier 2001, 194). Considerable variation between populations living in different environments demonstrates a substantial element of plasticity and adaptability in red deer dietary behaviour (Gebert and Verheyden-Tixier 2001, 196). Clutton-Brock and Albon (1989) observed Highland deer populations in Scotland feeding in six to ten bouts of activity, interspersed with rest and rumination periods, with total grazing time amounting to 10–12 hours per day.

Elk diet consists of highly nutritious low-toxin foliage and browse. Submerged and aquatic plants also play an important role in the diet of elk, especially during the spring and summer months, leading to a concentration of elk in wetland areas during this time of the year (Albright and Keith 1987). These foods are believed to be an important source of minerals, which is essential for the synthesis of new tissue and the re-establishment of body mass during the summer. During the winter, elk will also exploit mineral licks (Geist 1998, 226). Food scarcity in winter leads adult elk to break sizeable branches and stems in search of the living plant tissue within (Geist 1998, 237). They are also capable of rearing up on their hind legs, or pulling trees down, to access new growth in the canopy – which may have originally stood up to 6 m above ground level (Whitehead 1993, 224). Due to the toxic nature of many of the plant species available in the environments that elk inhabit, they actively favour newly growing forage that has not reached the stage of maturity required to produce toxins (Geist 1998, 226).

Elk have been described as 'concentrate feeders', in that they roam in search of pockets of food and, once located, remain in these areas until the forage resources are totally exhausted. This strategy has implications for the mobility of individual elk as they stay confined to these areas when they are exploiting them and do not 'roam' from them, but between them (Geist 1998, 225). When faced with higher quality browse resources, elk become more mobile and active in their foraging but less intensive of their exploitation of one set resource (Sæther and Reidar Andersen 1990).

Roe deer diet shares several similarities with that of elk, both being noted to switch between concentrate feeding strategies in the summer months to high-fibre foraging in the winter (Geist 1998, 302). It is also characterised by a favouring of early succession plant communities (Geist 1998, 303) and a subsequent attraction to areas affected by localised ecological or anthropogenic disruption. The smaller stature of roe deer limits the height of browse that these animals are able to exploit, and as such the feeding damage of roe deer tends to be focused around 1.2 m above ground level (The Deer Initiative 2008b).

The behaviour and physiology of cervids changes throughout the course of the year (Figure 5.2). All species of deer grow antlers, clean them of velvet at the end of the growing period and then shed them. The mating (or rutting) season also varies between deer, as do the gestation periods, calving and seasonal coat changes.

86                                     Ben Elliott

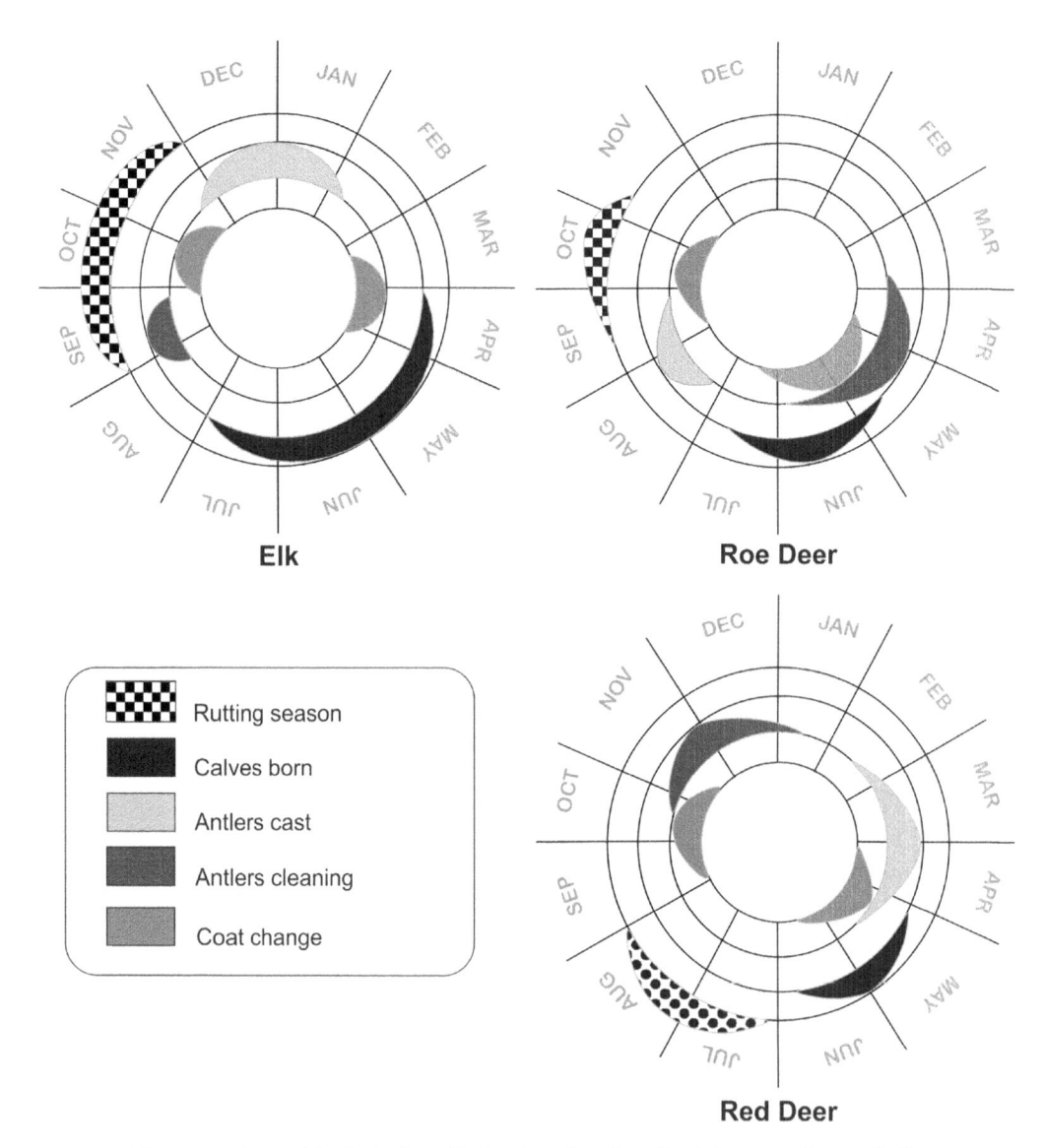

*Figure 5.2. Annual biological and behavioural cycles of red deer, roe deer and elk.*

The social structure of red deer changes on a yearly cycle, corresponding with hormone-driven reproductive behaviour. Mature males will separate themselves from females and young for the majority of the year, and during this separation matriarchal and patriarchal groups coexist amicably, moving around daily ranges with degrees of overlap. This pattern transforms during the rut, when males become aggressively territorial and compete for the right to breed with females. Competition between the males is played out through roaring, parading, trotting alongside one another and finally rushing, where stags lower their antlers and charge towards each other in a contest of strength (Clutton-Brock et al. 1982, 105–117).

Red deer behaviour also varies in accordance with environmental conditions. Animals living in open conditions and at high altitudes are known to aggregate into large herds of up to forty individuals, and migrate between upland to lowland in the autumn and spring (Clutton-Brock et al. 1982, 227–229). However, when inhabiting more forested landscapes, red deer do not form the larger groups seen in the open. In the mixed forest and agricultural landscapes of southern Sweden, Ahlen (1965) found that the modal group size for females consists of two to three mature does and one to two young, whilst stags are most commonly found to move in isolation.

Roe deer have an intricate social structure that is dictated by the delayed impregnation of does during the autumn and early winter. One key factor of roe deer social structure is the establishment of both male and female territories in the spring, as a precursor to the summer rut (Geist 1998, 304). Bucks become gradually more aggressive and intolerant of other deer as their antlers develop during the winter (Geist 1998, 313). By spring they actively begin to compete for territories that offer good feeding grounds and cover from predators (Carne 2000, 14). These areas are established through visual markings and scenting. During the establishment of these territories, young, weak or older males are often displaced and forced to exploit less favourable habitats for the remainder of the rut. These disorientated and exposed individuals subsequently become vulnerable to predation (Geist 1998, 311).

Following the rut, the enforcement of territories loosens somewhat, and deer revert to a solitary lifestyle in forested areas and form herds in open environments (Geist 1998, 305). Occasionally, however, there is a resumption of rutting behaviour by some males during October in the 'false rut' – thought to be linked to hormonal changes. Following the casting of antlers, bucks become much more passive and coexist more peacefully and in closer proximity to other bucks and does. This coexistence is interrupted by the birth of fawns during May/June and the re-establishment of territorial behaviour on the part of the does.

Elk are, for the most part, solitary foragers that can roam up to 130 km from their place of birth and still return (Geist 1998, 225). They form herds only in very snowy conditions and on open ground (Geist 1998, 227). Individuals establish home ranges between 200–400 hectares in size, although considerable overlap between these ranges has been observed (Albright and Keith 1987). Studies of elk populations in Newfoundland have concluded that elk prefer to exploit different areas of the home range seasonally, with high-fibre twigs and bark being sought in more densely forested areas during winter and aquatic resources being sought in the summer. They also select specific roaming routes to coincide with rough terrain as a deterrent for would-be predators, and rarely cross large areas of open ground (Geist 1998, 225). At the beginning of the rut, yearling elk are driven away from their mothers and establish their own home ranges in adjacent territories (Geist 1998, 227).

During the rut, males (bulls) compete for breeding rights through dominance displays:

> ... the bull approaches slowly, tips its antlers left and right, and calls in rhythm with its steps. The hair on the back of the neck, croup and withers is raised a little; the ears slightly lowered. The approach is not direct, but at a tangential angle. Eye aversions by both bulls at close ranges appear to 'display' the antlers in profile. A bull may also tip its antlers in rhythm with its steps when walking after a female. The dominance display may be interrupted by horning of bushes by one or both partners. (Geist 1998, 239)

Following the rut, bulls become less aggressive and return to their usual movements through the home range. Although they do not live in close groups, neighbouring elk will signal to each other through roaring when a threat is perceived. This noise is notably different to the calls of other deer, and sounds much more like that of a large carnivorous mammal than an ungulate (Geist 1998, 237). Female elk (cows) become territorial immediately before birth, selecting areas of rich forage such as creek mouths with abundant aquatic plants as nursery ranges. Other elk will be driven away from these areas (Geist 1998, 228). Following birth, cows can become highly aggressive if disturbed – much more so than the bulls during the rut (Geist 1998, 224) – and will attack any perceived threats by flailing with the front legs, kicking with the hind legs and goring with antlers (in the case of bulls) (Geist 1998, 235).

## Three British classics

Since the pioneering work of Clark, Godwin and Walker in the 1940s, British Mesolithic Studies have been characterised by the consistent integration of archaeology and palaeo-environmental research. This tradition has provided evidence for a rich and dynamic series of environment types that were present across Britain during the period, and which responded to changes in climate, the influx and disappearance of new floral and faunal species, the ongoing development of interstadial soil formation and human action. However, relating archaeological material directly to specific environment types has proven notoriously difficult. Factors such as the differential rates of preservation for different types of environmental evidence, sampling biases and the multi-scalar temporal ranges that many palaeo-environmental techniques work at (Spikins 1999) make it difficult to contextualise specific episodes of human activity to any one of the environmental types evidenced within the regional record. Due to these difficulties, this paper will use three case study types, selected based on their prominence within the literature concerning the British Mesolithic, to consider the character of non-hunting encounters between people and deer.

### *Birch-pine 'Pre-Boreal' environments*

Due to the prominence of Star Carr within the Mesolithic cannon, much academic attention has previously focused on the exploitation of birch-based environments of the pre-boreal period (Walker and Godwin 1954). These are often viewed as transition communities that were able to colonize the rapidly warming areas of Britain during the initial stages of the Holocene. They are characterised by scrub vegetation, featuring spaced and open areas of *Juniperus* (juniper), *Betula* (birch) and *Salix* (willow) trees and underlying grasses (Walker *et al.* 2003). In southern Britain, high pine pollen values show a balanced pine/birch woodland, whilst more sporadic pine values in samples from northern England and Scotland have been interpreted as more birch-dominated areas with occasional stands of pine. High *Corylus* (hazel) pollen values in samples from northern England and Scotland indicate that hazel also formed a significant component of the initially expanding birch-pine forest communities in the higher latitudes of northern England and Scotland (Godwin 1975, 457). Low background pollen levels of *Quercus* (oak) and *Ulmus* (elm) are present across Britain, indicating their minor role in the composition of these birch-pine forests. A similar pattern is noted for *Alnus* (alder), although with higher levels in west-central Scotland, indicating a more prominent role in forest composition within this localised area (Godwin 1975, 459).

Within these birch-pine woodland environments, elk would enjoy a variety of food resource, and an abundance of understory cover over which to evade predators. Both birch and pine are known to play a prominent role in the diet of elk, particularly during the winter (Sæther and Andersen 1990), and so elk can be expected to have inhabited these environments, albeit at the relatively low population densities that are observed in elk today. As a consequence, the chances of a direct encounter between people and elk may have been quite low within birch-pine woodlands. Yet the tracks and markings that elk create may have advertised their presence to the people who also moved through these environments, leading to an indirect form of people/elk encounter. The distinctively large tracks, wallows, damage to high-level vegetation and characteristic grunts and roars of the species would have meant that, even at low densities, elk would have advertised their presence within these birch-pine landscapes. Seasonal variations in elk behaviour, such as an increase in wallowing and roaring during the autumn rut, the rubbing of velvet from newly grown antlers in late summer, the shedding of elk antler in mid-winter and the appearance of elk calf prints during mid-spring to mid-summer time would have varied the nature of these tracks throughout the year. The nature of direct encounters may also have varied, with increased levels of aggression from bulls in the autumn and cows in mid-spring to mid-summer in correspondence to the rut and calving seasons respectively.

Red deer would have also found open birch-pine woodland conditions favourable. In these conditions dispersed and small social units would have enjoyed cover from the elements and an abundance of diverse food resources. As such, large body sizes may have been obtained by red deer living in these conditions. The potential abundance of these large ungulates within the birch-pine woodland of Mesolithic Britain may have led to more frequent direct encounters with people. The nature of these encounters may have changed throughout the year, with males becoming increasingly aggressive during the rut, whilst females become particularly flighty and elusive during the initial stages of pregnancy in early winter. As well as direct, face-to-face encounters between people and red deer, the distinctive tracks and markings created by the activities of red deer may also have allowed people to observe their presence within birch-pine woodland through indirect encounters. Tracks and mid-level browse damage to flora, as well as the calls of the animals themselves, would have alerted people to the presence of red deer. Similarly to that of elk, the nature of these indirect human/red deer encounters would have varied seasonally. The roaring and marking of trees associated with the rut would be confined to autumn, the appearance of removed velvet to late summer, whilst doe tracks would vary during pregnancy and fawn tracks would have appeared after the early summer. Shed red deer antler would also have been accessible in late winter/early spring.

Roe deer living within the birch-pine woodland would have benefited from the open nature of the forest composition, and consequent abundance of shrubs and understory browse. The territorial behaviour of roe deer would lead to the regular dispersal of individuals within these types of environments, although their reclusive nature may have resulted in a low frequency of direct encounters with people. However, the behaviour of these animals would create a distinctive suite of tracks and markings that would have alerted humans to their presence. Low-level browse damaged vegetation and tracks would have been visible throughout the year, but the demarcation of territories by tree marking, distinctive buck barking and the creation of scenting scrapes in the early summer would have also been visible to those inhabiting the birch-pine woodland areas during the Mesolithic on a seasonal basis. The behavioural changes of the rut would also result in the creation of the iconic chase tracks around certain trees and shrubs, whilst this late summer period would also be marked by an increase in the calling of does and bucks and fights between competing bucks. Shed roe deer antler would have been accessible in late autumn/early winter.

## High altitude peat moors

Palaeo environmentalists have long noted the advent of peat formation in the Early Holocene in high altitude areas of Britain (Simmons 1996; 2001, 39), with the steadily ameliorating climate mooted as a trigger for peat-forming conditions to occur in areas where water collects. It has been suggested that further intervention would be required for peat to form on convex slopes, and that fire may have been used to remove deciduous tree cover and increase the quantities of water present in the soil. Although the role of human agency within the occurrence of upland fires has been debated (Simmons 1996; Brown 1997), the subsequent peat deposits gave rise to specific communities of vegetation, which Simmons describes as:

> heather moors, accumulating more humus and becoming seasonally waterlogged (with underlying soild and ongoing gleying) and invaded by wet-tolerant sedges and Sphagnum, cotton-sedge mires, Sphagnum bogs, open hazel and birch scrub with a variety of wet-tolerant ground flora species and a high proportion of dead trees. (Simmons 2001, 40)

The occurrence of these open moorland environments would have had a profound influence on deer behaviour. It could be argued that these colder, high-altitude environments offered favourable conditions for refugia elk populations during the warmer lowland climes of the Atlantic climatic optimum. However, moorland environments would not offer the types of tree-based browse favoured by elk. Additionally, elk avoid travelling through open landscapes due to the lack of cover and opportunities to escape predators in adverse terrain. Consequently, it may have been less likely for people to encounter elk in these open moorland environments.

Analogies with modern populations suggest a different behavioural response from red deer. Red deer are known to inhabit heather moorland in Britain today. However, the exposed nature of moorland can lead to a reduction in the body size of individual animals (Clutton-Brock *et al.* 1982), and exploitation of open landscapes over mixed forests tends to occur as a result of a shortage of the high-quality browse, or as of a product of population pressure (Clutton-Brock *et al.* 1982). Consequently, the nature of human/red deer encounters on open moorland may have varied throughout the Mesolithic. When red deer populations existed at higher densities, individuals may have spent more time grazing on the forbes associated with the heather environments. As a consequence, these red deer may have had lower body masses than animals living in adjacent forested areas. At other times in the Mesolithic, when predation or disease drove local red deer populations down, it would have been less common to encounter these animals in a moorland context.

Modern-day roe deer populations generally avoid open moorland environments (Cornelis *et al.* 1999). This is due to a combination of factors – principally a lack of cover from predators, exposure to the elements and a general scarcity of preferential browse (de Nahlik 1987, 169). However, the occurrence of scrub and open birch woodland conditions at higher altitudes in the Mesolithic period may have allowed roe deer populations to exist throughout the year. Year-round roe deer presence may have therefore have been restricted to these specific areas of high-altitude peat moor environments. There is also the possibility that roe bucks that were unable to secure territories before the rutting season may have been driven into unfavourable peat moor areas, and thus became a seasonal presence in these areas.

## *Mixed deciduous woodland*

The environment most commonly associated with Mesolithic Britain is that of the mixed deciduous forest, or 'wildwood'. In broader prehistoric narratives, this is often portrayed as a static and stable climax community that covers the majority of the British Isles during the Mesolithic period. However, palaeo-environmental data has shown variations in the composition of these forests and in particular the dominant tree species at certain locales (Simmons 1996, 13). Oak, lime, ash and alder have all been observed to be dominant tree species within the mixed deciduous forest communities at different points in time and space during the Mesolithic (Godwin 1975, 464; Bennet 1989;

Simmons 2001). More recent approaches to reconstructing Mesolithic environments have tended to view these deciduous climax woodland as 'mosaic' forests (Brown 1997). This has been prompted by the acceptance of the limitations of pollen analysis in giving high-resolution data on the density, layout and age of trees within a forest community (Clare 1995). As an alternative, palaeo environmentalists have looked to *in situ* plant macrofossil remains recovered from submerged peat deposits at coastal locations (Clapham *et al.* 1997), and also buried below alluvial floodplain deposits (Brown and Keough 1992). These have revealed an uneven distribution of tree species within mixed deciduous woodlands, with dense stands of older trees being surrounded by areas of thinner, more open distributions of younger trees and shrubs. Small openings in the forest canopy are also noted to occur (Clare 1995).

Deer behaviour within these mosaic woodland habitats has some implications for the ways in which people may have encountered and interacted with them during the Mesolithic. These types of conditions would offer feeding opportunities and understory obstacles for elk, but their patchy distribution could lead to quite specific responses in foraging strategies and movements. Areas of more open woodland and clearings may have been avoided by elk, as they lack the obstacles required to evade predators. Instead, elk may have restricted their movements to denser areas of forest. Their preference for difficult terrain could lead to the establishment of set routes that elk followed through the Mesolithic woodland in search of food resources, resulting in a concentration of tracks and markings along these routes. The distribution of these denser areas of closed woodland may have been particularly important for cows during calving, as cover and browse are essential resources for the early, sedentary stages of the calf's life. This could lead to higher chances of human/elk encounters in such areas, and even make these types of habitats a danger to people during the fiercely territorial period of calving during the spring and early summer.

However, elk behaviour may have varied in response to openings within the forest canopy. As noted above, the growth of plant communities associated with clearings do play an important role within the diet of elk, and so these clearings may have attracted individuals into areas that they would not otherwise frequent. As such, there may have also been a higher chance of people directly encountering elk at the edges of forest clearings and in the initial stages of their re-growth, due to improved levels of visibility in these environments.

Red deer behaviour within the mixed deciduous woodland may have been similar to that expected within birch-pine or boreal woodland habitats. The preference for browsing on forbes may have resulted in both male and female red deer being attracted towards more open areas of forest and small clearings, and as such there being a higher chance of direct people/red deer encounters at these locales.

Roe deer would also have thrived in these mixed deciduous woodland habitats. The quality of territories within this habitat varied in terms of its ability to provide browse and cover, and so the level to which territoriality was displayed may have varied within the forest itself. In particular, the new growth communities associated with areas of clearings may have been particularly attractive, and as such the focus of tree marking, scent scraping and barking during the spring.

As in other habitats, the elusive nature of roe deer behaviour may have meant lower chances of direct encounters between people and roe, although their presence would have been attested through their tracks, sound and impact on browse flora. Less favourable areas of forest, with little understory cover or browse, may have been inhabited more seasonally by the displaced bucks during the late spring and summer rutting season. In these areas, the lack of cover would have potentially increased the chances of direct encounters between people and roe deer due to increased visibility within these environments.

## Conclusions

The above discussion of deer behaviour demonstrates the rich levels of detail that current research into the behaviour and ecology of modern-day cervid populations can offer archaeologists who wish to understand how people may have coexisted within environmentally varied Mesolithic landscapes. There is the potential here to generate more nuanced and balanced accounts of human and deer relations that stress the character and frequency of human/animal encounters – points of contact both direct and indirect – that help to underpin both individual and collective understandings of animals within a landscape. These three case study 'types' are by no means exhaustive, and there is further scope to model deer behaviour within a much wider range of Mesolithic environments. Whilst this style of narrative does little to directly challenge the problematic gender-biases associated with hunting in twenty-first-century Western society, by shifting the focus away from such activities they implicitly create more inclusive accounts of the relationship between people and deer. Accounts such as these highlight the significance of animals in the lives of people who were not involved in hunting for whatever reason – as well as providing a vital context for the hunting encounters that did occur.

However, there are limits to this approach. A fundamental assumption here is that animal behaviour observed today can be taken as a direct analogy for animal behaviour in the deep past. This is far from certain, and the plasticity of cervid behaviour in response to the introduction of new predators in North America highlights the complex historical and ecological factors that can govern dietary habits and patterns of movement (*e.g.* Laudré *et al.* 2001). There are also issues with the reconstruction of past environments, and the integration of archaeological data within these models in areas that lack organic preservation and *in-situ* archaeological material. As such, these accounts remain 'floating' – describing possible encounters within landscapes without being able to tie these to specific times and places with any level of accuracy or confidence. The absence of hunting in these accounts is also problematic. As outlined in the introduction, there is direct evidence for these practices within the archaeological record, and this is not referred to or discussed here.

These factors necessitate a specific role for accounts such as these within Mesolithic research. We cannot ignore the growing body of knowledge concerning animal behaviour emerging from biological sciences – and this can prove a rich source of detail for our understanding of how people and animals interacted within environmentally diverse Mesolithic landscapes. These accounts should therefore be used as a starting point for discussions of the relationship between people and animals; the underlying context within which future discussions of hunting practices can be situated, and considerations of the social interactions between people and deer can be built from. This approach cannot replace the explicit critique of contemporary attitudes towards hunting, and the implications these have more generally for archaeological narratives concerning hunter-gatherers. However, they can work alongside these critical discourses to demonstrate that interactions between people and deer were diverse, multi-faceted and driven, in part, by the actions of animals themselves.

## Bibliography

Ahlen, I. (1965) Studies on the Red Deer, *Cervus elaphus* L. *Swedish Wildlife Research* 3, 177–376.

Albright, C. and Keith, L. (1987) Population Dynamics of Moose, *Alces alces*, on the South-Coast Barrens of Newfoundland. *Canadian Field Naturalist* 101, 373–387.

Bennet, K. (1989) A Provisional Map of Forest Types for the British Isles 5000 Years Ago. *Journal of Quaternary Science* 4, 141–144.

Bevan, L. (2003) Stag Nights and Horny Men: Antler symbolism and interaction with the animal world during the Mesolithic. In: L. Bevan and J. Moore (eds) *Peopling the Mesolithic in a Northern Environment*, pp. 35–44. British Archaeological Report International Series 1157. Oxford: Archaeopress.

Bishop, H. (1914) An Oransay Shell-Mound – A Scottish Pre-Neolithic Site. *Proceedings of the Society of Antiquaries of Scotland* 48, 52–108.

Brittain, M. and Overton, N. (2013) The Significance of Others: A prehistory of rhythm and interspecies participation. *Society and Animals* 21, 132–149.

Brown, T. (1997) Clearances and Clearings: Deforestation in Mesolithic/Neolithic Britain. *Oxford Journal of Archaeology* 16, 133–146.

Brown, T. and Keough, M. (1992) Palaeochannels and Palaeolandsurfaces: The geoarchaeological potential of some Midland floodplains. In: S. Needham and M. Macklin (eds) *Alluvial Archaeology in Britain*, pp. 185–196. Oxbow Monograph 27. Oxford: Oxbow Books.

Burkitt, M. (1926) *Our Early Ancestors: An introductory story of Mesolithic, Neolithic and Copper Age cultures in Europe and adjacent regions*. Cambridge: Cambridge University Press.

Carne, P. (2000) *Deer of Britain and Ireland: Their origins and distribution*. Shrewsbury: Swan Hill Press.

Chatterton, R. (2003) Star Carr Reanalysed. In: L. Bevan and J. Moore (eds) *Peopling the Mesolithic in a Northern Environment*, pp. 69–80. British Archaeological Report International Series 1157. Oxford: Archaeopress.

Clapham, A., Clare, T. and Wilkinson, D. (1997) A Plant Macrofossil Investigation of a Submerged Forest. In: A. Sinclair, J. Gowlett and E. Slater (eds) *Archaeological Sciences 1995: Proceedings of a conference on the application of scientific techniques to the study of archaeology, Liverpool, July 1995*, pp. 265–270. Oxbow Monographs 64. Oxford: Oxbow Books.

Clare, T. (1995) Before the First Woodland Clearings. *British Archaeology* 8, 6.

Clark, G. (1932) *The Mesolithic Age in Britain*. London: Cambridge University Press.

Clark, G. (1954) *Excavations at Star Carr: An early Mesolithic site at Seamer near Scarborough, Yorkshire*. Cambridge: Cambridge University Press.
Clark, G. (1972) *Star Carr: A case study in bioarchaeology*. Addison-Wesley Module in Anthropology 10. Menlo Park, USA: Cummings.
Clutton-Brock, J. (1991) Extinct Species. In: G. Corbet and S. Harris (eds) *Handbook of British Mammals*, pp. 571–575. Oxford: Blackwell Scientific Publications.
Clutton-Brock, T. and Albon, S. (1989) *Red Deer in the Highlands*. Oxford: BSP Professional Books.
Clutton-Brock, T., Guinness, F. and Albon, S. (1982) *Red Deer: Behaviour and ecology of two sexes*. Edinburgh: Edinburgh University Press.
Cobb, H. (2005) Straight Down the Line? A queer consideration of hunter-gatherer studies in north-west Europe. *World Archaeology* 37, 630–636.
Conneller, C. (2004) Becoming Deer: Corporeal transformations at Star Carr. *Archaeological Dialogues* 11, 37–56.
Conneller, C. (2011) *An Archaeology of Materials: Substantial transformations in Early Prehistoric Europe*. Oxford: Routledge.
Cornelis, J., Casaer, J. and Hermy, M. (1999) Impact of Season, Habitat and Research Techniques on Diet Composition of Roe Deer (*Capreolus capreolus*): A review. *Journal of Zoology* 248, 195–207.
De Nahlik, A. (1987) *Wild Deer: Culling, conservation and management*. Southampton: Ashford Press.
Elliott, B. (2013) Antler Working Practices in Mesolithic Britain. Unpublished PhD thesis, University of York.
Elliott, B. (2015) Time of the Deer. *Deer* 17, 20–23.
Finlay, N. (2000) Deer Prudence. *Archaeological Review from Cambridge* 17, 67–79.
Finlayson, B. (1995) Complexity in the Mesolithic of the Western Scottish Seaboard. In: A. Fischer (ed.) *Man and Sea in the Mesolithic. Coastal settlement above and below the present sea level*, pp. 261–264. Oxford: Oxbow Books.
Gebert, C. and Verheyden-Tixier, H. (2001) Variations of Diet Composition of Red Deer (*Cervus elaphus* L.) in Europe. *Mammal Review* 31, 189–201.
Geist, V. (1998) *Deer of the World: Their evolution, behaviour and ecology*. Mechaniesburg, USA: Stackpole.
Godwin, H. (1975) *The History of the British Flora: A factual basis for phytogeography*. Cambridge: Cambridge University Press.
Grigson, C. and Mellars, P.A. 1987. The Mammalian Remains from the Middens. In: P.A. Mellars (ed.) *Excavations on Oronsay. Prehistoric Human Ecology on a Small Island*, pp. 243–289. Edinburgh: Edinburgh University Press.
Kitchener, A. (2010) The Elk. In: T. O'Connor and N. Sykes (eds) *Extinctions and Invasions: A social history of British fauna*, pp. 36–42. Oxford: Windgather Press.
Kitchener, A. and Bonsall, C. (1997) AMS Radiocarbon Dates for Some Extinct Scottish Mammals. *Quaternary Newsletter* 83, 1–11.
Laudré, J., Hernández, L. and Altendorf, K. (2001) Wolves, Elk, and Bison: Re-establishing the 'landscapes of fear' in Yellowstone National Park, USA. *Canadian Journal of Zoology* 79, 1401–1409.
Maroo, S. and Yalden, D. (2000) The Mesolithic Mammal Fauna of Great Britain. *Mammal Review* 30, 243–248.
Mellars, P. (1976a) Settlement Patterns and Industrial Variability in the British Mesolithic. In: G. Sieveking, I. Longworth and K. Wilson (eds) *Problems in Economic and Social Archaeology*, pp. 375–400. London: Duckworth.
Mellars, P. (1976b) Fire Ecology, Animal Populations and Man: A study of some ecological relationships in prehistory. *Proceedings of the Prehistoric Society* 42, 15–45.
Mithen, S. and Finlayson, B. 1991. Red Deer Hunters on Colonsay? The implications of Staosnaig for the interpretation of the Oronsay middens. *Proceedings of the Prehistoric Society* 57, 1–8.
Munro, R. (1908) On the Transition between the Palaeolithic and Neolithic Civilizations in Europe. *Archaeological Journal* 65, 205–244.

Myers, A. (1987) All Shot to Pieces? Inter-assemblage variability, lithic analysis and Mesolithic assemblage 'types'; some preliminary observations. In: A.G. Brown and M.R. Edmonds (eds) Lithic Analysis and Later British Prehistory: Some problems and approaches, pp. 137–153. British Series 162. Oxford: British Archaeological Reports.

Overton, N. (2016) More than Skin Deep: Reconsidering isolated remains of 'fur bearing species' in the British and European Mesolithic. *Cambridge Archaeological Journal* 26, 561–578.

Overton, N. and Hamilakis, Y. (2013) A Manifesto for a Social Zooarchaeology: Swans and other beings in the Mesolithic. *Archaeological Dialogues* 20, 111–136.

Sæther, B. and Reidar Andersen, E. (1990) Resource Limitation in a Generalist Herbivore, the Moose *Alces alces*: Ecological constraints on behavioural decisions. *Canadian Journal of Zoology* 68, 993–999.

Simmons, I. (1996) *The Environmental Impact of Later Mesolithic Cultures: The creation of moorland landscape in England and Wales*. Edinburgh: Edinburgh University Press.

Simmons, I. (2001) *An Environmental History of Great Britain: From 10,000 years ago to the present*. Edinburgh: Edinburgh University Press.

Simmons, I. and Dimbleby, G. (1974) The Possible Role of Ivy (*Hedera helix* L.) in the Mesolithic Economy of Western Europe. *Journal of Archaeological Science* 1, 291–296.

Spikins, P. (1999) *Mesolithic Northern England: Environment, population and settlement*. British Archaeological Report British Series 283. Oxford: British Archaeological Reports.

The Deer Initiative. (2008a) *Species Ecology: Red Deer* (available online: http://www.thedeerinitiative.co.uk/uploads/guides/168.pdf).

The Deer Initiative (2008b) *Species Ecology: Roe Deer* (available online: http://www.thedeerinitiative.co.uk/uploads/guides/169.pdf).

Viveros de Castro, E. (1998) Cosmological Dieixis and Amerindian Perspectivism. *Journal of the Royal Anthropological Institute, New Series* 4, 469–488.

Walker, D. and Godwin, H. (1954) Lake Stratigraphy, Pollen Analysis and Vegetational History. In: G. Clarke (ed.) *Excavations at Star Carr: An early Mesolithic site at Seamer near Scarborough, Yorkshire*, pp. 25–69. Cambridge: Cambridge University Press.

Walker, M., Coope, G., Sheldrick, C., Turney, C., Lowe, J., Bockley, S. and Harkness, D. (2003) Devensian Lateglacial Environmental Changes in Britain: A multi-proxy environmental record from Llanilid, South Wales. *Quaternary Science* 22, 475–520.

Whitehead, G. (1993) *The Whitehead Encyclopedia of Deer*. Shrewsbury: Quiller.

Yalden, D. (1999) The History of British Mammals. London: T. and A.D. Poyser.

# Chapter 6

# Man's best friend? A critical perspective on human-animal relations from Natufian and Pre-Pottery Neolithic mortuary practices

*Gabrielle Borenstein*

**Abstract**

*No living creature escapes its inevitable fate – death. Human responses to death, however, vary dramatically across time, landscapes and cultures. Provisions are carried out for the dead, but these practices are generally not so much about the dead themselves as they are about the living, who process the remains of the dead within a mortuary context (Pearson 1999). Funerary rites are performances undertaken by the living that utilise objects, beings and actions, and convey social knowledge through the participants' social relations with the dead (Rowlands 1993; Watts 2013). These acts, carried out for the dead, also serve to reinforce and renegotiate the community identity of the living and their relationship(s) with the natural (Bloch and Parry 1982; Huntington and Metcalf 1991; Kuijt 2000; Laneri 2007). This paper examines the emergence and increased inclusion of animals in mortuary contexts in the Southern Levant from the Natufian through Pre-Pottery Neolithic (PPN) periods. This is achieved through an exploration of the social and symbolic implications of incorporating animals into burial practices to evaluate the renegotiation of economic, social, and political roles during this period.*

The Natufian period (12,500–10,200 BP) is widely posited as the time in which people took their initial steps towards sedentary and agricultural life (Byrd 1989; Tchernov 1991; Byrd and Monahan 1995; Bar-Yosef 1998; 2004; Belfer-Cohen *et al.* 2000). In this period, individuals erected substantial structures, began manipulating wild plants and animals and developed a diversity of lithic, bone and ground stone artefacts (Belfer-Cohen 1991; Boyd 1992; 2006). These innovations are frequently regarded as the precursors to the dramatic socioeconomic developments of the subsequent Neolithic period, distinguishing them from the cultural practices of the preceding Geometric Kabaran Epipalaeolithic (Grossman 2013). Despite the possible links to Neolithic society, it is necessary to recognise the Natufian as a distinct cultural entity and evaluate their symbolic and agricultural practices without an exclusively proto-Neolithic transitionary lens (Belfer-Cohen and Goring-Morris 2013).

The archaeological record shows that at most sites in the Levant there is a hiatus of more than 1,000 years between Natufian and Neolithic settlements (Boyd 2006). The Natufian modality was distinctly that of a culturally complex hunter-gatherer society. Natufian subsistence strategies – though varying in accordance with particular environmental characteristics – were not concerned with plant cultivation and domestication. While there was a heavy emphasis on plant processing, any degree of relative sedentism occurred independently of the development of an agricultural way of living in the Near East. Belfer-Cohen *et al.* (2000) explain that, from its inception, the Natufian can be defined as a complex society of specialised hunter-gatherers and/or collectors. This particular social system influenced and modified much of Natufian behavioural make-up: social structure, social behaviours and subsistence-acquisition practices. Information regarding any sort of sedentism that occurred during the Natufian remains somewhat elusive in the archaeological record; however, sedentism can be very difficult to identify via archaeological remains (Belfer-Cohen and Bar-Yosef 2000). Features typically assumed to be evidence of permanent occupations or residences, such as stone architecture, heavy-duty material culture (such as silos or large ground stones) and cemeteries, are not always guaranteed markers of long-term occupation (Bar-Yosef and Belfer-Cohen 1989; Valla 1999; Boyd 2006).

The Natufian mode of existence combined year-round occupation of sites with short, interspersed, seasonal spells of anticipatory mobility of both task groups and entire communities (Belfer-Cohen and Bar-Yosef 2000). While the Natufian period can be seen to bridge both mobile and sedentary ways of life, the motivation for this shift is not visible vis-à-vis agriculture in and of itself. In this paper, I consider the discernable symbolic links that evidence an apparent commonality of practices. As Bar-Yosef and Belfer-Cohen explain, 'the role of the direct ancestors of the Natufians, and their social and economic decisions taken around 13,000 BP, proved to be crucial for the ensuing history of the entire Near East' (1992, 40). While striving to avoid considering the Natufian through the lens of the Neolithic, it is nevertheless possible to critically investigate the possibility of symbolic continuity between these two periods.

Architectural remains and material culture, as well as botanical and zooarchaeological evidence, suggest that early traces of sedentary agricultural life (or its precursors) appear in the Natufian period (Garrod 1957; Valla 1995; Belfer-Cohen and Bar-Yosef 2000; Goring-Morris and Belfer-Cohen 2008). Emphasis is often placed on changes in methods of subsistence and dwelling as causative factors that facilitated the shift from foraging to farming. It is equally important to consider the other changes in human behaviour that occurred alongside – and quite possibly in reaction to – these changes. I argue that the budding domestication or 'neolithisation' of plants, animals and the landscape was accompanied by another innovation: the domestication or 'neolithisation' of the human.

Profound changes in cultural and symbolic practice, as evidenced in mortuary contexts, demonstrate that the onset of agricultural life was not an exclusively economic phenomenon. The presence of animals, both wild and domestic, in burial practices suggests that changes in human-animal relations were not singularly linked to the transition from hunting to methodological farming (Russell 2012). The material traces, as evidenced in human-animal interments at sites such as Hillzon Tachtit, Mallaha, Hayonim Terrace and the later pre-pottery Neolithic site of Kfar HaHoresh, demonstrate that concurrent with the advent of agrarian life was a crucial shift in human perspective regarding animals. The symbolism of burials in the Levantine Natufian period through to the Pre-Pottery Neolithic illustrates how the changing roles of animals in the world of the living warranted address and representation in the world of the dead. The novelty of these practices and the broader ideology from which they were derived are indicative of what Cauvin referred to as the 'revolution of symbolism' (1994).

Multiple lines of archaeological evidence point to a change in the belief systems of individuals inhabiting the Mediterranean region of the Southern Levant during the Natufian Period. The increased frequency of artistic manifestations such as figurines, bone objects incised with patterns, and beads manufactured from marine shells accompanying burial contexts are representative of a material shift from the unembellished graves of the Epipaleolithic and Early Natufian (Bar-Yosef 2002; Dosseur and Marechal 2013). The period is also marked by a higher concentration of human burials, both in quantity and spatial density. More than 400 individuals have been recovered from Natufian sites, signifying a dramatic intensification in the number of dead recovered in comparison to any preceding cultural period in this region. The paralleled increase in number of cemeteries – or exclusionary burial areas – supports the idea of a visibly different type of commitment to the deceased. For the first time, it appears that select sites in this region were functioning primarily as cemeteries (Grosman and Munro 2007; 2016). Investigation of the mortuary practices associated with these burials demonstrates that death and dying prompted heightened collective activity in this period, inspired by sociopolitical need or perhaps by a new sense of cultural and/or spiritual conviction (Kuijt 1996).

Cauvin (1994) famously defined the Neolithic as the culmination of a series of changes that transmuted nearly every sector of human life. During the Neolithic, individuals not only changed the landscape and differently utilised material resources, they also altered their own perceptions and understanding of nature and their place within it. I propose that this shifted relationship between human and environment took root slightly earlier and worked to establish the relevant preconditions for settled, large-scale agricultural communities. The presence of the animal – particularly the wild animal – in a ritualised context had the capacity both to reinforce certain norms in human-animal relations as well as to challenge them (Alexander 1997; Turner 2006).

By the Late Natufian period, the increased evidence of funerary rituals also suggests that these practices became increasingly public. The variety of burial modes is diverse, ranging from single to multiple, primary to secondary and articulated to partial, including evidence of skull removal. While certain diachronic trends can be identified, these are not all-encompassing (Belfer-Cohen and Goring-Morris 2013). The intentional co-association of human and animal remains appears to be limited only to sites in the Galilee (Davis and Valla 1978; Tchernov and Valla 1997). It is for this reason that this paper critically investigates the aforementioned sites, probing what this co-association signifies in the broader context of Natufian identity, social structure and practice.

Human burials associated with animal remains from the Late Natufian cave site of Hilazon Tachtit in northern Israel demonstrate an early example of elaborate, animal-inclusive human burial practice in the Levant. The site contained the remains of at least twenty-eight individuals (Grosman *et al.* 2008). Grosman *et al.* (2016) reason that the primary role of this site was for human interment and associated mortuary activities. The site proffered primary burials and a number of pits containing the collective burials of individuals of various sexes and ages. These individuals were originally interred in primary position, but were later disturbed when the graves were reopened so that the long bones and skulls could be removed (Grosman and Munro 2016). Among the primary burials, one context was particularly striking and provides strong evidence for community engagement in ritual practice. Bioarchaeological analysis and interpretation of the skeleton suggest that the individual was a petite, elderly woman who was interred with ten large stones placed directly above her head, pelvis and arms. The individual was positioned on its side with the spinal column, pelvis and right femur resting against the curved southern wall of the oval-shaped grave. The legs were spread apart and folded inward at the knee (Grosman *et al.* 2008). In addition to this aberrant placement, the woman was interred with a complete articulated human foot – which was not her own – and over fifty complete tortoise carapaces. Given that some of the plastrons of these were found broken, it appears that a number of the tortoises were removed from their shells prior to deposition, possibly for consumption as part of a feast surrounding the interment of the deceased. This burial also contained over thirty tortoise limb bones, suggesting that entire tortoises, not just their shells, were transported to the cave (Grosman *et al.* 2008; Grosman and Munro 2016).

These provisions would have required a considerable investment of time and resources. Tortoises are predominantly solitary animals. While it is possible that these animals could have been collected and confined by humans for a period preceding the event, it is clear these burial accoutrements were not without forethought and intentionality. This grave also included the body parts of several other animals that rarely occur in contemporaneous assemblages. Two stone marten skulls, the carpometacarpus and first phalanx of a golden eagle, several articulated caudal vertebrae from the tail of an aurochs, the near-complete pelvis of leopard, the forearm of a wild boar and a complete male gazelle horn were also found carefully arranged in relation to this individual's remains (Tchernov and Valla 1997; Grosman et al. 2008).

The Hilazon Tachtit burial marks the most diverse Natufian interment to date. The grave goods are substantially more numerous and varied. The mixed incorporation of multiple wild animals and the sheer volume of the remains has led several scholars to deduce that the deceased was a shaman-like figure, one who readily engaged with different animals during life (Grosman et al. 2008; Grosman and Munro 2016). The term 'shaman' is imbued with myriad cultural associations, which tend to emphasise individuals as mediators between mortal and supernatural planes while also propagating the binary between these spheres. Rather than focusing exclusively on the particularities of the individual, perhaps it is better to critically examine the societal implications of such practices. What possible ideological impetus might compel individuals to bury the human with the animal? How might this practice foreground and create the preconditions for changes in human-animal relations? In what ways might this represent changing conceptions of personhood? Perhaps this type of mortuary instalment evidences an assertion of human power and control over the wild (Ingold 1987; Russell 2012). Alternatively, the presence of unmodified animal parts here, prior to the first instances of domestication, can be viewed as evidence for a deeply entrenched, general belief in either the spiritual properties of animals or the desire for their company in that which followed death. These ideological enactments – which are fundamentally communal – integrate communities, reduce anxiety, negotiate relationships and convey important social information related to power (Russell 2012; Watts 2013).

It is clear from the assemblage at Hilazon Tachtit that this Natufian community wanted to commemorate the relationship between this individual and different animals, either as they were during life, or through their abstract and referential properties (Preucel 2006; Kockelman 2007; Crossland 2009). The inclusion of the animal in the mortuary sphere is suggestive of a socio-ideological relationship that goes beyond predator-prey. It would appear that animals were more than just economic resources from which food and other items could be taken and modified into tools, clothing or decorations, they were codified into symbolic thought (Maher et al. 2011). Partial inclusions are frequently regarded as funerary offerings. The fragmentary nature of some of these finds, from shells to skulls, a pelvis, forearm and horn perhaps demonstrates the Natufians' symbolic capacity for metonymy wherein the fragment of the animal could have been used in place of the whole item. It is representative of the object from which it was derived and in association with part of something else is thought to signify relationships the two respective wholes take part in (Croucher 2012, 209). If such were the case, the rest of the animal likely would have been utilised amongst the living community (Russell 2012, 265). Regardless of the specific meaning affixed to the different faunal remains, Hilazon Tachtit is demonstrative of an important societal shift – that the animal was welcomed into the human realm. The incorporation of the wild into the cultural suggests that categorically the wild

– as a memento of place, of human power or dependence – was a communal priority. The growing imperative to include the animal(s) in these definitively human spheres of activity represents a social categorical shift.

Data from Mallaha (Eynan) and Hayonim Terrace similarly evidence a unique human-animal relationship in burial contexts. In contrast to Hilazon Tachtit, these sites contain finds of what are interpreted to be domesticated canids (Davis and Valla 1978, 608). At Mallaha, located in the Upper Jordan Valley, two Natufian occupation levels were uncovered that contained numerous burials. One individual, interpreted as an adult female, from the later occupation was found with her left wrist resting on the thorax of a four- to six-month old canine. Referred to as the 'puppy burial', the canid remains were found in extremely close proximity to those of the human, suggesting a uniquely close relationship between the two species (Davis and Valla 1978, 608). Similarly, at Hayonim Terrace, Late Natufian layers yielded three human burials (H7, H8, H10) that included two interred dogs that displayed morphological evidence of domestication (Tchernov and Valla 1997). Domesticates, however, were not the only animals discovered in these burial contexts. There are also examples of comingled domesticates with non-domesticates, as exemplified by a collective burial on Hayonim Terrace where gazelle horn cores were found in association with two tortoise carapaces and two adult canids. This site also proffered two burials where human remains were exclusively deposited with gazelle remains (Boyd 1992, 24–25). Some burials at Mallaha similarly contained exclusively wild animal remains, as evidenced by gazelle horn cores found in the grave-pit of the collective burial containing five individuals. Animal bones were associated with two additional pit burials, one of which contained a cervid antler. Hayonim Cave, Grave 10, likewise yielded only a wild boar tusk. It seems that, while domesticated and wild animals were both subject to inclusion in the ritual milieu, they were neither treated nor presented equally. Whereas the dogs were interred in their entirety, the remains of the cervid, boar, gazelle and tortoises were merely partial.

The puppy burial at Mallaha suggests that dogs occupied a unique place in Natufian society. The interment of a complete puppy exceeds purely pragmatic provisioning or considerations. This animal was not utilised as a food resource. The nature of deposition suggests that dogs were regarded by Natufian individuals with a kind of care that signifies friendship, potentially symbolic of a concurrent afterlife (Morey 2006, 166). Perhaps, as Morey (2006) suggests, this sort of companion status and privilege could only be bestowed on animals that had been domesticated, and thus transgressed the category of wild, so as to be understood as 'tamed'.

Mallaha and Hayonim Terrace, like a number of Late Natufian sites, illustrate a deeply rooted commitment to include animal remains in human burials. What remains striking, however, is the lack of homogeneity in these practices. While the sample size is limited, incorporation over time does not seem to adhere to any standardised behaviours, especially outside of the Galilee (Belfer-Cohen and Goring-Morris 2013). However, there is a notable consistency in the prioritisation of associated animal remains in mortuary contexts rather than utilitarian objects (Croucher 2012). While this burial assemblage demonstrates the propensity for an array of wild animals, much like Hilazon Tachtit, the inclusion of the entire puppy marks a profound departure from earlier Natufian burial customs. Complete, articulated animal skeletons are rare in mortuary contexts (Maher *et al.* 2011, 8; Russell 2012). It appears, in this intimate association, that an affectionate rather than gastronomic relationship existed between the puppy and the buried person (Davis and Valla 1978, 610). Unlike the fragmented remains of the wild animals, the dog was treated preferentially to a complete and deliberate interment.

The exact nature and meaning of this relationship between human and dog is difficult to decipher. There are very few criteria to recognise 'pets' in the archaeological record. The term pet itself dates to seventeenth-century Britain (Amato 2015). A defining quality of pets relates to their positionality regarding understood taboos. Russell (2012) explains that animals treated as pets – or with affection – are culturally recognised as that which is not eaten. Archaeologically, their bones are not processed for food (Russell 2012, 264). Another key quality is that these animals are brought into the human family, treated as quasi-kin. This status may be reflected in the treatment of dead pets as though they were people, with similar burials (Ojoade 1990, 217). The dogs included in the burials at Mallaha and Hayonim Terrace are consistent with these principles. Their skeletons are fully articulated and their presence adjacent to humans is definitely distinct. Whether or not these dogs were killed at the time of burial of their owner remains unknown. Faunal analysis did not reveal any evidence of blunt force trauma; however, this alone is not enough evidence to rule out sacrifice. Animals buried with people are most likely killed to accompany their owner. It is, however, possible that these animals died from disease. Regardless of the nature of their death, it appears that the incorporation of the dog in the burial context served as a symbol of continued companionship beyond death. It is clear that dogs entertained an ideologically distinct, ritualistic role in the animal kingdom (Pearson 1999).

Mallaha and Hayonim Cave offer a unique type of insight into symbolic animal expression in Natufian mortuary rituals. These burial procedures represent increased notions of human symbolic enculturation of the animal. The use of animal elements and complete animals in practice marks a pronounced exploitation of wild resources and is perhaps indicative of selective hunting and/or gradual manipulation of gazelles. Evidence of dog domestication has implications beyond the ritual context. This would have had implications in daily life and encounters. It requires a mediation of the structurally opposed wild and domestic spheres (Boyd 1992). The ritualised moment of burial provides an arena for the convergence of categories – a liminal space where human and animal can be united (Insoll 2009). The moment of ritual is telling of – and permeates into – daily life. From Natufian mortuary practices it becomes evident that their complex spiritual outlooks, which weighed heavily on changing human-animal relations, were inextricably linked to dynamic negotiations of the natural and the social.

While I have identified what was included in burials during this period (animal remains, dentalium, beads, *etc.*), it is also important to address what was not. There is a complete absence of utilitarian objects such as bone tools, chipped stone and ground stone. Mundane materials are extremely rare in Natufian funerary contexts (Byrd and Monahan 1995, 271). Existing evidence suggests that, though Natufian burial practices were not remarkably standardised, the materials with which Natufian individuals endowed their deceased were not of an explicitly utilitarian nature. This could be used to corroborate notions of symbolic intentionality behind the mortuary deposits.

The propensity for including animals in mortuary contexts intensifies throughout the Southern Levant during the subsequent Pre-Pottery Neolithic period. Even without imposing a social evolutionary model, I argue that human-animal relationships demonstrate some sort of ideological continuity between Natufian and Neolithic. The site of Kfar HaHoresh, in the lower Galilee of Israel, is just one example of the way in which intentional human-animal deposition intensified in the Pre-Pottery Neolithic. This site contained a large number of primary, and especially secondary, human internments, often in direct and unique co-association with animal remains (Goring-Morris 2000, 110). While these remains were sometimes partial or complete articulation, the multitude of such, in contrast to the aforementioned Natufian sites, suggests a more developed and standardised ritual practice for linking the perceived identity of an individual with that of the animal or natural world within the mortuary context. Goring-Morris succinctly states that the provision of the animal offerings 'all require labor' (2000, 114). At Kfar HaHoresh, the use of prolific oblations – irrespective of their cost – represent the ceremonial nature of the activities directly associated with the deceased in contrast to assemblages from earlier sites. Both time- and resource-intensive, these burials reveal that among this group of individuals it was necessary to not only transport the corpse from the location of death to this particular site for primary burial, but also to subsequently return to the burial site in order to perform additional funerary treatments and rituals.

The increased prevalence of these efforts reflects an intensification of the metaphorical link between humans and ancestors that began to materialise during the Natufian. However, at Pre-Pottery Neolithic sites such as Kfar HaHoresh, wild animals were not only interred, but also interred in the same manner as humans. The wild carcass of a gazelle was found complete, but headless. Likewise, plastered gazelle skulls were also found in a neighbouring region of the site (Goring-Morris 2000). Moreover, the common mortuary treatment of humans and animals during the Pre-Pottery Neolithic suggests that these relationships cannot be simply classified as hunter-hunted and domesticator-domesticated. These burials seem to address conceptual aspects of kin relations and common ancestry between the two groups rather than change in subsistence arts and economics as they did during the Natufian period. These can be understood to represent the mutually entangled history that has pervaded human-animal relationships (Ingold 1987). Here, it is clear that human identity was implicitly understood as closely related to that of animals. During the Pre-Pottery Neolithic, animals not only of a domesticated nature were regarded as more than entirely economic entities. These mortuary practices, supplemented with the increased sense of place and landscape laden to sedentary life, uphold the idea that animals were another form of people whose lives had an important impact upon humanity. Pre-Pottery individuals conceived of animals as ancestors of and ancestral to human population, and their mortuary practices can be seen as a reflection of the development of a series of ritual events organised for the veneration or worshipping of ancestors of multiple biological species (Kuijt 1996, 331). This materially expressed belief system was founded upon rituals that emphasised the identity of the community with regard to its shared ancestors: animals.

Both Natufian and Neolithic mortuary rituals can thus be seen as social mechanisms employed by members of the community in order to structure not only their own social relations, but also those among the living, the dead and the animals. In other words, burial practice provided the framework for greater community and landscape cohesion amidst a period of potentially fissive social, environmental and economic change. The surge in animal symbolism – especially visible at more contemporary sites across the Near East from Gobekli Tepe to Çatalhöyük and 'Ain Ghazal – can all be viewed as representative of a common phenomenon. Communities called upon animals and animal symbolism to abet the tensions of larger, more complex, sedentary societies. It seems that animals may not merely be a friend to man, but also his means of self-identification for relating to – and understanding – his place within both his natural and constructed landscape.

## Bibliography

Alexander, B. (1997) Ritual and Current Studies of Ritual: Overview. In: S.D. Glazier (ed.) *Anthropology of Religion: A handbook*, pp. 139–60. Westport, Connecticut: Greenwood.

Amato, S. (2015) *Beastly Possession: Animals in the Victorian consumer culture*. Toronto: University of Toronto Press.

Bar-Yosef, O. (1983) The Natufian of the Southern Levant. In: T. Cuyler Young, P.E.L. Smith and P. Mortesen (eds) *The Hilly Flanks and Beyond: Essays on the prehistory of southwestern Asia presented to Robert J. Braidwood, Nov. 15. 1982*, pp. 11–42. Chicago: University of Chicago Press.

Bar-Yosef, O. (1998) The Natufian Culture in the Levant, Threshold to the Origins of Agriculture. *Evolutionary Anthropology* 7, 159–177.

Bar-Yosef, O. (2002) Natufian: A complex society of foragers. In: B. Fitzhugh and H. Junko (eds) *Beyond Foraging and Collecting: Evolutionary change in hunter-gatherer settlement systems*, pp. 91–149. New York: Kluwar Academic/Plenum Publishers.

Bar-Yosef, O. (2004) Guest Editorial: East to West – Agricultural origins and dispersal into Europe. *Current Anthropology* S1–S3.

Bar-Yosef, O. and Belfer-Cohen, A. (1989) The Origins of Sedentism and Farming Communities in the Levant. *Journal of World Prehistory* 40, 447–498.

Belfer-Cohen, A. (1989) The Natufian Issue: A suggestion. In: O. Bar-Yosef and B. Vandermeersch (eds) *Investigations in South Levantine Prehistory*, pp. 297–307. British Archaeological Reports International Series 497. Oxford: BAR.

Belfer-Cohen, A. (1991) The Natufian in the Levant. *Annual Review of Anthropology* 20, 167–186.
Belfer-Cohen, A. (1995) Rethinking Social Stratification in the Natufian Culture: The evidence from burials. In: S. Campbell and A. Green (eds) *The Archaeology of Death in the Ancient Near East*, pp. 9–16. Edinburgh: Oxbow Monographs.
Belfer-Cohen, A. and Bar-Yosef, O. (1992) From Foraging to Farming in the Mediterranean Levant. In: A.B. Gebauer and T.D. Price (eds) *Transitions to Agriculture in Prehistory*, pp. 21–48. Madison: Prehistory Press.
Belfer-Cohen, A., Bar-Yosef, O. and Kuijt, I. (2000) Early Sedentism in the Near East: A bumpy ride to village life. In: I. Kuijt (ed.) *Life in Neolithic Farming Communities: Social organization, identity, and differentiation*, pp. 19–37. New York: Kluwer/Plenum Publishers.
Belfer-Cohen, A. and Goring-Morris, N. (2013) Breaking the Mold: Phases and facies in the Natufian of the Mediterranean zone. In: O. Bar-Yosef and F.R. Valla (eds) *Natufian Foragers in the Levant: Terminal Pleistocene social changes in western Asia*, pp. 544–561. New York: Berghahn Books.
Bloch, M. and Parry, J. 1982. Introduction: Death and the regeneration of life. In: M. Bloch and J. Parry (eds) *Death & Regeneration of Life*, pp. 1–44. Cambridge: Cambridge University Pres.
Boyd, B. (1992) The Transformation of Knowledge: Natufian mortuary practices at Hayonim, western Galilee. *Archaeological Review from Cambridge* 11, 19–38.
Boyd, B. (2004) Agency and Landscape: Abandoning the 'nature/culture' dichotomy in interpretation of the Natufian and the transition to the Neolithic. In: C. Delage (ed.) *The Last Hunter-Gatherer Societies in the Near East*, pp. 119–136. British Archaeological Reports International Series 1320. Oxford: BAR.
Boyd, B. (2006) On 'Sedentism' in the Later Epipalaeolithic (Natufian) Levant. *World Archaeology* 38, 164–178.
Byrd, B. and Monahan, C. (1995) Death, Mortuary Ritual, and Natufian Social Structure. *Journal of Anthropological Archaeology* 14, 251–287.
Byrd, B.F. (1989) The Natufian: Settlement variability and economic adaptations in the Levant at the end of the Pleistocene. *Journal of World Prehistory* 3(2), 159–197.
Byrd, B.F. (2000) Households in Transition: Neolithic social organization within southwest Asia. In: I. Kujit (ed.) *Life in Neolithic Farming Communities: Social organization, identity, and differentiation*, pp. 63–98. New York: Kluwer Academic/Plenum.
Cauvin, J. (1994) *The Birth of the Gods and the Origins of Agriculture*. New York: Cambridge University Press.
Crossland, Z. (2009) Of Clues and Signs: The dead body and its evidential traces. *American Anthropologist* 111, 69–80.
Croucher, K. (2012) *Death and Dying in the Neolithic Near East*. Oxford: Oxford University Press.
Davis, S. and Valla, F. (1978) Evidence for Domestication of the Dog 12,000 Years Ago in the Natufian of Israel. *Nature* 276, 608–610.
Dosseur, G. and Marechal, C. (2013) Bone Ornamental Elements and Decorated Objects of the Natufian from Mallaha. In: O. Bar-Yosef and F.R. Valla (eds) *Natufian Foragers in the Levant: Terminal Pleistocene social changes in western Asia*, pp. 293–311. New York: Berghahn Books.
Garrod, D.A.E. (1957) The Natufian Culture: The life and economy of a Mesolithic people in the Near East. *Proceedings of the British Academy* 43, 211–227.
Goring-Morris, N. (2000) The Quick and the Dead: The social context of aceramic Neolithic mortuary practices as seen from Kfar HaHoresh. In: I. Kujt (ed.), *Life in Neolithic Farming Communities: Social organization, identity, and differentiation*, pp. 103–136. New York: Kluwer/Plenum Publishers.
Goring-Morris, N. and Belfer-Cohen, A. (2008) A Roof Over One's Head: Developments in Near Eastern residential architecture across the Epipalaeolithic–Neolithic transition. In: J.P. Bocquet-Appel and O. Bar-Yosef (eds) *The Neolithic Demographic Transition and its Consequences*, pp. 239–286. Dodrecht: Springer Verlag.

Grosman, L. (2013) The Natufian Chronological Scheme – New insights and their implications. In: O. Bar-Yosef and F.R. Valla (eds) *Natufian Foragers in the Levant: Terminal Pleistocene social changes in western Asia*, pp. 622–637. New York: Berghahn Books.

Grosman, L. and Munro, N. (2007) The Sacred and the Mundane: Domestic activities at a Late Natufian burial site in the Levant. *Before Farming* 4, 1–14.

Grosman, L. and Munro, N. (2016) A Natufian Ritual Event. *Current Anthropology* 57, 311–331.

Grosman, L., Munro, N. and Belfer-Cohen, A. (2008) A 12,000-Year-Old Shaman Burial from the Southern Levant (Israel). *Proceedings of the National Academy of Sciences* 105, 17665–17669.

Huntington, R. and Metcalf, P. (1991) *Celebrations of Death: The anthropology of mortuary ritual*. Cambridge: Cambridge University Press.

Ingold, T. (1987) *The Appropriation of Nature: Essays on human ecology and social relations*. Manchester: Manchester University Press.

Ingold, T. (1994) *Animals and Society: Changing perspectives*. London: Routledge.

Insoll, T. (2009) Materiality, Belief, Ritual: Archaeology and material religion: An introduction. *Material Religion* 5, 261–264.

Jakobsen (1999) *Shamanism: Traditional and contemporary approaches to the mastery of spirits*. New York: Berghahn Books.

Kinnes (1981) Dialogues with Death. In: R. Chapman, I. Kinnes and K. Randsborg (eds) *The Archaeology of Death*, pp. 83–92. Cambridge: Cambridge University Press.

Kockelman, P. (2007) Agency: The relation between meaning, power, and knowledge. *Current Anthropology* 48, 375–401.

Kuijt, I. (1996) Negotiating Equality Through Ritual: A consideration of Late Natufian and Prepottery Neolithic A period mortuary practices. *Journal of Anthropological Archaeology* 15, 313–336.

Kuijt, I. (2000) People and Space in Early Agricultural Villages: Exploring daily lives, community size and architecture in the Late Pre-Pottery Neolithic. *Journal of Anthropological Archaeology* 19, 75–102.

Laneri, N. (2007) Burial Practices at Titriş Höyük, Turkey: An interpretation. *Journal of Near Eastern Studies* 66, 241–266.

Latour, B. (2010) *On the Modern Cult of the Factish Gods*. Durham: Duke University Press.

Maher, L., Stock, J.T., Heywood, J.N., Miracle, P.T. and Banning, E.E. (2011) A Unique Human–Fox Burial from a Pre-Natufian Cemetery in the Levant (Jordan). *PLoS ONE* 6, e15815.

Morey, D. (2006) Burying Key Evidence: The social bond between dogs and people. *Journal of Archaeological Science* 33, 158–175.

Ojoade, K.O. (1990) Nigerian Cultural Attitudes to the Dog. In: R. Willis (ed.) *Signifying Animals: Human meaning in the natural world*, pp. 228–234. London: Unwin Hyman.

Pearson, M.P. (1999) *The Archaeology of Death and Burial*. College Station: Texas A&M University Press.

Pettitt, P. (2011) *The Paleolithic Origins of Human Burial*. New York: Routledge.

Preucel, R. (2006) *Archaeological Semiotics*. Malden: Wiley-Blackwell Press.

Rowlands, M. (1993) The Role of Memory in the Transmission of Culture. *World Archaeology* 25, 141–151.

Russell, N. (2012) *Social Zooarchaeology: Humans and animals in prehistory*. Cambridge: Cambridge University Press.

Tchernov, E. (1991). Biological Evidence for Human Sedentism in Southwest Asia during the Natufian. In: O. Bar-Yosef and F.R. Valla (eds) *Natufian Foragers in the Levant: Terminal Pleistocene social changes in western Asia*, pp. 315–340. New York: Berghahn Books.

Tchernov, E. and Valla, F. (1997) Two New Dogs, and Other Natufian Dogs from the Southern Levant. *Journal of Archaeological Science* 24, 65–95.

Turner, T. (2006) Structure, Process, Form. In: J. Kreinath, J. Snoek and M. Stausberg (eds) *Theorizing Rituals Volume 1: Issues, topics, approaches, concepts*, pp. 207–246. Leiden: Brill.

Valla, F. R. (1995) The First Settled Societies – Natufian (12,500–10,200 BP). In: T.E. Levy (ed.) *The Archaeology of Society in the Holy Land*, pp. 170–187. London: Leicester University Press.

Valla, F. R. (1999) The Natufian: A coherent thought? In: W. Davies and R. Charles (eds) *Dorothy Garrod and the Progress of the Palaeolithic. Studies in the prehistoric archaeology of the Near East and Europe*, pp. 224–241. Oxford: Oxbow Books.

Watts, C. (2013) Relational Archaeologies: Roots and routes. In: C. Watts (ed.) *Relational Archaeologies: Humans, animals and things*, pp. 1–20. New York: Routledge.

Winkelman, M.J. (1990) Shamans and other 'Magico-Religious' Healers: A cross-cultural study of their origins, nature, and social transformations. *Ethos* 18, 308–352.

# Chapter 7

# Empathy, cognition and the response to death in the Middle Palaeolithic: The emergence of postmortemism

*Suzi Wilson*

**Abstract**

*The cognitive developments that occurred in the* Homo *genus ultimately enabled more expansive forms of consciousness, facilitated increased creative capacities and, in so doing, allowed hominins to consider concepts that were previously unimaginable. The evidence - both scientific and archaeological - suggests that these advancements are rooted in social origins, possibly extending back to the australopithecines, if not further. Such cognitive developments are reflected in the first burials of the dead; however, the possibility of human burial during the Middle Palaeolithic has been fiercely debated, largely over whether or not humans during this period were cognitively advanced enough to express spiritual concepts symbolically through the performance of burial. But why must these burials be interpreted as symbolic expressions associated with 'religious' concepts? I argue that these burials do not necessarily indicate the provenance of spirituality or the belief in an afterlife or after-person, but rather a shift in thinking, primarily with respect to the corpse - one that I have termed 'postmortemism'.*

*Postmortemism is a response to death that transforms the corpse into something other than waste, thereby affording it special treatment, possibly as a means to honour the dead, mourn them, memorialise them or perpetuate their existence within the community. At the same time, mortuary treatment acted as a cohesive social device for the community following the tragedy of death. It is from postmortemism that mortuary practices developed, and as these habitual actions took root-spiritual beliefs later emerged from these embodied practices.*

## Cognitive development

Archaeologists often infer cognitive development through cultural materials and taphonomic evidence in the archaeological record that appear to demonstrate 'unique' or 'advanced' behaviour. Yet, what behaviours are truly exclusive to the *Homo* genus, specifically *Homo sapiens* and *Homo neanderthalensis*? The primatologist Frans de Waal has effectively illustrated how all *emotionally* based behaviours can be observed throughout the animal kingdom with parallels between human and animal behaviour (de Waal 2009; Swaab 2014). Likewise, the neuroscientist D. F. Swaab, founder of the Netherlands Brain Bank and former director of the Netherlands Institute for Neuroscience, argues that the precursors to the five modern characteristics common to all cultures – language, toolmaking, music, art and religion – can be found on some level throughout the world of animals, with religion as the only apparent exception (2014). While religion may be the only apparent exception to these modern cultural characteristics, why is it so often assumed that religion must be associated with, if not a prerequisite to, human mortuary practice? Although it is possible that the first burials *may* have indicated the provenance of religion or spirituality, it is a long leap to move from an atheist perspective to one of *belief* that incorporates, as Gamble and colleagues suggest, the 'concept of an after-person, the idea that the dead still had power to affect the living' (Gamble *et al.* 2014, 174). Suppose instead that the first intentional burials do *not* necessarily indicate the presence of belief, but rather the presence of what I have termed 'postmortemism'.

Postmortemism is an emotional response to death, rooted in empathy, that requires and results in a mortuary action or performance that aids in ameliorating anguish among the living through honouring/memorialising the dead by extending special treatment to the corpse. Postmortemism and its attendant practices demonstrate a change in awareness and perhaps consciousness among these early humans, and as various traditions of postmortemism practices emerged across communities, consistent patterns developed regarding the treatment of the dead. Over time, these habitual actions became part of a shared culture – a shared embodied empathy among the community, and only later did beliefs emerge from these embodied communal practices.

## The empathetic, emotional response

John Barrett describes empathy as the emotional response between one individual (observer) and another (target) where the observer acknowledges some general quality manifested in a particular object or condition that the target individual is feeling, and recognises that this particular object or condition would evoke the same feeling in herself under similar circumstances (2013). He refers to this as an 'embodied disposition', which might include the avoidance of pollution or the respect of silence in certain situations, as well as a show of reverence towards authority. An embodied disposition might also include the grief or loss that one feels with another following the death of someone in the community, as well as a demonstration of respect for the dead. According to Barrett, 'an embodied disposition ... will unite the innate responses of the biological body with circumstances in ways that have been learnt from birth. We would normally regard this learnt behaviour amongst humans as expressing cultural values' (2013, 8).

These 'responses' would be paramount in enhancing socialisation and binding a community, and such empathetic reflection could produce a need to cope with grief both *as* individuals *for* other individuals as well as for the group. Accordingly, postmortemism developed as a mechanism for processing both the sentiments felt toward the deceased as well as the impact death had on the community at large. The postmortemism response manifested itself in terms of how the deceased's corpse was treated, providing glimpses of evidence in these early burials that relate to our cognitive development from the social foundation that ultimately led to the expansion of our consciousness and, ultimately, cognitive advancement.

## Social origins and cognitive cognition

In 1965 at the annual meeting of the American Anthropological Association in Denver, Ralph Holloway presented a paper arguing that 'selection for social behavioural complexity was what had driven the evolution of the hominid brain' (2008, 5), which was later published as 'The Evolution of the Human Brain: Some notes toward a synthesis between neural structure and the evolution of complex behavior' (1967). Following Holloway, various other theories involving how social complexity may have advanced cognitive abilities were published, such as Leslie Brothers' social brain hypothesis (1990), Byrne and Whiten's Machiavellian Intelligence theory (1988) and Robin Dunbar's version of the social brain hypothesis (1998). Dunbar emphasises the effect of group *size* on social relationships (Gamble *et al.* 2014), and although size would certainly would have had an impact on social relations, social complexity, perhaps the 'quality' of social relationships would have likewise played an important, if not greater, role in cognitive development.

Although these two factors probably had a coetaneous influence, it also seems likely that environmental and ecological challenges served as additional catalysts for driving the evolution of the brain. Certainly, the biological physical changes, and bipedalism in particular (see below), would have intensified social relationships, thereby requiring a cognitive adaptation. As the brain evolved and adapted to these enhanced social situations, relationships were then able to increase further in their complexity, thereby requiring a further adaptation for the brain, and so on and so forth. In this manner, social abilities and cognition had a symbiotic relationship that developed somewhat concomitantly, although it was the social conditions, I argue, that provided the initial kick.

It is possible that our social origins extend back over 50 million years to the early primates of the Eocene, who abandoned their nocturnal lifestyle when it became safer to band together against predators and, as a result, started living in social groups

(Stringer 2011; Swaab 2014). During the Miocene, the *Homo* ancestral lineage broke with that of the chimpanzees (between approximately 5 and 7 million years ago (Gamble *et al.* 2014; Sept 2015)), and a number of physical changes later ensued – the most prominent being bipedalism. Although there are arguments for early bipedalism such as the anterior shift in the position of the foramen magnum in *Sahelanthropus tchadensis* (to adjust the head for a more 'upright' posture), which is dated to between 7 and 6 million years ago (Lee-Thorp *et al.* 2012; Stringer 2012), as well as the femur of *Orrorin tugenensis* dated to between 6 and 5.8 million years ago (Stringer 2012; Martin 2015), these two isolated samples alone are not convincing. At present it seems more likely that bipedalism developed in stages. Certainly, however, by the time of *Australopithecus* (approximately 4.2 million years ago), bipedal locomotion was employed on a regular basis (Cartmill and Smith 2009; Hunt 2015). Subsequently, regular bipedalism would have resulted in other physical adjustments and changes, which would in turn have contributed to enhanced social situations as well as provide for expansion of the brain. According to the neuroscientist and biologist Gerald Edelman, for example, bipedalism would have been a prerequisite for cortical enlargement, thereby accommodating a larger cortex by lifting the craniofacial morphology (2004). With respect to its effect on social relations, habitually standing upright would have resulted in closer full-body proximity between two individuals, thereby contributing to potentially intense social situations.

In addition to bipedalism, other physical changes included the waning of the pigment in the sclera of the eyes, which would have further impacted social relations now that hominins could track gaze direction and intensity. Also highly relevant in increasing social complexity was the development of a complex facial musculature (Barrett 2013). Although the timing of these developments cannot be anatomically determined, it is among these regularly bipedal Australopithecines that a deepened socialisation developed, which would ultimately serve to stimulate brain development. However, such brain developments were not limited to an increase in volume (Holloway 1967; 1996; *et al.* 2004; Holloway and Coste-Lareymondie 1982; Deacon 1997), and Holloway stresses how there could be several possible scenarios for the way brains changed through time, including reorganisation, hierarchy (or maturation), hemispheric asymmetry or neuroreceptor distribution. From his study of cranial endocasts, Holloway argues that there were three major reorganisational changes that occurred in early hominin brains:

1. Reduction of the primary visual striate cortex (Brodmann area 17) and relative enlargement of extrastriate parietal cortex (areas 18 and 19), angular gyrus (area 39), and supramarginal gyrus (area 40) of the inferior parietal lobe. This represents the first major change from pongid to human brain organisation, and occurred between 3 and 4 million years ago.

2. A reorganisation of the frontal lobe occurred mainly involving the third inferior frontal convolution, known as Broca's area, toward a definitely human, external morphology, most fully evidenced in the KNM-ER 1470 specimen of *H. habilis*, which probably occurred between 2.5 and 1.8 million years ago.
3. In addition to brain enlargement (mostly as an allometric relation to body size), there was a change from a pongid pattern of minimal cerebral asymmetries to a human pattern involving a higher degree of left-occipital and right-frontal petalial enlargements, associated with greater hemispheric specialisation. This appears most clearly in *H. habilis*, but may have occurred earlier in *Australopithecus africanus*, 2 to 3 million years ago (Holloway and de Lacoste-Lareymondie 1982). (see Holloway 1996, 43)

Over the course of these potential brain reorganisations, there would have also been at least five episodes of brain volume increase (Holloway 1996). Furthermore, Swaab suspects the brain has continued (and is continuing) to evolve, as evidenced through genetic analysis (2014). For example, a mutation in the ASPM gene, which is essential for normal mitotic spindle function in embryonic neuroblasts, and affects brain/cortex size across species, accelerated after the split between humans and chimpanzees. Defective forms of the ASPM gene are associated with autosomal recessive primary microcephaly. According to Swaab, a genetic variant of the ASPM gene is believed to have originated only 5,800 years ago and then spread rapidly through the population (2014, 380). Another example is the variant of the microcephalin gene (D allele of MCPH1) that regulates brain size, which is believed to have originated in *Homo sapiens* DNA only 37,000 years ago and is carried by approximately 70% of the world's population today (Swaab 2014, 380).

## Self-awareness/consciousness and social interaction

Both Darwin and de Waal stress that there was a powerful evolutionary advantage to complex social interaction within a group, and Swaab notes the importance of social interaction and self-awareness (Darwin 1859; de Waal 2009; Swaab 2014). By observing and constantly interpreting one's own experiences as compared with the experiences of others, a forum is provided for learning and growing from each other. Swaab and de Waal note that self-awareness is not unique to the *Homo* genus, as it has been demonstrated that various species such as chimpanzees, orang-utans, dolphins and elephants recognise themselves in mirrors (de Waal 2009; Swaab 2014). However, although a rudimentary form of consciousness can be found in every living organism, it is unlikely that other organisms are conscious in the same respect as humans (Edelman 2004; Swaab 2014). According to Swaab, there are three brain structures essential for consciousness and, thus, self-awareness and the awareness of others for negotiating social situations: the cerebral cortex, the thalamus and the nerve fibres (*i.e.* 'white matter') that link these two structures (2014).

## The cerebral cortex, thalamus and cerebral networking

Swaab speculates that the increase in brain size during evolution was primarily due to an increase in the number of neurons in the cerebral cortex (2014). These are grouped in functional units called columns. The encephalisation quotient (ratio of brain weight to body) is largely determined by the cerebral cortex which, in turn, is driven by its number of columns (Swaab 2014). Although the cerebral cortex grew exponentially over the course of evolution, the cross sections of the columns remained almost identical, around half a millimetre, and thus it was an increase in the number of columns that caused our brains to grow bigger and the cortex to become convoluted in the process (Swaab 2014).

The cerebral cortex covers the cerebrum and contains at least 30 billion neurons (nerve cells) and one million billion synapses, or 'connections' (Edelman 2004, 15–16). These neurons are connected to each other within a dense network and they communicate over longer distances via the nerve-fibre tracts. The cortex is divided into six layers and subdivided into regions that control various sensory modalities, and the area of the cerebral cortex where the stimulus arrives must be able to communicate with the other areas of the brain (Carter *et al.* 2009; Swaab 2014).

All sensory information, with the exception of smell, is received and routed to the cerebral cortex by the thalamus, which lies in the centre of the brain (Carter *et al.* 2009; Swaab 2014). The thalamus and the cerebral cortex must not only be intact but also in contact with one another in order for consciousness to arise (Edelman 2004; Swaab 2014). A functional connection with the frontoparietal (*i.e.* the prefrontal and lateral cortices) network is also required for consciousness (Swaab 2014). Consciousness can be viewed as an 'emergent characteristic generated by the joint functioning of specific areas of the huge network of neurons in our heads' (Swaab 2014, 170). These various regions of the brain must be linked and communicate well with one another. Sensory information must be relayed back and forth by the neurons in the prefrontal and parietal cortices to the cerebral cortex via the thalamus.

## Social awareness and conformity

Some of the earliest evidence as to how our personalities are affected by various portions of the brain was ascertained through an 1848 railroad excavation accident to a young man, Phineas Gage, in Vermont. Phineas was 25 years old at the time, and reputed to be intelligent, responsible and socially well-adapted with a good work ethic (Damasio *et al.* 1994; Pinker 2002; Carter 2009). He was excavating the terrain for future railroad tracks by drilling holes into the rocks to be removed, then inserting explosive powder into the hole, followed by sand, which would then be ignited via a fuse and tamping iron to trigger the explosion. Gage was momentarily distracted and failed to realise that his assistant had not covered the explosive powder with sand when Gage started tamping the iron rod directly into the explosive powder. The ensuing explosion sent the 109 cm long and 3 cm thick iron rod directly through Gage's left cheek and through his brain, and then exited the top of his skull and landed several metres away (Damasio *et al.* 1994). Although stunned, he remained fully conscious. The impalement left him blind in his left eye, but his intelligence, perception, memory, language skills and motor functions appeared to be intact. However, Gage became rude, unreliable and shiftless (Pinker 2002; Carter 2009; Swaab 2014). He no longer cared for social conventions, often using profanity and offending others, and he had no sense of responsibility (Damasio *et al.* 1994). According to Damasio *et al.* 'Gage exemplified a particular type of cognitive and behavioural defect caused by damage to ventral and medial sectors of prefrontal cortex' (1994, 1103).

The prefrontal area of the brain together with the limbic system (the seat of emotions, which include the thalamus, mentioned previously, and the hippocampus) recognise the consequences of one's actions and therefore consider the appropriate behaviour for various circumstances and situations (Pinker 2002). However, it is important to note that, aside from whatever damage the penetration itself may have caused, the man additionally lost a portion of his brain in the process, as well as a number of cortical connections as the iron rod was propelled through his crania. Furthermore, it is also likely that Gage would have suffered from at least *some* level of psychological post-traumatic stress disorder, which could have also contributed to his change in behaviour.

## The perception of moral awareness and empathy

Moral awareness and empathy arose from social instincts in order to promote the survival of the group, and Swaab emphasises how important the prefrontal cortex is for this process as it plays a crucial role in expressing personality and taking initiative, as well as ensuring that one conforms to social norms (2014):

> Moral precepts serve to promote cooperation and support within social groups; they also act as a social contract, imposing restraints on the individual to benefit the community at large ... Darwin's theory of moral psychology (1859) traced the emergence of ethical behaviour not to selfish competition between individuals but to social solidarity within the group. As they evolved, humans developed altruistic behaviour ... Such behaviour, the product of millions of years of evolution, was ultimately made the cornerstone of human morality, a code of beliefs that was only recently incorporated into religions, a mere couple of thousand years ago. (Swaab 2014, 248)

Accordingly, empathy and altruism long preceded religion, and evidence of such behaviour; embodied empathy among the Middle Palaeolithic people is implicit in the early burials. However, one should not assume that lack of burial implies lack of empathy and/or altruism among these people, as such qualities have also been observed in a number of non-human species who do not, to our knowledge, engage in burial practices.

## Animals and empathy

In addition to Barrett's (2013) technical definition of empathy, it can also be more simply considered as the capacity to recognise and share the feelings of others as the basis for moral behaviour – behaviour which Darwin described in detail, noting how moral awareness in *Homo* developed from social instincts that were crucial for the survival of the group (1871; Swaab 2014). According to de Wall, empathy engages brain areas that are more than 100 million years old (2009), and is demonstrated among many species – especially those that need to work together, such as primates, elephants, wolves and rats. Some species have even been evidenced to feel and express empathy towards *other* species, such as dolphins protecting swimmers in shark-infested waters, or one particular incident involving a bonobo who attempted to comfort and assist a stunned bird that had hit the glass wall of her enclosure (de Wall 2009).

Although we presume that they do not bury their dead, certain animal species have been known to engage in mortuary behaviour towards the corpse. Goodall believes that the behaviour exhibited by extant chimpanzees often reflects the behaviour of earlier hominids, and her studies provide ample evidence that chimpanzees are acutely aware of death (Goodall 1990). Boesch and Boesch-Achermann illustrate this awareness in *The Chimpanzees of the Taï Forest*, where they provide a detailed account of the funerary activities conducted by a group of chimpanzees over the death of a 10-year-old female, 'Tina', who had been killed by a leopard (Boesch and Boesch-Achermann 2000). Following Tina's death, the adult chimpanzees examined her corpse thoroughly, then continued to interact with it for nearly seven hours. These acts included smelling her, grooming her and even occasionally holding her hand. During this time, there were always adult chimpanzees either holding watch over her body or touching her corpse in a tender manner. The infant chimpanzees were not allowed in the general vicinity of the corpse, with the exception of Tina's younger brother, who was allowed to approach and even caress her body. This social interaction with the corpse lasted for 6 hours and 50 minutes, after which the corpse was abandoned and ultimately reclaimed by the leopard.

Elephants likewise seem to have an awareness of death, demonstrated by their frequent visits to the bones of their dead companions. They have been known to remain at the site of the remains for as long as an hour either standing solemnly over the bones or examining them while gently turning them over, smelling them and sometimes carrying them off (de Waal 2009).

## Other empathetic hominins?

Prior to 400,000 years ago, there are, in fact, a few rare instances where it would appear that mortuary treatment was extended to the bodies of conspecifics. The Bodo skull, a hominin cranium dating to approximately 600,000 years ago, was found in the Ethiopian Awash river valley with 25 cut marks in 17 places (White 1986), thereby suggesting the deliberate defleshing of the skull after death.

Another example of Early Palaeolithic mortuary treatment is presented in the extraordinary case of probable postmortemism caching at Sima de los Huesos (the pit of bones) in Atapuerca, Spain where over 6,500 fossil remains from at least 28 individuals were discovered (Bischoff *et al.* 2007, 763; Arnold *et al.* 2014, 85). Although initially believed to be Neanderthal ancestors, DNA extracted from a femur bone from the site suggests a possible link to the Denisovans, known to have occupied the south-western Siberia region (Callaway 2013). Genetic research is, however, ongoing and species determination remains uncertain. Regardless, the dates for these undetermined hominin remains range from between 427±12 kya and *c.* 780 kya based on two semi-independent extended-range luminescence dating techniques (Arnold *et. al* 2014, 104). The pit that the bodies were deposited into lies approximately half a kilometre from the main entrance to the karstic system, and in the opposite direction of a large gallery that was once used as a Bronze Age funerary chamber (Arsuaga *et al.* 1997).

The passageway slopes downward and is very narrow, only allowing for one or two individuals in some parts, making it particularly difficult to negotiate. It could not have been a simple task to carry and deposit the corpses, most likely requiring several people. Although the remains were likely deposited via human intervention, Pettitt argues that the accumulation occurred over a potentially long period of time with the corpses initially deposited either inside the cave or its exterior, perhaps near the original entrance yet to be discovered, rather than directly into the pit (2011). He speculates that, over time, the remains made their way to the pit through faunal disturbance or other natural causes such as mud flows. Pettitt also notes that most of the individuals displayed evidence of disease and/or trauma, so it is possible that the bodies were believed to be polluted and required separation from the living in order to avoid infection. He additionally warns that Sima de los Huesos should not be considered a 'proto-cemetery', but rather a possible mortuary landscape that became known as a 'place of the dead', certainly in terms of disposal and potentially in terms of liminality and danger, associated with decay and disease (2011). Perhaps it is this association that ultimately gave rise to the Bronze Age funerary chamber near the Cueva Major entrance. It is also possible that these early interactions with the dead were postmortemism reactions to the complex sentiments associated with death and loss.

Most recently, 15 individuals of an Archaic hominin species named *Homo naledi* were discovered within the Rising Star Cave in South Africa (Dirks *et al.* 2015). The Dinaledi chamber where the hominin remains were discovered is approximately 30 m below the surface and accessed via a narrow 12-m vertical column, as narrow as 0.20 m in places (Dirks *et al.* 2015, 4). Approximately 1,550 hominin fossils were found in the Rising Star Cave during November of 2013 and March of 2014, of which 1,250 were recovered from a small excavation pit in the Dinaledi chamber, while 330 were collected from the surface of the chamber (2015, 4). No faunal remains were discovered among the hominin fossils, although the remains of six birds and several rodents were found elsewhere in the Rising Star cave. Accordingly, Dirks *et al.* asserted that the 'preliminary evidence is consistent with deliberate body disposal in a single location, by a hominin species other than *Homo sapiens*, at an as-yet unknown date' (2015, 1). However, this claim remains to be assessed by the greater archaeology community and most published debate centres on two issues: (i) whether or not corpse deposition was intentional; and (ii) if so, what these intentions might indicate regarding cognitive ability.

These two issues are commonly the core of debate over Middle Palaeolithic burial, with the cognitive advancement argument focused on the ability to conceptualise symbols. However, the emergence of postmortemism suggests a transitional stage in *Homo* cognitive development – one where the brain was evolving as a result of enhanced social relations, but perhaps had not yet reached the level of symbolic thinking. Such an argument might extend to these early hominin groups, as well as empathetic animals who demonstrate practices of morbidity – morbidity being an enquiring concern with the injured, diseased or dead body, whether or not this derives from a desire to understand the nature or cause of death of an individual (Pettitt 2011).

## Middle Palaeolithic burials

The range for Middle Palaeolithic burials extends from approximately (arguably) between 130,000 years ago in the Levant (Mercier *et al.* 1993; Grün *et al.* 2005) and up to c. 40,000 years ago in Europe (Pettitt 2011, 86–91). According to Hovers and Belfer-Cohen, there could be as many as 58 cases of Middle Palaeolithic burials, of which 35 are Neanderthals, and 23 are *Homo sapiens* (Hovers and Belfer-Cohen 2013, 635). However, the controversy over these burials with respect to intentionality remains in debate. In 1989, Gargett published an article providing alternative sedimentological and taphonomic explanations for six Neanderthal burial sites which he concluded did not represent intentional burials (Gargett *et al.* 1989). Ten years later, he published a follow-up article where he critiqued additional Middle Palaeolithic burials, including the *Homo sapiens* burials at Qafzeh, providing his own criteria for determining an intentional burial and arguing against the possibility of any deliberate burials during the Middle Palaeolithic (Gargett 1999).

Gargett insists that the burials were the result of natural causes such as sedimentation, fluvial depositions and/or faunal intervention. While there is merit to some of his reassessments, Teshik Tash in particular (Gargett *et al.* 1989, 168–169), his consistent argument against deliberate burial in favour of deposition via natural causes does not seem likely in a number of cases. For example, at Regourdou in the Dordogne of southern France, Gargett and colleagues described the site's various features as 'explained by bedrock breakdown, slope transport, and possibly water erosion' (Gargett *et al.* 1989, 174), yet it is difficult to conceive how the neat, seemingly constructed walls could have been formed without human intervention. With respect to Gargett's dismissal of La Chappelle-Aux-Saints as a deliberate burial, also in the Dordogne of France, Rendu recently reassessed the funerary context and human remains, and provided detailed and convincing evidence for intentional burial as opposed to deposition via fluvial or other natural causes (Rendu *et al.* 2014, 81–86). Belfer-Cohen and Hovers have suggested that Gargett holds Neanderthal burials to a higher standard of evidence than other burials (1992). When Gargett ruled out the Amud 7 infant burial in the Levant (1999), Hovers argued that sedimentary processes could not have produced comparable taphonomic evidence, and effectively illustrated how all aspects of the case met Gargett's criteria for intentional burial (Hovers *et al.* 2000).

Regardless of whether any of Gargett's various arguments for natural deposition are valid, the debate continues as to what any evidence of intentional burial might indicate with respect to cognition. The question as to whether or not Middle Palaeolithic people – and the Neanderthals in particular, as our formerly closest living relative – were cognitively capable of conceiving concepts of spirituality or afterlife that would have prompted them to bury their dead. Many argue that Neanderthal intellectual ability was *not* inferior to that of Homo sapiens (Holloway 1985; d'Errico *et al.* 2003; 2009; Renfrew 2009), while others insist that the Neanderthals were incapable of a fully syntactic, semantic language, as well as the ability to think symbolically (Mithen 1996; Lewis-Williams 2002; Edelman 2004; Dunbar 2014). According to Mithen and Lewis-Williams, without the ability to create, interpret and process symbols, there can be no conception of spirituality and/or afterlife (Lewis-Williams 2002; Mithen 2009).

However, Barrett argues that cognitive development theories, such as Mithen's cognitive fluidity, or Foder's mental modularity, place too much emphasis on the brain's ability to download certain concepts into external storage as symbols (Barrett 2013). He agrees that humans make and use representations in language, imagery and text, but he argues against the idea that human consciousness should be based on the 'operation of representations' (2013, 6). Instead, he argues that cognition is derived 'not from mental representations of the world but from an embodied empathy with others' (2013, 2), and he demonstrates how 'things gain a non-representational significance by means of embodied practice' (2013, 7). Accordingly, these Middle Palaeolithic people, through the postmortemism response to death, began to bury their dead as an embodied act of community empathy (as opposed to a symbolic expression of religious concepts).

## Conclusion

I argue that the first burials were not performed as the result of spiritual beliefs in an afterlife or a concept of divinities, and therefore did not require the cognitive ability to create and process symbols. Instead, these burials were the postmortemism response to death that compelled Middle Palaeolithic humans to take action as a community for the living, as well as for the dead. Postmortemism emerged because of the way they felt for one another, the way they felt *about* the dead, and because of the effect that death had on the living – both on an individual basis and on the society as a whole. And thus, the resulting performance in response to this embodied empathy by the community was burial. As burial became more habitual, beliefs began to emerge from these embodied practices – not the other way around. The mortuary response began with postmortemism.

## Bibliography

Arnold, L.J., Demuro, M., Parés, J.M., Arsuaga, J.L., Aranburu, A., Bermúdez de Castro, J.M. and Carbonell, E. (2014) Luminescence Dating and Palaeomagnetic Age Constraint on Hominins from Sima de los Huesos, Atapuerca, Spain. *Journal of Human Evolution* 67, 85–107.

Arsuaga, J.L., Martínez, I., Gracia, A., Carretero, J.M., Lorenzo, C., García, N. and Ortega, A.I. (1997) Sima de los Huesos (Sierra de Atapuerca, Spain). The site. *Journal of Human Evolution* 33, 109–127.

Barrett, J.C. (2013) The Archaeology of the Mind: It's not what you think. *Cambridge Archaeological Journal* 23, 1–17.

Belfer-Cohen, A. and Hovers, E. (1992) In the Eye of the Beholder: Mousterian and natufian burials in the Levant. *Current Anthropology* 33, 463–471.

Bischoff, J.L., Fitzpatrick, J.A., León, L., Arsuaga, J.L., Falgueres, C., Bahain, J.J. and Bullen, T. (2007) Geology and Preliminary Dating of the Hominid-Bearing Sedimentary Fill of the Sima de los Huesos Chamber, Cueva Mayor of the Sierra de Atapuerca, Burgos, Spain. *Journal of Human Evolution* 33, 129–154.

Boesch, C. and Boesch-Achermann, H. (2000) *The Chimpanzees of the Täi Forest: Behavioural ecology and evolution.* Oxford: Oxford University Press.

Brothers, L. (1990) The Neural Basis of Primate Social Communication. *Motivation and Emotion* 14, 81–91.

Byrne, R.W. and Whiten, A. 1988. *Machiavellian Intelligence. Social expertise and the evolution of intellect in monkeys, apes, and humans.* Oxford: Clarendon Press.

Callaway, E. (2013) Hominin DNA Baffles Experts. *Nature* 504, 16–17.

Carter, R., Aldridge, S., Page, M. and Parker, S. (2009) *The Human Brain Book.* New York: DK Publishing.

Cartmill, M. and Smith, F.H. (2009) *The Human Lineage.* Hoboken, NJ: Wiley-Blackwell.

Damasio, H., Grabowski, T., Frank, R., Galaburda, A.M. and Damasio, A.R. (1994) The Return of Phineas Gage: Clues about the brain from the skull of a famous patient. *Science* 264, 1102–1105.

Darwin, C. (1859) *On the Origins of the Species.* Mineola, NY: Dover Publications.

Darwin, C. (1871) *The Descent of Man and Selection in Relation to Sex.* London: J. Murray.

Deacon, T.W. (1997) *The Symbolic Species.* New York: W.W. Norton.

d'Errico, F. (2009) The Archaeology of Early Religious Practices: A plea for a hypothesis-testing approach. In: C. Renfrew and I. Morley (eds) *Becoming Human*, pp. 104–122. New York: Cambridge University Press.

d'Errico, F., Henshilwood, C., Lawson, G., Vanhaeren, M., Tillier, A., Soressi, M., Bresson, F. and Bruno, M. (2003) Archaeological Evidence for the Emergence of Language, Symbolism, and Music – An alternative multidisciplinary perspective. *Journal of World Prehistory* 17, 1–70.

De Waal, F. (2009) *The Age of Empathy.* New York: Three Rivers Press.

Dirks, P.H.G.M., Berger, L.R., Roberts, E.M., Kramers, J.D., Hawks, J., Randolph-Quinney, P.S., Elliott, M., Musiba, C. M., Churchill, S.E., Ruiter, D.J.D., Schmid, R., Backwell, L.R., Belyanin, G.A., Boshoff, P., Hunter, K.L., Feuerriegel, E.M., Gurtov, A., Harrison, J.D.G., Hunter, R., Kruger, A., Morris, H., Makhubela, T.V., Peixotto, B. and Tucker, S. (2015) Geological and Taphonomic Context for the New Hominin Species *Homo naledi* from the Dinaledi Chamber, South Africa. *eLife* 4, 1–37.

Dunbar, R.I. (1998) The Social Brain Hypothesis. *Evolutionary Anthropology* 6, 178–190.

Dunbar, R. (2014) *Human Evolution.* London: Pelican Group.

Edelman, G. (2004) *Wider Than the Sky, the Phenomenal Gift of Consciousness.* New Haven, CN: Yale University Press.

Gamble, C., Rowlett, J. and Dunbar, R. (2014) *Thinking Big: How the evolution of social life shaped the human mind.* London: Thames and Hudson.

Gargett, R.H. (1999) Middle Paleolithic Burial is Not a Dead Issue: The view from Qafzeh, Saint-Césaire, Kebara, Amud, and Dederiyeh. *Journal of Human Evolution* 37, 27–90.

Gargett, R.H., Bricker, H.M., Clark, G., Lindly, J., Farizy, C., Masset, C., Frayer, C.W., Montet-White, A., Gamble, C., Gilman, A., Leroi-Gourhan, A., Martinex Navarret, M.I., Ossa, P., Trinkaus, E. and Weber, A.W. (1989) Grave Shortcomings, the Evidence for Neandertal Burial. *Current Anthropology* 30, 157–190.

Goodall, J. (1990) *Through a Window: My thirty years with the chimpanzees of Gombe.* Boston: Houghton Mifflin.

Grün, R., Stringer, C., McDermott, F., Nathan, R., Porat, M., Robertson, S., Taylor, L., Mortimer, G., Eggins, S. and McCulloch, M. (2005) U-Series and ESR Analyses of Bones and Teeth Relating to the Human Burials from Skhūl. *Journal of Human Evolution* 49, 316–334.

Holloway, R.L. (1967) The Evolution of the Human Brain: Some notes toward a synthesis between neural structure and the evolution of complex behaviour. *General Systems* 12, 3–19.

Holloway, R.L. (1985) The Poor Brain of *Homo sapiens neanderthalensis*: See what you please ... In: E. Delson (ed.) *Ancestors: The hard evidence. Proceedings of the symposium held at the American Museum of Natural History April 6–10, 1984 to mark the opening of the exhibition 'Ancestors, four million years of humanity'*, pp. 319–324. New York: Alan R. Liss.

Holloway, R.L. (1996) Toward a Synthetic Theory of Human Brain Evolution. In: J. Changeux and J. Chavaillon (eds) *Origins of the Human Brain*, pp. 43–52. Oxford: Oxford University Press.

Holloway, R.L. (2008) The Human Brain Evolving: A personal perspective. *Annual Review of Anthropology* 37, 1–19.

Holloway, R.L., Broadfield, D. C. and Yuan, M. S. (2004) *The Human Fossil Record*, 3. Hoboken: John Wiley & Sons.

Holloway, R.L. and de la Coste-Lareymondie, M. C. (1982) Brain Endocasts Asymmetry in Pongids and Hominids: Some preliminary findings on the paleontology of cerebral dominance. *American Journal of Physical Anthropology* 58, 101–110.

Hovers, E. and Belfer-Cohen, A. (2013) Insights into Early Mortuary Practices of *Homo*. In: S. Tarlow and L.N. Stutz (eds) *The Oxford Handbook of the Archaeology of Death and Burial*, pp. 631–642. Oxford: Oxford University Press.

Hovers, E., Kimbel, W.H. and Rak, Y. (2000) The Amud Skeleton – Still a burial. Response to Gargett. *Journal of Human Evolution* 39, 253–260.

Hunt, K.D. (2015) Bipedalism. In: M.P. Muehlenbein (ed.) *Basics in Human Evolution*, pp. 103–112. London: Academic Press.

Lee-Thorp, J.A., Likius, A., Mackay, H.T., Vignaud, P., Sponheimer, M. and Brunet, M. (2012). Isotopic Evidence for an Early Shift to $C_4$ Resources by Pliocene Hominins in Chad. *Proceedings of the National Academy of Sciences* 109, 20369–20372.

Lewis-Williams, D. (2002) *The Mind in the Cave.* London: Thames & Hudson.

Martin, R.D. (2015) Primate Evolution. In: M.P. Muehlenbein (ed.) *Basics in Human Evolution*, pp. 31–41. London: Academic Press.

Mercier, N., Valladas, H., Bar-Yosef, O., Vandermeersch, B., Stringer, C. and Joron, J.L. (1993) Thermoluminescence Dating for the Mousterian Burial Site of Es-Skhūl, Mount Carmel. *Journal of Archaeological Science* 20, 169–174.

Mithen, S. (1996) *The Prehistory of the Mind: The cognitive origins of art, religion and science.* London: Thames and Hudson.

Mithen, S. (2009) Out of the Mind: Material culture and the supernatural. In: C. Renfrew and I. Morley (eds) *Becoming Human*, pp. 123–134. New York: Cambridge University Press.

Montgomery, S.H., Mundy, N.I. and Barton, R.A. (2014) ASPM and Mammalian Brain Evolution: A case study in the difficulty in making macroevolutionary inferences about gene-phenotype associations. *Proceedings of the Royal Society* 281, 1–3.

Pettitt, P. (2011) *The Paleolithic Origins of Human Burial.* New York: Routledge.

Pinker, S. (2002) *The Blank Slate: The modern denial of human nature.* London: Penguin Books.

Rendu, W., Beauval, C., Crevecoeur, I., Bayle, P., Balzeau, A., Bismuth, T., Bourguignon, L., Delfour, G., Faivre, J., Lacrampe-Cuyaubere, F., Tavormina, C., Todisco, D., Turq, A. and Maureille, B. (2014) Evidence Supporting an International Neanderthal Burial at La Chapelle-aux-Saints. *Proceedings of the National Academy of Sciences* 11, 81–86.

Renfrew, J.M. (2009) Neanderthal Symbolic Behaviour? In: C. Renfrew and I. Morley (eds) *Becoming Human*, pp. 50–60. New York: Cambridge University Press.

Sept, J. (2015) Early Hominin Ecology. In: M.P. Muehlenbein (ed.) *Basics in Human Evolution*, pp. 85–101. London: Academic Press.

Stringer, C. (2011) *The Complete World of Human Evolution.* China: Everbest Printing.

Stringer, C. (2012) *Lone Survivors: How we came to be the only humans on earth.* New York: Times Books.

Swaab, D.F. (2014) *We Are Our Brains*, trans. J. Hedley-Prôle. New York: Spiegel & Grau.

White, T.D. (1986) Cut Marks on the Bodo Cranium: A case of prehistoric defleshing. *American Journal of Physical Anthropology* 69, 503–509.

# Chapter 8

# Seeking the body: The nature of European Palaeolithic cave art and installation art

## Takashi Sakamoto

**Abstract**

*In Upper Palaeolithic cave-art research, the reason why most works are located in the deep interior of caves remains an enigma. I will consider this issue by looking into environmental properties of caves from the perspective of installation art, a format of contemporary art, whose primary interest is multisensory interactivity between viewers and artistic environment. Based upon analogy from modern examples and analysis of the environmental constraints of cave, we will learn that caves inevitably enhance bodily engagement and heighten human senses/ attention, which is the precondition to view/produce visual works of cave art. Accordingly, a meaningful link between the site-specific multisensory experience and the reason for the site selection will be suggested. After the examination, I will argue the significance of cave-installation art view, indicating further research focusing on human-art interaction in the space of cave-installation and its broad connectivity to other recent approaches.*

## Introduction: A traditional question

This paper explores a traditional question in the research into cave art: *why did Palaeolithic people select caves as places for art?* Archaeologists agree that caves are universally used for dwellings throughout prehistoric society; but that the cave entrance was the actual living area – use of the dark zone of the cave for inhabitation is rare due to the inconvenience that the absence of the natural light causes (Straus 1990; Moyes 2012). However, where most works of cave art are found is in such an inconvenient 'dark zone'. This site selection must have been deliberate: humans in Upper Palaeolithic preferred the interior of caves despite there having been plenty of free space nearer in the cave mouth (living area) for depicting images – a brighter place, more practical than the deep interior for both activities of image-making or seeing an image

(Pettitt 2014). Accordingly, researchers, presuming a hidden link between cave art and cave space itself, have sought to understand the reason why Palaeolithic artists produced art in such a remote location.

In this context, interpretations regarding caves and art have been proposed: Burkitt (1933) claimed caves as shrines; Leroi-Gourhan (1968a; 1968b) viewed that the combination of painting and cave environment as a medium to transmit/represent ideology of Upper Palaeolithic society (so-called 'mythogram'); Pfeiffer (1982) and Mithen (1988) suggested caves might have been an educative facility, like a school, where necessary knowledge for survival was transmitted over generations; and Lewis-Williams (2002) proposed that cave interior of Upper Palaeolithic represents a shamanic cosmological domain where shamans could obtain deep trance state of consciousness (known as an altered state of consciousness: see Lewis-Williams and Dowson 1988). Although each view has its limitations and drawbacks (discussed in detail elsewhere, and thus not examined in this paper), it is undeniable that they have enriched our understanding on the nature of cave art.

The common notion in these explanations is that caves are simply passive geological features. However, is it really correct? Gibson (1979) proposed 'affordance theory', which is an idea that any possible actions animals can take in an environment are defined by physical-cognitive capacity of an animal species and environmental features. For example, if there is a bridge across a river, one can walk on the bridge; if not, one has to walk or swim across. Thus, possible actions humans can conduct differ by environmental features, and in this sense 'activities' transform into 'interactivities' that the certain environments may or may not make possible. Considering this affordance, caves are not passive, but rather active agents to govern any human actions in their environments. With regard to the dark zone of caves, as well as concepts of permanent darkness, these spaces are filled with rich variety of unique spatial elements such as silence, resonant capacity, smell (often of calcite) and unpredictable topography of the floor. These novel stimuli constantly address our different sensory channels. Adopting the view of the 'active cave', we can consider that there must have been specific interactions between Palaeolithic humans and these spatial properties, and therefore it can be hypothesised that these specific environmental components of cave are crucial factors for the site selection. Namely, cave environments offer humans multisensory site-specific experience (White 2003).

Based upon the above hypothesis, this paper will examine the environmental significance of cave and the multisensory experience. Although some researchers take account of the environmental conditions (darkness and the use of light source: Groenen 2000; Pettitt 2014; Pettitt *et al.* 2017, and the topography of cave and human tactility: Petitt *et al.* 2014) and suggest that interactivity with environmental constraints is attributable to the production of certain images, I will focus on human-cave relations without the artistic contents of cave art, because this relation must have preceded creation of any imagery left in caves. Logically speaking, there must have been a special regard to 'cave space' itself first of all, which led Palaeolithic humans to the formation of a particular association between the location and art – otherwise we might reason that it would have made more sense to create art in the open air, such as at Fos Coa valley in Portugal (Baptista 2009), or in rockshelters, such as with the Spanish later-prehistoric Levantine art (Beltran 1982). Crucially, the uniquely multisensual setting of the cave interior signifies one's precondition to view/produce works of visual art (Leroi-Gourhan 1968a; 1968b; White 2003; Nowell 2006). Taking this point into account, it is not hard to assume that visual works left in caves are only a part of the entire experience of 'cave art'.

To examine human-cave multisensory interaction, I will introduce a concept, 'installation art', that is able to draw a meaningful line between a site and site-specific experience. Installation art is an art format of contemporary art that aims to bodily engage viewers with an artificially constructed artistic environment and to offer them a unique multisensory experience (Reiss 1999; Bishop 2005). Passive viewers are 'installed' into installation art space, and consequently transformed into active participants (Bishop 2005). From this perspective, I will argue that cave environment is essentially analogous to installation art, and that the precondition for cave art never allows one to see it as a mere collection of visual art. For this purpose, I will demonstrate how cave environmental components engage humans in a multisensory way and encourage them to participate with the space, focusing on the topography of the floor surface, luminal condition and auditory setting. In fact, analogies from contemporary installation examples allow us to describe possible human reactions to cave interiors, which reveal that bodily engagement and heightened attention/alternative senses (auditory, olfactory and tactile) are absolute conditions of one's physicality and cognition. After examining this, I will introduce two major possibilities of the cave-installation art perspective for the cave-art research.

## What is installation art?

Installation art is a format of expression in contemporary art, which is also known as environmental art (Reiss 1999). In this discipline, artists construct a unique environment that viewers can explore. The central feature of installation art is to force viewers to interact with an artistically constructed space; while conventional fine art requires audiences to be passive recipients of visual information transmitted from artworks such as paintings and sculptures, installation art rejects such a one-way relationship (Reiss 1999; Bishop 2005). Precisely, as Bishop (2005, 6) expresses, 'installation art presupposes an *embodied* viewer whose sense of touch, smell and sound are as heightened as their sense of vision'. For this purpose, artists aim to establish an environment full of elements enhancing one's multisensory experience, and, importantly, in order to experience an installation work, viewers need to physically *walk into* it (Reiss 1999). This is the most salient contrast to conventional art, where one *walks around* paintings or statues. Thus, the core idea of installation art is as an embodiment of viewers and to offer 'theatrical' and 'immersive' experiences, beyond the scope of traditional means of expression (Bishop 2005). Once a viewer enters into a work, he/she is no longer a passive recipient/consumer of the art, but becomes an active participant: the viewer becomes a part of the art; in other words, the installation work is only complete when its viewers are installed within it (Bishop 2005). In short, installation art is a multisensory novel environment to alter viewers (objective) into explorers (subjective) by forcing them to interact with its space.

This art began in the 1960s with an aim to resist institutionalisation of art (Reiss 1999) and developed with the postmodernism movement (Ran 2009). Modern art galleries are a place to preserve artworks, to archive relevant documents and thus to 'histor-ify' all activity related to modern art in order to allow audiences to communicate with both works and their history. However, this institutionalisation defines modern art as such, despite modern art itself originating in antithesis to conventional art institutions (Reiss 1999). For this reason, artists of that period held their criticism towards the archiving nature of art institutions and began artistic practice to avoid being recorded, so that they might emphasise the temporality and ephemerality of the viewer's experience. Installation art is one of the results of this movement (Reiss 1999). Indeed, one's multisensory experience escapes any attempts to record it due to its subjective nature. Further to this, taking a different position, the impression offered from the space of installation work is never fixed, because in installation art there is no single point to view the entire space – the viewer is surrounded by a single work of art in the environment itself. These multiple viewpoint potentials in combination with multisensory experiences highlight the temporality and ephemerality of installation art.

Overall, what I have so far mentioned about installation art can be summarised as following two points: interactivity with environmental constraints and multisensory experiences and their temporality/ephemerality. These two features define installation art and differentiate it from conventional notions of fine art. Keeping this in mind as the definition of this very contemporary art-form, we may now examine the installation-art nature of the cave environment.

## Cave as installation art

European Upper Palaeolithic cave art constitutes some of the greatest cultural heritage of *Homo sapiens*, spanning over 25,000 years (Bahn and Vertut 1997; Lewis-Williams 2002; Pettitt 2014). During this vast amount of time, Palaeolithic humans explored their artistic potential and consequently left naturalistically painted and engraved images of animals, geometric signs, hand stencils and prints, sculpture, finger flutings (doodling-like lines left by fingers on cave walls of soft clay) and, although relatively rare, sometimes, anthropomorphic figures (Bahn and Vertut 1997; Clottes and Lewis-Williams 1998; Vialou 1998; White 2003). Today, we can find these images on various media. They are displayed in catalogue books, on computer monitors or on clothing; images photographically taken out of their original location under a certain lighting condition that is suitable to visually inform what humans of thousands of years ago depicted. Thanks to the recordable nature of visual art, archaeologists and art historians may study cave art, and the general public can see and communicate with it.

However, when actually standing in the caves and viewing the original works, we will recognise that they are far from identical to what we see through such media, because in photographic images the significance of the site-specific experience from the cave environment is lost (Pettitt *et al.* 2017). White epitomises this point:

> Photographs ... do not capture the dynamic, non visual qualities of cave images and indeed of the caves themselves; Leroi-Gourhan described as 'the cave as participants.' In other words, one cannot hope to enter the 'ancient dialogue with caves' without experiencing the images in all the multisensorial richness of the cave themselves. Add fear; uncertain footing, flickering lamplight; moving shadows; sounds of dripping water, the cave floor underfoot, children's cries; the smell of humid limestone confronted by smoldering, sizzling, juniper wick of fat burning lamp or torch, and one begins to resemble the original cloak of the context, meaning and state of mind that wrapped itself around the visual perception of paintings and engravings. (2003, 117)

The author here mentions that one's experience in caves is a highly complicated internal phenomenon, interwoven with multisensory stimuli (vision, audition, olfaction and tactility) and emotion. Cave art would have been experienced under such various conditions. Such an experience is incomparable to the uni-sensory experience of vision – it does not allow us to have a definable impression of visual form of the cave art. We should remember that this is the primary context in which to view and produce images of cave art.

Thus, one of the two definitions of installation art raised in the previous section is applicable to cave art. Their spatially unique topography and acoustics constitute caves as novel, multisensory environments, capable of providing a temporal/ephemeral site-specific experience. However, this is still a general description – below I examine caves from the consideration of the other defining feature of installation art: the interactivity between humans and the caves. The topography, luminary conditions and auditory settings of caves involve bodily engagement and heightened senses/attention.

## Cave topography and human engagement

The topography of a cave should form the starting point for investigation. Caves may be formed in a variety of conditions, including those of sandstone, volcanic and even glacial circumstance – those with Palaeolithic art, at least in Europe, however, are most famously associated with limestone (or karstic) geologies, the nature of which contributes to the formation of natural hollows (Waltham 1974). It is generally known that the configuration of cave floor is never flat – this is attributed to its formation process. In the beginning, a cave is a microscopic level fissure running through this limestone land. However, carbon-dioxide-enriched rainwater is infiltrated into the narrow fracture of limestone, and the fissure is gradually widened over time (Waltham 1974; Straus 1990). Once a conduit/channel reaches a certain size by erosion of subterranean water, internal collapse begins taking place. Repetition of crumbling of cave ceiling enlarges inside a cave, and the water flow eroding/transferring debris creates sediments of complicated configurations on the cave floor. Water, percolated through the limestone, dissolves calcite to create uniquely textured surfaces (Gillieson 2009). The whole process for cave formation requires tens of millennia (Gillieson 2009)

As many researchers (*e.g.* White 2003; Pettitt *et al.* 2014) have remarked, venturing inside the cave interior is often not an easy task, and even shallow caves could present difficulties or dangers due to this unpredictable topography; even speleologists with modern equipment may struggle in such conditions (Waltham 1974). An explorer needs to pay constant attention to the nature of the cave floor in order to navigate, and a certain degree of flexibility may be required to traverse some areas of the cave or even just to retain balance. As the shape of the cave wall changes, unpredictably, inwards and outwards, space can become so narrow that minor acts of bodily contortion may be necessary to proceed (Pastoors and Weniger 2011). Thus, bodily awareness is the first way in which a visitor is installed into the cave environment, constituting a significant impact on their awareness of their surroundings as physical and physiological responses that present an 'overall multisensory-motor experience' (Bacci and Pavani 2014, 26).

Recent installation artworks may be used to understand how such experiences can be constituted, and from these one can elucidate how humans engaged experientially with caves. A series of architectural works by Shusaku Arakawa and Madeline Gins serves as an informative example of a visitor's role within such an environment. These artists produced provocative architectures, the significance of which is discussed at present in the field of philosophy and contemporary art. The salient characteristic of their work is its highly complicated topography. The 'Sites of Reversible Destiny' in Yoro Park in Japan (1995) is a large hemispherical depression of approximately 18,000 m$^2$. The depression has a 25° tilt from rim to centre and consists of a number of small mounds that contribute to irregular topography. Although trees and narrow paths are situated within the work's geography, the experience of these runs contrary to everyday perception: a path viewed from a specific point appears to run through flat ground, for example, but upon traversing the path it becomes clear that it is actually on highly tilted ground (Kaji-O'Grady 2002). All information encountered within this environment seems to run against our normative expectations, including unusually convex and concave floors, meaning explorers can lose their balance or fall when suddenly encountering a steep slope if they are not expecting it. In order to avoid discomfiture and accidents, one must carefully comprehend the environment, involving observation, presumption and hypothesis-testing in terms of body use. In fact, being forced into such a condition requires a more direct and critical engagement with one's perception for surroundings, and through the unusual use of the body it is possible to recover, discover or educate the function of the human body (Baron 2008; Keane 2013). In the same vein as this architecture, Richard Serra's 2006 sculptural installation work 'Sequence' also requires that participants use their bodies in ways distinct from those of everyday life. The installation consists of randomly curved walls that contribute to the convexity and concavity of the space, and participants often encounter narrow points through which they cannot walk with any ordinary posture. In order to explore the work, therefore, they are forced to twist their body or occasionally to crawl. Consequently, these actions 'provoke a dizzying sensation of steel and space in motion' (Bacci and Pavani 2014, 24).

Aside from the cave floor, wall and ceiling (the three often contiguous and thus further adding to the abnormal sense of space), the very nature of the physical environment is distinct: numerous stalagmites and stalactites present a unique and unusual visual impression (Till 2014). Stalagmites (forming from the floor up) and stalactites (from the ceiling down), along with calcite flowstones can easily create the illusion that everything appears upside-down. The effect could further be exaggerated with the reflections cast by still pools of water. A second work of Arakawa and Gins (from 1994) illustrates this effect: 'Ubiquitous Site' in the Contemporary art Museum of Okayama prefecture (Ryoanji in Nagi, Japan). Here, the traditional Japanese Zen garden in Ryoanji is reconstructed on both interior sides of a tube-like space. In the middle of the 20 m long space, see-saws are located on both the ground and the ceiling. Keane (2013a) notes that such a mirror-like-environment easily hampers visitors' spatial orientation; they lose their proper positioning within the installation. Given that in quotidian, Upper Palaeolithic life such disorienting upside-down architectures did not exist, the cave environment must have strongly drawn attention from explorers, perhaps stimulating questions of *where am I?* or *where is here?*

Thus, as these installation works exemplify, cave topography forms an essential factor for engaging a visitor with the environment. To state this concisely, *passive audiences* in such environments are forced to become *active participants*. The combination of unusual bodily control and spatial disorientation through the mirror-like surroundings offers significant levels of multisensory experience.

## Darkness and light

In human culture, darkness tends to be associated with fear, because risks and dangers in most activities during darkness simply increase (Edensor 2013). This dark-related fear transforms uncertainty into the devils, monsters or supernatural beings that in most societies are believed to lurk in the darkness. For this reason, caves are likely associated with fear, the unknown and other worlds (Ucko and Rosenfeld 1967; Pfeiffer 1982; Arias and Ontañón 2012; Figueiredo 2013). It would be remiss to claim, without supporting evidence, that Palaeolithic hunters necessarily feared darkness. Ethnographic examples such as the forest-dwelling Mbuti of the Congo regard the darkness of the forest as a positive element (*e.g.* Turnball 1976; Akombo 2016); however, we cannot deny the possibility that darkness was also a hostile factor for Upper Palaeolithic hunters. Instead, we should consider the universality of our physiology and, therefore, our autonomic physiological response to the dark environment.

In deep caves, beyond the daylight-zone, permanent darkness envelops everything. As long as this is the primary condition of the cave, human actions are therefore governed by darkness, and the use of artificial light sources is essential (Moyes 2012; Pettitt *et al.* 2017). Unlike modern electric lighting, however, the light sources available during the Upper Palaeolithic were either stone lamps or torches fuelled by animal fat and twigs (de Beaune 1987), which provided only low illumination of about 10 watts/1850 kelvin, *i.e.* about the level of a candle (Delluc and Delluc 2009). With such lighting, the visible area around the light source is profoundly limited (approximately ~4 m diameter: Pastoors and Weniger 2011). The dim light is constantly moving and thus constantly alters the impression of surroundings (Pettitt 2014; Pettitt *et al.* 2017). Thus, as the explorers progressed along their path, the darkness would 'open up' before them and close in again behind them (Groenen 2000; Pettitt 2014; Pettitt *et al.* 2017).

Vision is our primary sense. The eyes receive light from external objects and transmit the information as electric pulses to the visual cortex of the brain (Murra and Di Lazzaro 2010; Di Lazzaro *et al.* 2013). The human eye consists of a cornea, pupil, lens and retina, and two type detectors on the surface of the retina: cones and rods. The cones are responsible for colour detection. On the other hand, the rods react to light levels and become active; especially so when light is scarce. During daylight, the cones are activated, processing the colours of visual information, but in the darkness the rods play the important role of distinguishing and processing forms. The number and distribution of the cones and the rods differ: around 5–6 million cones concentrate on the central area of retina, whereas over 100 million rods are located on peripheral region. As the function of these detectors depends on light levels, humans are able to distinguish objects seen between the illumination level of 0.001 lux and 100,000 lux (*e.g.* 0.001 lux is approximately equivalent to moonless clear night sky, and 100,000 lux represent direct sunlight); thus humans can perceive in various circumstances within a wide range of luminosity.

Given this, humans are not well adapted to low illumination environments, as we are mainly diurnal. Although we have a good sense of distance under daylight conditions, during darkness the location of distance becomes far more ambiguous and is ultimately lost. In total darkness, individuals are isolated perceptually, and it becomes very difficult to visually confirm events that may be happening (Bishop 2005; Morris 2011).

A closely analogous sensory experience to that of the deep caves occurred among the participants of the 'Storr' installation project (2005). NVA (Nacionale Vite Activa), an art charity institution, built an installation using a hilly landscape of 30 m$^2$ on the Isle of Skye, Scotland. It was designed to allow participants to experience how their perception and awareness alters in the night-time landscape, or in darkness, and demonstrated that even familiar surroundings, once covered by darkness, could transform into strange, unfamiliar and mysterious places (Morris 2011). The conditions given to the participants were simple: participants were instructed to walk through the installation. Their experiences were assessed by a structured interview, by direct observation and by an online feedback form. In the Storr, participants were provided with a head torch and told to walk a fixed route of rough topography. As a result, during the walking, they were exposed to a constant worry that anything might have suddenly appeared from out of the darkness. It therefore became necessary for the participants to be able to distinguish between artificial sounds that were 'part' of the installation from natural sounds or the footsteps of other participants. As their eyesight was so profoundly limited (they could not see beyond a few metres) their sense of hearing was noticeably heightened, and this altered sensation substituted for their visual sense. Consequently, their awareness became so sensitive that they responded even to the softest of noises. Furthermore, the absence of light forced them to refine not only their auditory sense, but also their olfactory and tactile senses. They reported that they perceived rustling leaves, the smell of the wet ground, and the cold wind, all as vivid experiences. Being in such an environment, one cannot help being extremely 'attentive' (Morris 2011, 322). Within darkness, therefore, one's awareness concentrates in an exaggerated way on all components of the environment.

In such an invisible place, as experienced by the project's participants, one necessarily relies on alternative senses in order to collect information about surroundings. This supplementary response of alternative senses to a reduced visual sense has been acquired during the trajectory of human evolution. The world is perceptively constructed by input from multiple senses (Levent and Pascual-Leone 2014). One perceives, for example, water as 'water' through a combination of colour, smell, sound, textural sensation (cold or hot) and taste. Such a combination of different sensory channels is essential for survival as it maximises the chances that dangers or opportunities have been correctly identified: for instance, even if visual data are unavailable, one may distinguish predators/prey by their footsteps. Humans rely in particular on 'tele-receptive senses' (visual, audial and olfactory), which detect sensory information from both the near and distant environment (Aglioti and Pazzaglia 2010). Therefore, once the visual sense deteriorates, the other two senses are automatically activated and become critical for detecting information about the environment.

As Upper Palaeolithic cave explorers had to rely on non-electric light, such an importance of the audial and olfactory realms is very clear; as the light source available to them was far less bright than electric lamps, their visual acuity must have been considerably limited. Given the combination of this limited eyesight and the complex topographic features of caves, it is easy to imagine that the Palaeolithic cave explorer needed to pay considerable attention to their multisensual surroundings in order to avoid misdirection and accidents. As well as tele-receptive senses, it has been suggested (Pettitt 2014; Pettitt *et al.* 2017) that the sense of touch was particularly important, because this allows one to keep balance and assist in a variety of body uses, such as twisting and lowering during exploration within complicate cave geographies. Touch would have played an important role in cave navigation. In cave exploration, therefore, the texture of surroundings, the sound of breathing of others and other noises, the scent in the air, all replaced the reduced visual perception. In this sense the cave becomes a very different experiential world.

## Acoustic properties in caves and in relation to human activity

Through the discussion above it can be justifiably thought that exploring caves required significant interaction between the explorer and the cave environment. Topography, darkness, disorientated spatial perception, activation of the non-visual senses and unfamiliar ways of body use combine to create a unique and unfamiliar perceptive environment. In addition to this, it is possible that acoustic properties added a further spectrum of interaction.

Deep caves are profoundly quiet places, given their isolation from major background noises in the outside world (*e.g.* wind, rustling of leaves and rain). In such acoustic isolation, even very low levels of sound become accentuated, such as footsteps and the sound of dripping water (Till 2014). Once a certain level of sound is made, the strong acoustic resonance of caves can considerably exaggerate noise (*e.g.* the cathedral-like Salon Noir of Niaux Cave). Reznikoff refers to this feature of cave as 'acoustic pipes' (1995, 543), describing details in a survey of three caves: Niaux, Fontanet and Le Portel (Reznikoff 1995; 2008; 2014). Reznikoff defines resonance by its strength (noise level) and length (duration), and measured this at various points along the caves' walls. In order to cause resonance, he used his voice, changing pitch from low to high (specifically C to G3), and found that lower sounds were more likely to generate strong resonance. He also noted a correspondence between the resonance of the body and resonance of the cave; sounds such as *mm* or *um* that cause cranial vibration through their enunciation also produce a vibration within the cave. As a result, it was with this sound that resonance could most effectively be measured. Additionally, the male voice is more suitable to producing a more pronounced echo than the female, because the sound of lower frequencies generates a stronger resonance (Reznikoff 2008; 2014).

Based on these observations, Reznikoff suggested that Upper Palaeolithic cave visitors must have utilised the resonance to measure distance as part of their exploration: since the interior of a cave is entirely dark, one could use their voice and resonance as a form of sonar navigation. As with the light sources available almost nothing can be seen over 1–2 m from the light source, sound resonance can be used to measure distances between the explorer and, for example, a dead end of a passage. Such a technique is well known as the 'echolocation' that visually impaired people use to perceive their surroundings by generating clicking sounds in their mouths (even non-blind individuals can acquire this skill through a few hours training, even if not to the extent of the visually impaired: Arnott and Alain 2014). It is therefore technically possible that Upper Palaeolithic people used echolocation as part of their exploratory apparatus. Reznikoff (1995) further argues that the positioning of cave art often remarkably corresponds to resonant places within those caves, adding support to the notion that Upper Palaeolithic artists were well aware of cave acoustics.

In this vein, the voice is a far more appropriate means of generation resonance as a form of echolocation than musical instruments. The pitch of the human voice can be quickly adjusted, whereas flutes, drums or hand clapping cannot; instruments furthermore require both hands to hold and operate, which becomes difficult when the explorer needs to hold a light source in one hand (Reznikoff 2008; 2014) and potentially to steady the body or feel the cave with the other. Of course, this view, unlike observable bodily reaction to environmental facts such as topography and luminary condition, cannot go beyond hypothesis. However, it is highly likely that visitors were engaged with the sound property of caves, and we can therefore assume that the auditory environment formed part of the installation of the cave art.

## Potential of cave-installation view

From the perspective of installation art, I have demonstrated that the cave environment defines human physical and cognitive conditions and encourages them to take a certain site-specific action. In consequence, it can be said that caves inevitably enhance interactivity and provide a temporal multisensory experience compatible with the definition of installation art.

Because of unique environmental constraints, one's experience in caves unavoidably differs from that of outside; indeed, this novel immersive experience is so-called 'alternate mental states of reality' (Moyes *et al.* 2017) or, in short, 'alternative reality' (Sakamoto 2014, 83). This experience is the absolute condition for Palaeolithic viewers/artists to see/produce visual works that now we call cave art, and considering the reason for entering into deep interior of caves to create art despite the difficult accessibility, we cannot help hypothesising that there was a meaningful link between this alternative reality and the visual art being made. In other words, Palaeolithic people selected the deep interior of caves as places for art so that it may be created deliberately within the wider experience of navigating this unique environment.

Capturing the essence of cave art through utilising the concept of installation art is of fundamental importance to understanding the experience of Palaeolithic artists. What will this view provide us? Specifically, there are two possibilities: one is that visual works of cave art can also be examined in light of installation art. It is reported that shadow/darkness play an essential role for some animal images (*e.g.* a deer-like natural hollow in Niaux: Bahn and Vertut 1997, so-called bison man in el Castillo: Groenen 2000, a vertically depicted bison in Niaux: Lewis-Williams 2002), and the disappearance/appearance of these images can be manipulated by the position of a light source. The interactivity under the environmental restriction is the essential element in these images. In the same vein, we can focus on facts of bodily engagement with artworks, rather than assuming cave art is a series of static visual information, through considering environmental components such as topography/size/position of cave walls, *etc*. Significantly, by exploring this, means of interactivity that have perhaps gone unnoticed may become detectable (*e.g.* Boado and Romero 1993; Sakamoto 2014).

The other possibility is that this approach contains a broad compatibility with other fields of research. After the 1990s, when mainstream archaeological theory was arguably lost, prehistoric archaeologists have often looked to cognitive and neuroscience disciplines for theoretical development (Hodgson 2000; 2003; 2006). Alternatively, some have favoured interpreting cave art on an individual case-by-case approach, *e.g.* forensic analysis on hand stencils or finger flutings (Sharpe and Van Gelder 2006; Snow 2013), morphological analysis on superimposed animal images (Azema and Rivere 2012) and contextual analysis on hand stencils (Pettitt *et al.* 2014). The cave-installation art perspective outlined here is a broad theoretical framework that considers the human-art-environment triad, which implies that it can support and connect to all of the above approaches. For instance, Pettitt *et al.* (2014) associate the production of hand stencils with the importance of the sense of touch (to keep balance and detect information) in the dark environments. This hypothesis is a probable reality of interacting with the space of cave-installation art. What is important here is that this compatibility may extend to wider issues of cave art, which may, as per Lewis-Williams (2002), in turn lead to more scientifically reliable explanations. Thus, these advantages secure the value of the cave-installation art interpretation, and hold further potential for contribution to our knowledge of European Upper Palaeolithic cave art.

## Conclusion

In conclusion, caves can be regarded as installation art that necessarily engages humans with interaction with its environmental elements. The very spatial properties define basic human action-cognition. The unusual multisensory experience offered from such a circumstance is the precondition of European Upper Palaeolithic cave art. The reason why Palaeolithic people selected caves as places for art can be referred to in association with this environmental significance. Case studies to show the interconnectivity between human, art and space are necessary to show how humans are actually installed into the cave-art space and better comprehend the nature and experience of cave art.

## Bibliography

Aglioti, S.M. and Pazzaglia, M. (2011). Sounds and Scents in (Social) Action. *Trends in Cognitive Sciences* 15, 47–55.

Akombo, D. (2016). *The Unity of Music and Dance in World Cultures*. North Carolina: Macfarland & Company.

Arias, P. and Ontañón, R. (2012) La Galma [Spain]: Long term human activity in a karst system. In: K.A. Bergsvik and R. Skeates (eds) *Cave in Context, the cultural significance of caves and rock shelters in Europe*, pp. 101–117. Oxford: Oxbow Books.

Arnott, S.R. and Alain, C. (2014) A Brain Guide to Sound Galleries. In: N. Levent and A. Pascual-Leone (eds) *The Multisensory Museum: Cross-disciplinary perspectives on touch, sound, smell, memory, and space*, pp. 85–108. Lanham, Maryland: Rowman & Littlefield.

Azema, M. and Rivere, F. (2012) Animation in Palaeolithic Art: A pre-echo of cinema. *Animation* 86, 316–324.

Bacci, F. and Pavani, F. (2014) 'First Hand', Not 'First Eye' Knowledge: Bodily experience in museum. In: N. Levent and A. Pascual-Leone (eds) *The Multisensory Museum: Cross-disciplinary perspectives on touch, sound, smell, memory, and space*, pp. 17–28. Lanham, Maryland: Rowman & Littlefield.

Bahn, P.G. and Vertut, J. (1997) *Journey Through the Ice Age*. London: Weidenfeld and Nicolson.

Baptista, A.M. (2009) *O paradigma perdido: o Vale do Côa ea arte paleolítica de ar livre em Portugal*. Porto: Edições Afrontamento.

Baron, R.M. (2008) The Role of Tentativeness in Perceiving Architecture and Art: A far-from-equilibrium ecological perspective. *Ecological Psychology* 20, 328–342.

Beltran, A. (1982) *Rock Art of the Spanish Levant.* Cambridge: Cambridge University Press.

Bishop, C. (2005) *Installation Art.* London: Tate Publishing.

Boado, F.C. and Romero, R.P. (1993) Art, Time and Thought: A formal study comparing palaeolithic and postglacial art. *World Archaeology* 25, 187–203.

Burkitt, M.C. (1963) [1933] *The Old Stone Age: A study of palaeolithic times.* New York: Atheneum.

Clottes, J. and Lewis-Williams, J.D. (1998) *The Shamans of Prehistory: Trance and magic in the painted caves.* New York: Harry N Abrams.

de Beaune, S. (1987) Palaeolithic Lamps and their Specialization: A hypothesis. *Current Anthropology* 28, 569–577.

Delluc, B. and Delluc, G. (2009) Eye and vision in Palaeolithic Art. In: P. Bahn (ed.) *An Enquiring Mind: Studies in honor of Alexander Marshack*, pp. 77–98. Oxford: Oxbow Books.

Di Lazzaro, P., Murra, D., and Schwortz, B. (2013) Pattern Recognition After Image Processing of Low-Contrast Images, the Case of the Shroud of Turin. *Pattern Recognition* 46, 1964–1970.

Edensor, T. (2013) Reconnecting with Darkness: Gloomy landscapes, lightless places. *Social & Cultural Geography* 14, 446–465.

Figueiredo, L.A.V. (2013) Cave and Karst at the Cinema: Cultural speleology and the geography of symbolic landscapes. In: M. Filippi and P. Bosk (eds) *16th International Congress of Speleology, Czech Republic, Brno, July 21-28, 2013 (volume 1)*, pp. 229–234. Brno: Czech Speleological Society.

Gibson, J.J. (1979) *The Ecological Approach to Visual Perception.* Boston: Houghton Mifflin.

Gillieson, D. (2009) *Caves: Processes, development and management.* Hoboken: John Wiley & Sons.

Groenen, M. (2000) *Sombra y luz en el arte Paleolitico.* Barcelona: Ariel.

Hodgson, D. (2000) Shamanism, Phosphenes, and Early Art: An alternative synthesis. *Current Anthropology* 41, 866–873.

Hodgson, D. (2003) The Biological Foundations of Upper Palaeolithic Art: Stimulus, percept and representational imperatives. *Rock Art Research* 20, 3–22.

Hodgson, D. (2006) Altered States of Consciousness and Palaeoart: An alternative neurovisual explanation. *Cambridge Archaeological Journal* 16, 27–37.

Kaji-O'Grady, S. (2002) National Identity at Arakawa & Gins' Site of Reversible Destiny – Yoro, Japan. *Fabrications* 12, 19–34.

Keane, J. (2013) Initiating Change: Architecting the body-environment with Arakawa and Gins. *Architectural Design* 83, 76–83.

Leroi-Gourhan, A. (1968a) *The Art of Prehistroric Man in Western Europe.* London: Thames and Hudson.

Leroi-Gourhan, A. (1968b) The Evolution of Paleolithic Art. *Scientific American* 218, 58–70.

Levent, N. and Pascual-Leone, A. (2014) Introduction. In: N. Levent and A. Pascual-Leone (eds) *The Multisensory Museum: Cross-disciplinary perspectives on touch, sound, smell, memory, and space*, pp. xiii–xxvi. Lanham, Maryland: Rowman & Littlefield.

Lewis-Williams, J.D. and Dowson, T.A. (1988) Signs of All Times: Entoptic phenomena in Upper Palaeolithic art. *Current Anthropology* 29, 201–245.

Lewis-Williams, J.D. (2002) *The Mind in the Cave: Consciousness and the origins of art.* London: Thames & Hudson.

Mithen, S.J. (1988) Looking and Learning: Upper Palaeolithic art and information gathering. *World Archaeology* 19, 297–327.

Morris, N.J. (2011) Night Walking: Darkness and sensory perception in a night-time landscape installation. *Cultural Geographies* 18, 315–342.

Moyes, H. (2012) *Sacred Darkness: A global perspective on the ritual use of caves.* Boulder: University Press of Colorado.

Moyes, H., Rigoli, L., Huette, S., Montello, D., Matlock, T. and Spivey, M. (2017) Darkness and the Imagination: The role of environment in the development of spiritual belief. In: C. Pappadopoulos and

H. Moyes (eds) *The Oxford Handbook of Light in Archaeology*, pp. 1-26. Oxford: Oxford University Press.

Murra, D. and Di Lazzaro, P. (2010) Sight and Brain: An introduction to the visually misleading images. In: P. Lazzaro (ed.) *International Workshop on the Scientific Approach to the Acheiropoietos Images, Conference at ENEA, Frascati, Italy*, pp. 31-34. Rome, Italian National Agency for New Technologies, Energy and Sustainable Economic Development.

Nowell, A. (2006) From a Paleolithic Art to Pleistocene Visual Cultures. *Journal of Archaeological Method and Theory* 13, 239-249.

Pastoors, A. and Weniger, G.C. (2011) Cave Art in Context: Methods for the analysis of the spatial organization of cave sites. *Journal of Archaeological Research* 19, 377-400.

Pettitt, P. (2014) The European Upper Palaeolithic. In: V. Cummings, P. Jordan and M. Zvelebil (eds) *The Oxford Handbook of the Archaeology and Anthropology of Hunter-Gatherers*, pp. 279-309. Oxford: Oxford University Press.

Pettitt, P.B. (2015) Darkness Visible. Shadows art and the ritual experience of caves in Upper Palaeolithic Europe. In: M. Dowd and R. Hensey (eds) *The Archaeology of Darkness*, pp. 11-23. Oxford: Oxbow Books.

Pettitt, P., Lelushko, S. and Sakamoto, T. (2017) Light, Human Evolution and the Palaeolithic. In: C. Popadopoulos and H. Moyes (eds) *The Oxford Handbook of Light in Archaeology*, pp. 1-29. Oxford: Oxford University Press.

Pettitt, P., Castillejo, A.M., Arias, P., Peredo, R.O. and Harrison, R. (2014) New Views on Old Hands: The context of stencils in El Castillo and La Garma caves (Cantabria, Spain). *Antiquity* 88, 47-63.

Pfeiffer, J.E. (1982) *The Creative Explosion. An inquiry into the origins of art and religion*. New York: Harper and Row.

Ran, F. (2009) *A History of Installation Art and the Development of New Art Forms: Technology and the hermeneutics of time and space in modern and postmodern art from cubism to installation*. New York: Peter Lang.

Reiss, J.H. (1999) *From Margin to Center: The spaces of installation art*. Massachusetts: MIT Press.

Reznikoff, I. (1995) On the Sound Dimension of Prehistoric Painted Caves and Rocks. In: E. Tarasti (ed.) *Musical Signification: Essays in the semiotic theory and analysis of music*, pp. 541-557. Berlin: Mouton de Gruyter.

Reznikoff, I. (2008) Sound Resonance in Prehistoric Times: A study of Paleolithic painted caves and rocks. *Journal of the Acoustical Society of America* 123, 3603.

Reznikoff, I. (2014) On the Sound Related to Painted Caves and Rocks. In: J. Ikaheimo, A.K. Salmi and T. Aikas (eds) *Sounds Like Theory 12 Nordic Theoretical Archaeological Group Meeting in Oulu 25-28.4.2012, Monographs of the Archaeological Society of Finland 2*, pp. 101-109. Helsinki: Archaeological Society of Finland.

Sakamoto, T. (2014) Upper Palaeolithic Cave Art as Multisensory Interactive Installation Art: Analysis of human-art-environment triad. Unpublished Master's dissertation, Durham University.

Sharpe, K. and Van Gelder, L. (2006) The Study of Finger Flutings. *Cambridge Archaeological Journal* 16, 281-295.

Snow, D.R. (2013) Sexual Dimorphism in European Upper Palaeolithic Cave Art. *American Antiquity* 78, 746-761.

Straus, L.G. (1990) Underground Archaeology: Perspectives on caves and rockshelters. *Archaeological Method and Theory* 2, 255-304.

Till, R. (2014) Sound Archaeology: Terminology, Palaeolithic cave art and the soundscape. *World Archaeology* 46, 1-13.

Turnbull, C.M. (1976) *Wayward Servants: The two worlds of the African pygmies*. Santa Barbara: Greenwood.

Ucko, P.J. and Rosenfeld, A. (1967) *Palaeolithic Cave Art*. New York: McGraw-Hill.

Vialou, D. (1998) *Our Prehistoric Past: Art and civilization*. London: Thames and Hudson.

Waltham, T. (1974) *Caves*. New York: Crown.

White, R. (2003) *Prehistoric Art: The symbolic journey of humankind*. New York: Harry N. Abrams.

# Chapter 9

# Reflecting Magdalenian identities: Considering a functional duality for Middle to Late Magdalenian antler projectile points

*Michelle C. Langley*

## Abstract
*Items of hunting weaponry are perfect for use in social-signalling as these artefacts are highly visible to persons both intimately familiar with the individual carrying the implement, as well as those encountered on the landscape during the course of subsistence or social activities. Magdalenian antler projectile points were no exception, being ubiquitous across the Magdalenian territory, carefully crafted and frequently beautifully decorated. These last two aspects have understandably drawn the attention of researchers over the past 150 years and resulted in their use to identify interaction between spatially distance sites (for example). This chapter uses archaeological and ethnographic data to explore whether the iconic, bilaterally barbed Magdalenian point, along with the ubiquitous bevel-based point, performed a functional duality, being both: (1) a subsistent; and (2) a social tool. It will be argued that, while regional communities are reflected in the form of the bevel edge, a wider Magdalenian identity may be contained within the bilaterally barbed points.*

## Introduction
Archaeological evidence suggests that a complex web of social and economic interconnections existed across Western and Central Europe during the Middle to Late Magdalenian (c. 21,000 to 14,000 cal. BP), with the apparent proliferation of both parietal and portable art argued to reflect an increase in social tensions and social competition at this time (*e.g.* Geist 1978; Conkey 1980; 1985; Bahn 1982; Sieveking 1991; Jochim *et al.* 1999). Included amongst the portable art lexicon of this period is an extensive array

of decorated antler, bone and ivory projectile points. Used to extract vital nutritional and raw material resources (potentially) from terrestrial, aquatic and avian species, these carefully crafted osseous weapon tips were also the perfect material culture item for use in social-signalling.

In this chapter, two aspects of Middle to Late Magdalenian antler projectile weaponry will be considered: (1) bevel-edge designs found on single and double bevel-based points (known as sagaie), and (2) the morphology and decoration of bilaterally barbed points (previously known as harpon). Situated in a framework of information exchange theory, and supported by ethnographic data, it is suggested that two forms of emblemic style are present within these artefacts: (1) regionally distinct communities as represented by the bevel-edge designs, and (2) a territory-wide symbol as represented by the bilaterally barbed points. Consequently, it will be argued that, while being fully operational hunting equipment, these implements were also social tools. In other words, that these weapon tips maintained a functional duality.

## Projectile point morphology, style and information exchange

In the archaeological literature, hunting weaponry is considered an excellent item for use in social-signalling, as not only do these artefacts have 'widespread social, economic, political and symbolic import' (Weissner 1983, 272), they are highly visible to persons who are both intimately familiar with the individual carrying the implement, as well as those encountered on the landscape during the course of subsistence activities (Tostevin 2007). Ethnographic data, as will be shown throughout this chapter, demonstrates that a multitude of information can and is stored and shared in projectile points through a process best described by information exchange theory.

Information exchange theory originated with the work of Wobst and Weissner during the late 1970s–1980s, and views style – those attributes which are the product of choices made by the artisan and selected from among a variety of possible solutions – that is, the chosen 'ways of doing things' resulting in different 'styles' in morphology and/or decoration of an artefact (Sackett 1973) – as the result of a conscious act of social communication aimed at various levels of society. Therefore, it can be argued to be an active process as opposed to the passive character of style advocated by social interaction theory (see Clark 1993; Barton et al. 1994). From this, style is argued to have its basis in a fundamental human behaviour where people create personal and social identity through comparison. According to this theory, the volume of style observed in the archaeological record can be used as a proxy for the amount of information that flowed across the landscape in prehistory. Put another way, 'style' is the vehicle by which information about the identity of the maker/owner of an artefact is transmitted to observers, with the amount of style invested into artefacts and their increased deposition in the archaeological record indicating the quantity of information being communicated between groups in a social network (*e.g.* Wobst 1977; Gamble 1980; 1982; Weissner 1983; 1984; 1985). For, as Dobres and Hoffman (1994, 213)

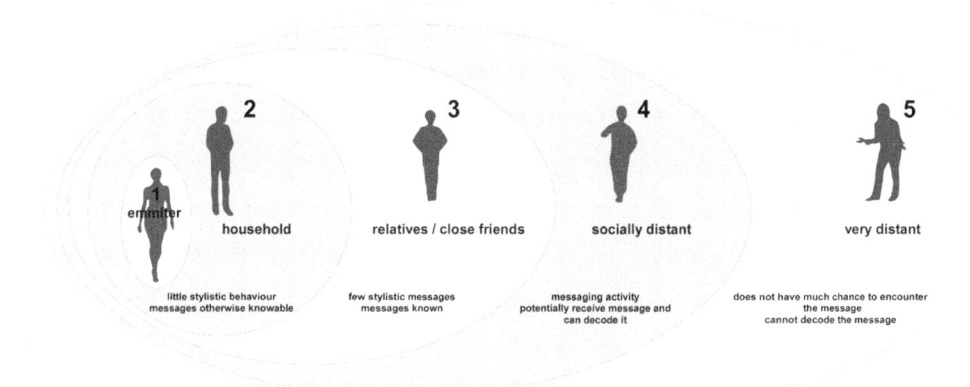

*Figure 9.1. Target groups for stylistic messages held in the design and display of material culture (altered after Wobst 1977, 325).*

rightly point out, 'technologies are not practiced in a cultural vacuum where physical laws take precedence', but, rather, are 'dynamic strategies often related to social identity and difference' (Dobres and Hoffman 1994, 219).

The use of artefacts to convey messages is considered to be most valuable when communicating information to those people in 'the middle distance'. That is, those people not so close to the emitter that the messages are already known, and therefore not needed (groups 2 and 3 in Figure 9.1), nor those so distant that the message cannot be correctly deciphered (group 5 in Figure 9.1). This 'middle group' (group 4 in Figure 9.1) instead consists of those people who are not encountered every day, but frequently enough that they understand the meaning of displayed symbols, and may include neighbouring groups, trading partners or other alliance members.

As Wobst (1977) explains, because stylistic messages are primarily aimed at 'the middle distance', these messages will mostly concern social integration and differentiation. Furthermore, as complex messages, or infrequently emitted messages, they require more energy to both make (emit) and interpret (receive); only simple and frequently used messages will normally be encoded in material culture. The types of messages that will therefore be commonly broadcast include: emotional state, identification (class affinity, social group affiliation, religious affiliation, rank, *etc.*), authorship and ownership.

So, why use artefacts in social-signalling? The use of material culture to transmit messages between the emitter and those in 'the middle distance' has a number of advantages for both parties, with the first being a reduction in stress during first encounters. This is achieved through potential advantages and disadvantages of the interaction being broadcast by the displayed artefacts before close (potentially dangerous) quarters are reached (Wobst 1977). An ethnographic example of this situation was given by Weissner (1983, 269), who reported that, while the San were afraid of strangers, it was 'said that if a man makes arrows in the same way, one could be fairly sure he shares similar values around hunting, land rights, and general conduct', while 'stylistic difference [in projectile point design] may signal another set of values and practices, if the two groups are known to each other, or if not, that its maker is foreign and his behaviour is unpredictable'.

The second major advantage of material social-signalling is the ability of these items to bind groups together in times of economic and/or social stress, allowing for and encouraging cooperation between related groups, resulting in better chances for the continued survival of all parties (Gamble 1982). Indeed, Conard (2008) has described such artefacts as the social and symbolic 'glue' that held together large and complex social groups during the Late Pleistocene.

A third advantage is that the emitter of the information (the person who made and/or owns the artefact) does not need to be present for the message to be transferred. Unlike vocal messages where the emitter and the receiver must be within 'earshot', messages held in artefacts have relative longevity, do not change rapidly and can be made portable, therefore broadcasting their information widely across the landscape and to people who are spatially distant to the emitter (Wobst 1977).

Additionally, while carried by the individual, an object's mode of production and morphology will be guided by its community of practice (Dobres and Hoffman 1994; Lave and Wenger 1991), and therefore should conform to cultural ideals regarding manufacturing techniques, form, decoration and use. As communities generally inhabit and exploit a certain territory (of varying sizes depending on their residential mobility strategy, resource richness, *etc.*), the 'style' of weapon carried by an individual can become indicative of that region and the people who occupy it. Therefore, because of the production and use of projectile points within cultural constraints, and because of the tendency of these weapons to be utilised in a certain way and in a certain (at least semi-)confined spatial area, hunting equipment has been identified as a prime item for the transmitting of messages (Weissner 1983; 1985; Tostevin 2007).

## Considering Middle to Late Magdalenian antler projectile points

Two aspects of the studied osseous projectile points in particular were considered to be potentially informative for investigating Magdalenian social interaction and organisation: the design of the bevel edge found on single and double bevel-based points and the morphological and decoration similarities of regionally dispersed bilaterally barbed points. Each of these technologies will be considered below in order to attempt to understand how the different styles apparent in these tools may have functioned within the Magdalenian social landscape.

Consideration of archaeological material from two central case studies (Isturitz, Pyrénées-Atlantiques and La Vache, Ariège), supplemented by smaller collections from another 22 sites located throughout France and southern Germany (Aurensan, Lorthet, Gourdan, Courbet, Montastruc, Laugerie-Basse, La Madeleine, Lyveyre,

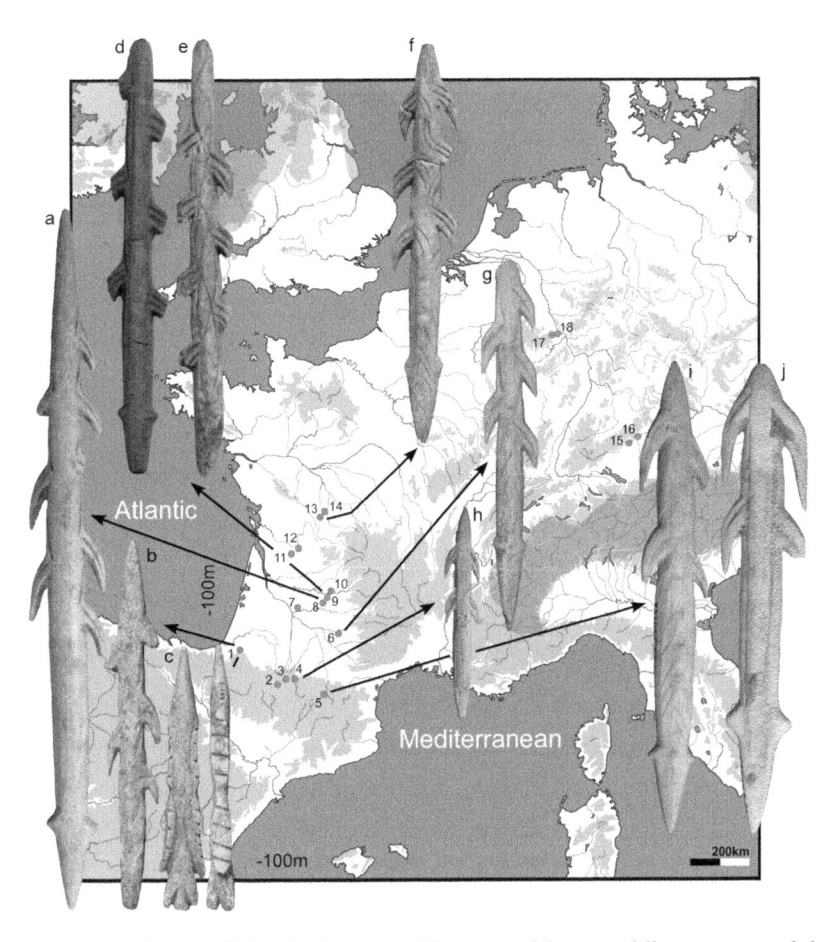

Figure 9.2. Examples of bilaterally barbed points and location of the 24 Middle to Late Magdalenian sites from which material was studied. Sites: 1) Isturitz; 2) Aurensan; 3) Lorthet; 4) Gourdan; 5) La Vache; 6) Courbet; 7) Montastruc; 8) Laugerie-Basse; 9) La Madeleine and Lyveyre; 10) La Tulière; 11) Chaire-à-Calvin; 12) La Placard, Abri de Fieux, and Grotte de l'Abbé; 13) Grotte du Bois-Ragot; 14) La Piscine, Grotte de La Marche, Fadets, and La Tannerie; 15) Hohle Fels; 16) Vogelherd; 17) Gönnersdorf; 18) Andernach-Martinsberg.

La Tulière, La Chaire-à-Calvin, Le Placard, Abri de Fieux, Grotte de l'Abbé, Bois-Ragot, La Piscine, La Marche, Les Fadets, La Tannerie, Hohle Fels, Vogelherd, Gönnersdorf and Andernach-Martinsberg) form the basis of the following discussion (Figure 9.2).

## Bevel edge design: reflecting regionally dispersed communities

Bevel-based points (consisting of both single- and double-bevelled varieties) are ubiquitous in Middle to Late Magdalenian osseous projectile point assemblages, with most examples exhibiting oblique, horizontal or cross-hatched striations incised into

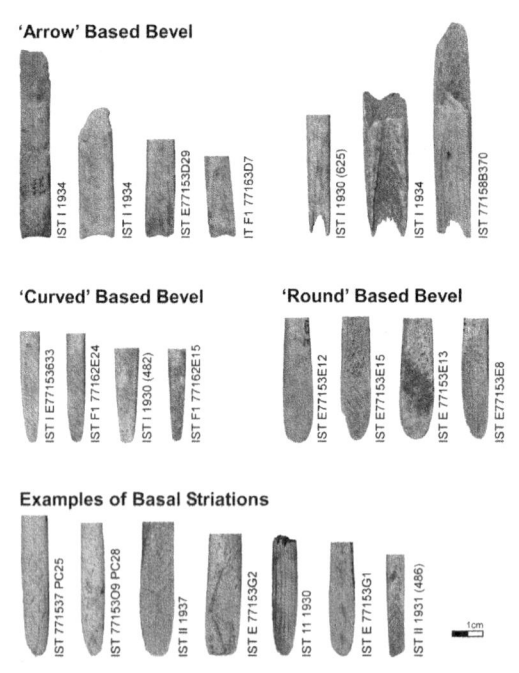

Figure 9.3. Proximal edge designs found in the Isturitz 'arrow' bevel-based point MAN collection.

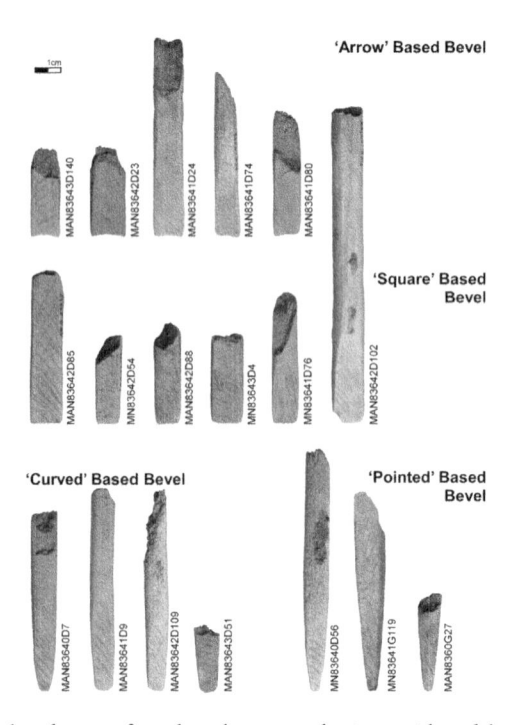

Figure 9.4. Proximal edge designs found in the La Vache 'arrow' bevel-based point assemblage.

the bevel face to assist in its secure hafting (Allain 1957; Leroi-Gourhan and Allain 1979; Allain and Rigaud 1986; 1989; 1992; Weniger 1992). While the arrangement of these striations may constitute a type of ownership mark, it is not these lines which are the topic of following discussion, though examples of the range of designs found at Isturitz and La Vache can be seen in Figures 9.3 and 9.4. Instead, we are concerned with the form of the proximal edge.

Examination of the Musée d'Archéologie Nationale (MAN) Isturitz material resulted in the identification of three types of basal edge designs present within this collection (Figure 9.3): the 'arrow' (which was also found on several whalebone implements with a slightly different character and which one might classify as a separate type), the 'curved' and the 'round' bevel edge. While the 'arrow' and 'curved' bevel design were found on both single and double bevel-based points, the 'round' edge form was only identified on single bevel-based points. Pétillon (2006, 67–68, fig. 40) has previously also noted these differences in bevel edge design in the Isturitz collection, dividing this same dataset into three more or less similar types: concave (arrow-based here), droite (square-based here) and lancéolée (curved-based here). The La Vache assemblage (also curated in MAN), on the other hand, produced four 'types' of basal edges (Figure 9.4): the 'arrow', the 'square', the 'curved' and the 'pointed' edge type.

Importantly, these bevel edge types were not found to correlate to a specific stratum, but were instead mixed together throughout the stratigraphy in both La Vache and Isturitz. Hence, the 'arrow' and 'curved' base edge forms are common to both La Vache and Isturitz, the 'round' type was unique to Isturitz, and both the 'pointed' and 'square' types were only found in the La Vache assemblage. While the absence of the 'round' type at La Vache may be simply explained by the fact that this site was not occupied during the Middle Magdalenian (as Isturitz was), and single bevel-based points were the dominant point form during this earlier phase, the complete absence of both the 'square' and 'pointed' basal types at Isturitz is perplexing.

Given that these different bevel-base forms are only visible when the point is not hafted, and would not have altered the performance of the weapon, we might suggest that these design elements reflect different communities of practice. That is, that these differing base types reflect the deposition of projectile points made by several groups who manufactured them according to their own distinct traditions of production. This hypothesis is logical for Isturitz, which is commonly agreed to have been an aggregation site – a location at which regionally dispersed groups would gather periodically to engage in economic and social activities. With different Magdalenian peoples coming together at the one locale, it would have been inevitable that broken equipment from groups who maintained their own design traditions would be discarded together. Alternatively, the mixed assemblage could be interpreted as implements made in different regions being traded between groups as part of an exchange system like that known as Hxaro in Southern Africa (Lee 1979; Weissner

1983; Wadley 1987; Mitchell 2003; Brooks *et al.* 2006; see Cattelain 1997 for a South American example of a similar exchange-based assemblage formation phenomena).

Similarly, the wider range of bevel-base forms represented in the La Vache assemblage might be explained if one accepts that this site was also a location where regionally dispersed peoples congregated for periods. As has been pointed out by Clottes (2003), La Vache displays all of the characteristics used by archaeologists to identify potential Palaeolithic aggregation sites (presence of exotic materials, shared art forms, dense deposit) except for one: its physical dimensions. Usually, aggregation sites are thought to be large spaces owing to the need to house a sizeable congregation of people (Conkey 1980; Bahn 1982). La Vache, though, is a small two-chambered cave. However, given that an array of exotics (including Pecten jacobeus shells likely from the Mediterranean, whale bone likely coming from the Atlantic coast and fossils from sites up to 200 km or more away (Bahn 1982; Pétillon 2008; 2013)), along with portable art, parietal art and lithic technology indicate connections between La Vache and sites located at the opposite end of the Pyrenees, the Périgord and the Dordogne (Delporte 1974; Bahn 1982; Gordon 1988), it is apparent that La Vache was part of a wide-reaching social and economic network during the Late Magdalenian.

Furthermore, the proximity of La Vache to the famous parietal-art site of Niaux (visible across the valley) may also play an important role in its use and formation of archaeological deposits. Investigations at Niaux have shown that both this site and La Vache are contemporaneous (Arnold *et al.* 1992), with evidence for both locations having been visited by people sharing similar paint recipes – pigments of similar mineral and chemical composition have been identified on both the parietal art in Niaux and on some of the portable art from La Vache (see Clottes *et al.* 1990a; 1990b; Pepe *et al.* 1991; Clottes 1993). Interestingly, Bahn and Vertut (1997) have observed that, while depictions of animal figures with 'missiles' on or near them are extremely rare in Magdalenian art (only around 3% or 4%), with some caves having not a single example of these images, around a quarter of the animals painted in Niaux have 'missiles' associated with them. The only other cave with this frequency of animal/'missile' imagery is Cosquer (Marseille) where around 28 of the 142 images are marked. Does this unusual association between animal and 'missile' imagery at Niaux suggest a connection with the projectile weapon rich deposit found in nearby La Vache?

Clearly, either individuals or groups of people visited La Vache from a number of locations in the surrounding region (as suggested by the exotics, art, lithics and bevel diversity), and it might be suggested that this site was not simply another winter base camp but an aggregation site for a much smaller (more select?) group of people who travelled to the site for meetings on the manufacture and use of osseous projectile weaponry. Certainly, the wide variety of stylistic forms of projectile weaponry present and their proximity to Niaux with its paintings of possible projectile weapons is quite suggestive.

Ethnographically, the design or style of projectile points are known to be identifiable to regionally distinct communities. For example, Griffin (1997) reports that certain metal arrows are recognised as belonging to particular Agta groups (such as the Dupangan), while others are shared across the wider eastern Luzon community. Similarly, Hitchcock and Bleed (1997) mention that Kalahari San recognise that different groups have different preferences in both the kinds of weapons utilised as well as the forms of the projectile points employed. Further inquiry regarding the morphology of their projectile points resulted in a response that they were made according to 'the way our ancestors made them' (Hitchcock and Bleed 1997, 350). In other words, the projectile forms were a product of traditions handed down from one generation to the next, or the community of practice in which they were made (see Hodder 1982 for a similar example with metal spear points made in the vicinity of Lake Baringo). Furthermore, such an argument has already been applied to European Palaeolithic technologies, with White (1992) suggesting that it is easy to imagine that split-based antler points acted to reflect or represent particular cultural or regional identities for Aurignacian groups; similarly, Conkey (1980) notes six core design elements engraved into Magdalenian portable osseous tools in the Cantabrian region.

The fact the bevel edge forms can play no role in overt social-signalling (as these differences are only visible when the point is not hafted and therefore not in active use) supports the notion that they reflect different communities of practice rather than individual ownership. Individual ownership marks may consist of carved or painted designs (Boas 1899; Reynolds 1989), or the form of the weapon itself ('each man makes arrows for himself, shaping the points ... with some slight distinction so that he will know them from the arrows of other men', Marshall 1961, 238) (Cundy 1989; Reynolds 1989; Allen 2011), with distinctions utilised to identify individual weapons when hunting in groups (Marshall 1961; Biesele 1975; Deacon 1992). Such a mark can indicate various levels of ownership, including the individual, household, family, task group, settlement or society (Reynolds 1989), and it is possible the bevel edge form in these two Magdalenian sites could have performed this task on a wider (community) level. Certainly, each bevel edge type appears to have been carefully crafted and are numerous enough in each of the two studied assemblages to represent communities rather than individuals.

Another interesting aspect of Isturitz's projectile weaponry which provides insight into the Magdalenian social world is the alteration of nine of the points for use as pendants. Each of these artefacts are shown in Figure 9.5 (a–d, f–j), along with a number of additional pendants that are of similar appearance to the pierced projectiles. These additional artefacts include two worked pieces of antler tine which are similar to the other artefacts (Figure 9.5: k–l), and a carefully worked linear pendant which is reminiscent of the baguettes demi-rondes examples (Figure 9.5: e).

Of the nine examples identified, seven originate from single bevel-based points. This observation is interesting as double bevel-based points are not rare at Isturitz (201 examined in this study), so the absence of a double bevel example appears

146     *Michelle C. Langley*

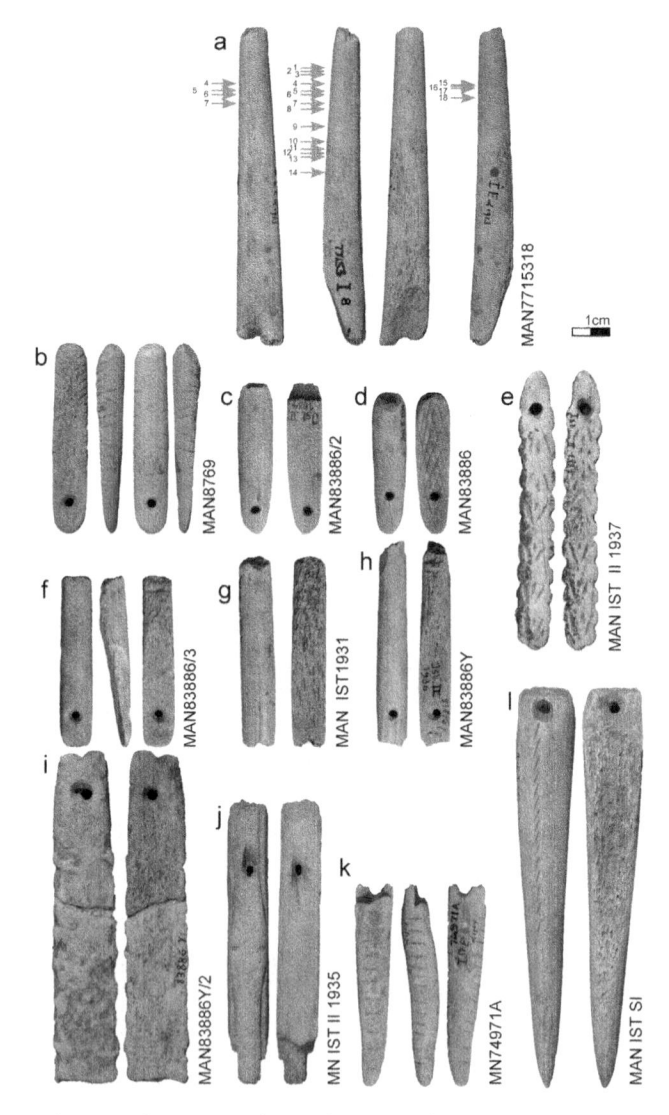

*Figure 9.5. Perforated projectile point and pseudo-projectile point ornamentation: A) Distal-mesial fragment with multiple retrieval cut marks (each being indicted by a red arrow); B-D, F-H) perforated single bevel based points; E) elongate form pendant; I-J), perforated Baguettes demi-rondes; K-L) worked antler tines.*

significant. Three of the perforated single bevels display clear impact fractures at their distal extremity (c, d, g), two were intentionally removed from a more complete implement by bifacially thinning an area before snapping the shaft via flexion (as evidenced by the chatter-marks and associated splinter fracture) (f and h), and the final example has been carefully worked to create a smooth and symmetrical tip (b), erasing any indication of whether it was fractured in use as in the first three examples or deliberately removed as in the next two. As these pendants are all of similar size, it is possible that those with evidence of deliberate removal (f and h, and possibly b) may have been cut to be consistent with others which fractured in use, and therefore had their size predetermined.

The holes used to string the ornaments were bifacially drilled (through superior and inferior surfaces) through the bevel of the implement in each case. Four out of the six implements have smoothed/rounded distal and proximal ends (b, c, d, f), while another has some rounding of the distal end, but the proximal extremity has been fractured and it cannot be determined whether this end was also rounded as in the other four examples (g). Only a single example (h) shows no signs of smoothing of the extremities; however, the proximal end has been fractured, removing any evidence of rounding, if present. While some post-depositional rounding of artefacts from this site was observed, and smoothing of beads and pendants commonly occurs through their use, in the case of MAN8769 (b), this feature is the result of a deliberate finish, either for aesthetic purposes or in order to prevent jagged or sharp edges from scratching exposed skin or catching on fabrics.

On these examples, there is no evidence that any additional decoration was added to the pendants. The striations and/or lines visible on the artefacts are all consistent with being original hafting striations (in the case of b–d, f–j), or retrieval cut marks (in the case of a and b).

While the smaller bevelled pieces (b–d, f–h) have been reported by de Saint-Périer (1936, 69–70, fig. 41) previously, the more complete point (Figure 9.5: a MAN7715318) appears to have not been identified. This pendant exhibits 18 retrieval cut marks (indicated by red arrows in Figure 9.5), along with an impact (splinter) fracture at its distal extremity. The hole was drilled from the superior surface, where a single curved striation resulting from the shoulder of the burin or other lithic used to make this feature can be seen. The proximal end has fractured and been post-depositionally rounded. Considering the large quantity of retrieval cut marks visible on this particularly piece – a great many more than usually present in the study sample (usually between one and four per artefact) – it seems reasonable to speculate as to whether this projectile point was regarded as particularly 'successful' or 'lucky' by the owner/user, resulting in its conversion into an ornament to be kept as a charm or talisman. Certainly, if this item was considered particularly 'lucky' it would account for its transformation into an item that could be worn on the body and kept over an extended period.

In addition to the bevel-based point pendants, two *baguettes demi-rondes* examples were also identified (Figure 9.5: i and j). These two weapon fragments are significantly longer than the other examples, with their perforations more crudely gouged than the carefully drilled bevelled pieces. Both exhibit impact (splinter) fractures on their extremities, demonstrating that they saw use before their transformation into a social technology.

Also examined from the Isturitz assemblage were two worked antler tines (k and l) featuring a series of parallel lines. De Saint-Périer (1936, pl. VII) presents photographs of these two artefacts along with several similar others, which, given their similarity to MAN7715318 discussed above, might be argued to have been modified to resemble projectile point pendants with the oblique line motif representing a simple reference to retrieval cut marks, a sign of a successful weapon. Along these lines, if authentic successful projectile point pendants constituted a commodity, imitations may have been produced much like the shell and animal tooth facsimile beads made from stone or ivory recovered from Aurignacian sites (White 2007). In this scenario, such artefacts may indicate that particularly successful weaponry held more importance than simply providing required food and raw materials.

## *Bilaterally barbed points: reflecting the Magdalenian identity*

The widespread similarity in the form and decoration of bilaterally barbed points is a widely discussed topic in the archaeological literature (*e.g.* Bahn 1982; Julien 1982; Gonzalez Sainz 1989; Straus 1992; Lefebvre 2011). In terms of how these similarities were maintained over a distance of some 1,000 km (north to south), Jochim *et al.* (1999, 134) have suggested that 'active visiting and exchange, and an ongoing emphasis on cultural ties, may have been used to counteract the effects of distance'. Examples of these weapons are shown in Figure 9.2.

A useful framework in which to consider the Magdalenian bilaterally barbed weaponry is Hayden's (1998) 'practical' verses 'prestige' technologies. While 'practical' technologies describe those items that solve problems of survival and basic comfort, 'prestige' technologies do not aim to perform a specific practical task, but instead act to display wealth, success and power. Their purpose is to solve social problems or accomplish a social task such as attracting mates, labour or allies, bonding members of social groups together via displays of success, or creating debt and reciprocal obligations (see also Peebles and Kus 1977; Earle 1978; Olausson 1983; Hodder 1986; Costin 1991; Perlès 1992; Hayden 1993).

It might be suggested that the Magdalenian bilaterally barbed points constitute a form of prestige technology as not only were these weapons capable of containing emblemic style (through overall morphology of barb, shaft, base and decoration), they appear to have been more carefully curated than their un-barbed counterparts (as suggested by their infrequency in the archaeological record, a total of only between 1,500–2,000 examples thus far recovered compared to many thousands of the un-barbed types), and required significantly more work to create and maintain than un-barbed points. Furthermore, when one considers that while a variety of barbed forms were technically available to the Magdalenian artisans only a very restricted range of types (in terms of barb shape, shaft section, point dimensions, *etc.*) and decoration techniques and motifs were selected. Similarly, remarkably simpler barbed point forms would have functioned just as effectively in hunting either terrestrial or aquatic game, with experiments demonstrating that self-barbed points (for example), which take significantly less time, effort and skill to produce, were extremely effective weapon tip forms. With more time and energy efficient projectile point forms available to the Magdalenians, why were such distinct and carefully crafted items produced if not to act to hold and transmit social information as well as capture game?

Along these lines, the strong morphological and decorative similarities may have acted to tie regionally dispersed groups together, making interactions out on the landscape less stressful, as was described above. Interestingly, Langlais (2009; 2011) has found an increase in regional variability of microlith form coinciding with the proposed increase in territoriality suggested by the increase in portable art and decorated osseous weaponry during the Middle Magdalenian (*e.g.* Bahn 1982; Conkey 1985; Buisson *et al.* 1996; Jochim *et al.* 1999). During this period, microlith technology becomes more diversified from what it was during the Early Magdalenian, as well as more distinct from domestic technologies. In particular, these lithic elements were hafted laterally or apically, with scalene bladelets being the dominant type in south-west France, pointed backed bladelets in the Pyrenees, and large pointed backed bladelets with a truncated base in the Poitou region (Lacombe 1998; Langlais 2011). Thus, it might be suggested that, while the different forms of microlith carried within composite antler/lithic weapon tips held and transmitted information regarding different regional identities, the osseous bilaterally barbed points may have been intentionally standardised in order to tie these same groups together under an overarching common 'Magdalenian' identity.

Alternatively, and for these very same reasons, these weapon tips may have functioned as weapons of war, their presence signalling to the observer the hostile intentions of the carrier(s). While lethal inter-group conflict among hunter-gatherers during the Late Pleistocene remains a controversial subject, with little agreement on either its extent or consequences (owing to a lack of evidence for its occurrence; see Keeley 1996; Ferguson 1997; Gat 2006), barbed spears and arrows have been recorded ethnographically to have been used in warfare in a number of ethnographic contexts. For example, by the Beothuk, Thule and Ingalik peoples of North America (Osgood 1940; McGhee 1977; Marshall 1996), as well as in Australia where they are reportedly used for both individual combat and inter-group conflict (including a specific type known as 'death spears') (Davidson 1934), and in the Matopos of Zimbabwe, Africa where several parietal images depict people attacking one another with fletched and barbed arrows (Walker 1995).

In more detail, Gould (1970, 20–21) observed encounters between Australian Western Desert groups where, in settling quarrels and social grievances, spears are noted as having a certain symbolic quality in these encounters. When the commotion begins, the relatives of the antagonists arrive, each armed with as many as six or seven spears, which they shake and rattle as they argue loudly for their side's cause. This is many more spears than one would ever need no matter how serious the conflict, and the purpose is clearly to daunt the opposition ... Spears in these cases are intended to represent a show of force.

He also reports that on occasions in which two groups come together with peaceful intentions (*e.g.* for ceremony),

the men from the visiting group approach the resident group in a body and alternately run and all together chanting and carrying their spears upright with the points facing down and clasping them near the points (a gesture of peaceful intent, since spears cannot possibly be thrown from this position) ... Thus the symbolic threat of force represented by the spear can, on certain occasions, be reversed to indicate a lack of hostility. However, it is worth remembering that the visitors and residents, despite their peaceful gestures, are still armed and give the appearance of being ready to fight if their peaceful overtures are spurned and trouble erupts. (Gould 1970, 21)

An event in which spears were being handled in this latter fashion is also shown in Tindale and Lindsay (1963, fig. 95). It is possible that the Magdalenian barbed points could have been utilised in such a fashion. Additionally, a number of ethnographies report that weapons were often deliberately discarded (and sometimes burnt) once they had killed an individual, providing an alternative explanation for the dearth of barbed points in Magdalenian assemblages.

In either of these scenarios, how intensively each individual barbed point was reduced before discard may have been influenced not only by its ability to effectively penetrate and hold game (that is, act as an effective hunting weapon), but also by their ability to transmit social messages. In other words, these implements were discarded once their form became too far removed from the commonly recognised form, and thus were considered unacceptable for further use. Experiments to determine their maximum utility are required in order to test this theory in the future.

## Conclusion

As Conkey (1985, 317) notes, 'if there is any one time during the Upper Palaeolithic at which such ritual communication increases in both quantity and diversity, it is by the Middle to Late Magdalenian'. Consequently, it is not surprising that projectile points, as a highly visible and ubiquitous item of hunter-gatherer material culture, were altered to effectively function in both social communication and in subsistence. Certainly, the Magdalenian antler projectile points discussed above were perfectly crafted to undertake such a functional duality, with information regarding both regionally dispersed groups as well as a wider Magdalenian identity potentially transmitted. Such information regarding the social organisation of peoples who lived some 21,000 years ago is hard to come by, to say the least, and future experimentation and examination of archaeological material is necessary if we are to investigate this line of inquiry further.

## Acknowledgements

The research undertaken in this paper stems from my DPhil project, undertaken at the Institute of Archaeology, University of Oxford. The Clarendon Fund (Oxford), Meyerstein Fund (Oxford) and the Boise Trust Fund (Oxford) are each thanked for funding this research, as are the staff of Musée d'Archéologie Nationale (St-Germain-en-Laye, France) for their generous time and assistance. I would particularly like to thank Nick Barton and Jean-Marc Pétillon for their guidance, as well as Meg Conkey for her stimulating discussion of Magdalenian antler projectile points during excavation digresses. Christophe Delage was kind enough to offer assistance with proofreading the manuscript. Finally, I would like to thank James Walker and Dave Clinnick for inviting me to participate in this volume.

## Bibliography

Allain, J. (1957) Contribution à l'étude des techniques magdaléniennes. Les navettes. *Bulletin de la Société Préhistorique Française* 54, 218–222.
Allain, J. and Rigaud, A. (1986) Décor et Fonction. Quelques exemples tirés du Magdalénien. *L'Anthropologie* 90, 713–738.
Allain, J. and Rigaud, A. (1989) Colles et mastics au Magdalénien. In: M. Olive and Y. Taborin (eds) *Nature et fonction des foyers préhistoriques*, pp. 221–223. Nemours: APRAIF Mémoires du Musée de Préhistoire d'Ile-de-France.
Allain, J. and Rigaud, A. (1992) Les petites pointes dans l'industrie osseuse de La Garenne: Fonction et figuration. *L'Anthropologie* 96, 135–162.
Allen, H. (2011) Thomson's Spears: Innovation and change in eastern Arnhem Land projectile technology. In: Y. Musharbash and M. Barber (eds) *Ethnography and the Production of Anthropological Knowledge: Essays in honour of Nicolas Peterson*, pp. 69–88. Canberra: ANU ePress.
Arnold, M., Cachier, H., Valladas, H. and Clottes, J. (1992) Des dates pour Niaux et Gargas. *Bulletin de la Société Préhistorique Française* 89, 270–274.
Averbouh, A. (2005) Collecte du bois de renne et territoire d'exploitation chez les groupes madgaléniens des Pyrénées ariégeoises. In: D. Vialou, J. Renault-Miskovsky and M. Patou-Mathis (eds) *Comportements des Hommes du Paléolithique Moyen et Supérieur en Europe: Territoires et milieux*, pp. 59–70. Liège: ERAUL.
Bahn, P.G. (1982) Inter-site and Inter-regional Links during the Upper Palaeolithic: The Pyrenean evidence. *Oxford Journal of Archaeology* 1, 247–268.
Bahn, P.G. and Vertut, J. (1997) *Journey Through the Ice Age*. Berkeley: University of California Press.
Barton, C.M., Clark, G.A. and Cohen, A. (1994) Art as Information: Explaining Upper Palaeolithic art in Western Europe. *World Archaeology* 26, 186–207.
Biesele, M.A. (1975) *Folklore and Ritual of !Kung Hunter-Gatherers*. Cambridge: Harvard University Press.
Boas, F. (1899) Property Marks of Alaskan Eskimo. *American Anthropologist* 1, 601–613.
Brooks, A.S., Yellen, J.E., Nevell, L. and Hartman, G. (2006) Projectile Technologies of the African MSA: Implications for modern human origins. In: E. Hovers and S.L. Kuhn (eds), *Transitions Before the Transition: Evolution and Stability in the Middle Paleolithic and Middle Stone Age*, pp. 233–256. New York: Springer.
Buisson, D., Fritz, C., Kandel, D., Pinçon, G. and Sauvet, G. (1996) Les contours découpés de têtes de chevaux et leur contribution à la connaissance du Magdalénien moyen. *Antiquités Nationales* 28, 99–128.
Cattelain, P. (1997) Hunting during the Upper Palaeolithic: Bow, spearthrower, or both? In: H. Knetch (ed.) *Projectile Technology*, pp. 213–240. New York: Plenum Press.

Clark, G.A. (1993) Paradigms in Science and Archaeology. *Journal of Archaeological Research* 1, 203-234.
Clottes, J. (1993) Paint Analyses from Several Magdalenian Caves in the Ariège Region of France. *Journal of Archaeological Science* 20, 223-235.
Clottes, J. (2003) Contexte géographique et archéologique. In: J. Clottes and H. Delporte (eds), *La Grotte de La Vache (Ariège)*, pp. 12-28. Paris: CTHS/RMN.
Clottes, J., Menu, M. and Walter, P. (1990a) La préparation des peintures magdaléniennes des cavernes ariégoises. *Bulletin de la Société Préhistorique Française* 87, 170-192.
Clottes, J., Menu, M. and Walter, P. (1990b) New Light on the Niaux Paintings. *Rock Art Research* 7, 21-26.
Conard, N.J. (2008) A Critical View of the Evidence for a Southern African Origin of Behavioural Modernity. *South African Archaeological Society* Goodwin Series 10, 175-179.
Conkey, M.W. (1980) The Identification of Prehistoric Hunter-Gatherer Aggregation: The case of Altamira. *Current Anthropology* 21, 609-630.
Conkey, M.W. (1985) Ritual Communication, Social Elaboration, and the Variable Trajectories of Paleolithic Material Culture. In: T.D. Price and J.A. Brown (eds) *Prehistoric Hunter-Gatherers: The emergence of cultural complexity*, pp. 299-323. San Diego: Academic Press.
Costin, C.L. (1991) Craft Specialization: Issues in defining, documenting, and explaining the organization of production. *Archaeological Method and Theory* 3, 1-56.
Cundy, B.J. (1989) *Formal Variation in Australian Spear and Spearthrower Technology*. British Archaeological Reports International Series 546. Oxford: British Archaeological Reports.
Davidson, D.S. (1934) Australian Spear Traits and their Derivations. *Journal of the Polynesian Society* 43, 143.
Deacon, J. (1992) *Arrows as Agents of Belief among the /Xam Bushmen*. Margaret Shaw Lecture 3. Cape Town: South African Museum.
Delporte, H. (1974) Le Magdalénien de la Grotte d'Aurensan à Bagnères-de-Bigorre (Htes. Pyr.). *Antiquités Nationales* 6, 10-25.
Dobres, M.-A. and Hoffman, C.R. (1994) Social Agency and the Dynamics of Prehistoric Technology. *Journal of Archaeological Method and Theory* 1, 211-258.
Earle, T.K. (1978) *Economic and Social Organization of a Complex Chiefdom: The Halelea district, Kaua'i, Hawaii*. Anthropological Papers 63. University of Michigan Museum of Anthropology.
Ferguson, B. (1997) Violence and War in Prehistory. In: D.L. Martin and D.W. Fraser (eds), *Troubled Times: Violence and Warfare in the Past*, pp. 321-354. London: Routledge.
Gamble, C. (1980) Information Exchange in the Palaeolithic. *Nature* 283, 522-523.
Gamble, C. (1982) Interaction and Alliance in Palaeolithic Society. *Man* 17, 92-107.
Gat, A. (2006) *War in Human Civilisation*. Oxford: Oxford University Press.
Geist, V. (1978) *Life Strategies, Human Evolution, Environmental Design. Toward a biological theory of health*. New York: Springer Verlag.
Gonzalez Sainz, C. (1989) El Magdaleniense superior final de la región Cantábrica. Unpublished PhD dissertation, Universidad de Cantabria.
Gordon, B. C. (1988) *Of Men and Reindeer Herds in French Magdalenian Prehistory*. British Archaeological Report International Series 390. Oxford: British Archaeological Reports.
Gould, R.A. (1970) Spears and Spear-Throwers of the Western Desert Aborigines of Australia. *American Museum Novitates* 2403, 1-42.
Griffin, P.B. (1997) Technology and Variation in Arrow Design Among the Agta of Northeastern Luzon. In: H. Knecht (ed.) *Projectile Technology*, pp. 267-286. New York: Plenum Press.
Hayden, B. (1993) The Cultural Capacities of Neanderthals: A review and re-evaluation. *Journal of Human Evolution* 24, 113-146.
Hayden, B. (1998) Practical and Prestige Technologies: The evolution of material systems. *Journal of Archaeology Method and Theory* 5, 1-55.

Hitchcock, R. and Bleed, P. (1997) Each According to Need and Fashion. Spear and arrow use among San hunters of the Kalahari. In: H. Knetch (ed.) *Projectile Technology*, pp. 345–368. New York: Plenum Press.

Hodder, I. (1982) *Symbols in Action. Ethnoarchaeological studies of material culture*. Cambridge: Cambridge University Press.

Hodder, I. (1986) *Reading the Past*. Cambridge: Cambridge University Press.

Jochim, M.A., Herhahn, C. and Starr, H. (1999) The Magdalenian Colonization of Southern Germany. *American Anthropologist* 101, 129–142.

Julien, M. (1982) *Les Harpons magdaléniens*. Supplément à Gallia Préhistoire 17. Paris: Editions du Centre National de la Recherche Scientifique.

Keeley, L. (1996) *War Before Civilisation*. Oxford: Oxford University Press.

Lacombe, S. (1998) Préhistoire des groupes culturels au Tardiglaciaire dans les Pyrénées centrales. Apports de la technologie lithique. Unpublished PhD thesis, Université de Toulouse-le-Mirail.

Langlais, M. (2009) Magdalenian Chronology and Territories Between the Rhone and the Ebro: The case of the lithic weapon elements. In: J.-M. Petillon, M.-H. Dias-Meirinho, P. Cattelain, M. Honegger, C. Normand and N. Valdeyron (eds) *Recherches sur les armatures de projectile du Paléolithique supérieur au Néolithique*. Colloque 83, XVe congres de l'IUSPP, Lisbonne, 4–9 Septembre 2006. P@lethnologie.

Langlais, M. (2011) Process of Change in Magdalenian Societies in the Pyrenean Isthmus (20–16 ky cal BP). *Antiquity* 85, 715–728.

Lave, J. and Wenger, E. (1991) *Situated Learning: Legitimate peripheral participation*. Cambridge, Cambridge University Press.

Lee, R.B. (1979) *The !Kung San: Men, women and work in a foraging society*. Cambridge: Cambridge University Press.

Lefebvre, A. (2011) Les pointes barbelées magdaléniennes. Étude typologique, géographique et chronologique. Unpublished PhD thesis, Université Toulouse le Mirail.

Leroi-Gourhan, A. and Allain, J. (1979) *Lascaux Inconnu*. Paris: CNRS.

Marshall, I. (1996) *A History and Ethnography of the Beothuk*. London: McGill-Queen's University Press.

Marshall, L. (1961) Sharing, Talking, and Giving: Relief of social tensions among !Kung Bushmen. *Africa* 31, 231–249.

McGhee, R. (1977) Ivory for the Sea Woman: The symbolic attributes of a prehistoric technology. *Canadian Journal of Archaeology* 1, 141–159.

Mitchell, P. (2003) Anyone for hxaro? Thoughts on the theory and practice of exchange in southern African Later Stone Age archaeology. In: P. Mitchell, A. Haour and J. Hobart (eds) *Researching Africa's Past*, pp. 35–43. London: Thames & Hudson.

Olausson, D. (1983) Flint and Groundstone Axes in the Scanian Neolithic: An evaluation of raw materials based on experiment. *Scripta Minora, Regiae Societatis Humaniorum Litterarum Lundensis 1982-1983*, p. 2. Royal Society of Letters at Lund: CWK Gleerup.

Osgood, C. (1940) *Ingalik Material Culture*. New Haven: Yale University Publications in Anthropology.

Peebles, C. and Kus, S. (1977) Some Archaeological Correlates of Ranked Societies. *American Antiquity* 42, 421–448.

Pepe, C., Clottes, J., Menu, M. and Walter, P. (1991) Le liant des peintures paléolithiques ariégeoises. *Comptes Rendus de l'Académie des Sciences Paris* 312, 929–934.

Perlès, C. (1992) Systems of Exchange and Organization of Production in Neolithic Greece. *Journal of Mediterranean Archaeology* 5, 115–164.

Pétillon, J.-M. (2006) *Des Magdaléniens en armes. Technologie des armatures de projectile en Bois de Cervidé du Magdalénien supérieur de la Grotte d'Isturitz (Pyrénées-Atlantiques)*. Treignes: Centre d'Etudes et de Documentation Archéologiques.

Pétillon, J.-M. (2008) First Evidence of a Whale-Bone Industry in the Western European Upper Paleolithic: Magdalenian artifacts from Isturitz (Pyrénées-Atlantiques, France). *Journal of Human Evolution* 54, 720–726.

Pétillon, J.-M. (2013) Circulation of Whale-Bone Artefacts in the Northern Pyrenees During the Late Upper Paleolithic. *Journal of Human Evolution* 65, 525–543.

Reynolds, G.L. (1989) Ownership Marks and Social Affinity in Northwest Alaska During Late Prehistoric Times. *Arctic Archaeology* 26, 88–107.

Sackett, J.R. (1973) Style, Function and Artifact Variability in Palaeolithic Assemblages. In: C. Renfrew (ed.) *The Explanation of Culture Change*, pp. 317–325. Pittsburgh: University of Pittsburgh Press.

Saint-Périer, de R.S.D. (1936) *La Grotte d'Isturitz: II: Le Magdalénien de La Grande Salle*. Paris: Masson et Cie, Éditeurs.

Sieveking, A. (1991) Palaeolithic Art and Archaeology: The mobiliary evidence. *Proceedings of the Prehistoric Society* 57, 33–50.

Straus, L.G. (1992) *Iberia Before the Iberians. The Stone Age prehistory of Cantabrian Spain*. Albuquerque: University of New Mexico Press.

Tindale, N.B. and Lindsay, H.A. (1963) *Aboriginal Australians*. Brisbane: Jacaranda Press.

Tostevin, G.B. (2007) Social Intimacy, Artefact Visibility and Acculturation. Models of Neanderthal-modern human interaction. In: P. Mellars, K.V. Boyle, O. Bar-Yosef and C. Stringer (eds) *Rethinking the Human Revolution*, pp. 341–357. Cambridge: McDonald Institute for Archaeological Research.

Wadley, L. (1987) *Later Stone Age Hunter-Gatherers of the Southern Transvaal: Social and ecological interpretation*. Oxford: Archaeopress.

Walker, N.J. (1995) *Late Pleistocene and Holocene Hunter-Gatherers of the Matopos*. Uppsala: Societas Archaeological Upsaliensis.

Weniger, G.C. (1992) Function and Form: An ethnoarchaeological analysis of barbed points from northern hunter-gatherers. In: A. Gallay, F. Audouze and V. Roux (eds) *Ethnoarchéologie: justification, problèmes, limites*, pp. 257–268. Juan-les-Pins: Editions APDCA. XII° Rencontres internationales d'archéologie et d'histoire d'Antibes.

White, R. (1992) Beyond Art: Toward an understanding of the origins of material representation in Europe. *Annual Review of Anthropology* 21, 537–564.

White, R. (2007) Systems of Personal Ornamentation in the Early Upper Palaeolithic: Methodological challenges and new observations. In: P. Mellars, K.V. Boyle, O. Bar-Yosef and C. Stringer (eds) *Rethinking the Human Evolution*, pp. 287–302. Cambridge: McDonald Institute for Archaeological Research.

Weissner, P. (1983) Style and Social Information in Kalahari San Projectile Points. *American Antiquity* 48, 253–276.

Weissner, P. (1984) Reconsidering the Behavioral Basis for Style: A case study among the Kalahari San. *Journal of Anthropological Archaeology* 3, 190–234.

Weissner, P. (1985) Style or Isochrestic Variation? A reply to Sackett. *American Antiquity* 50, 160–166.

Wobst, M.H. (1977) Stylistic Behavior and Information Exchange. In: C.E. Cleland (ed.) *For the Director: Research essays in honor of James B. Griffin*, pp. 317–342. Ann Arbor: Museum of Anthropology, University of Michigan.

# Chapter 10

# Concealing traces of 'untamed' fire: The Mesolithic pottery makers and users of Japan

*Makoto Tomii*

**Abstract**
*One of the hallmarks of the Jomon hunter-fisher-gatherers (15,000–2700 BP) of Japan is their pottery. These vessels are often decorated in an elaborate manor, compared to those of the Mesolithic pottery-makers of Eurasia. Prior to the advent of the Neolithic cultural complex (2700 BP), it is believed that such pottery was made using a simple open-firing technique, from which it was not uncommon to produce blackened discolouration and/or 'fire-clouds' – black-coloured patches on the surface of the vessels. These patches occur when smoky flame or burned fuel comes into contact with the pottery. They are often difficult to prevent in the open-firing process. Examination of the depositional context of some of these pots suggests that Jomon pottery users may have been conscious of these marks, perhaps as evidence of their inability to fully control the flame, and that they deliberately sought to hide these blemishes when engaging in acts of intentional deposition, even at the end of the vessel's practical use-life.*

## Introduction

Control of fire is something that humans mastered at some point in the Palaeolithic. Indeed, increasingly, evidence is accumulating to suggest that it pre-dates the emergence of anatomically modern humans in the fossil record (Gowlett 2016). Since this point, whenever it might have been, we might assume that this knowledge was maintained, passed on and developed, perhaps even forgotten and relearned at times, but ultimately with the result that throughout the interim past, whenever knowledge and conditions have been fit, humans have been able to start, manage and end fires at will.

In Japan, there is evidence that the controlled use of fire dates back to at least the end of the Palaeolithic, around 15,000 BP, through sites such as Nodai, on the main islands, where a stone-arranged hearth was constructed (Nagaizumi Town Board of Education 1986). Presumably, then, people from the Palaeolithic period in Japan were more than capable using fire for lighting, heating, burning, cooking and more.

In Japan, the Palaeolithic was followed by the Mesolithic – the 'Jomon' – which broadly dates from 15,000 to 2700 BP, prior to domesticate-reliant societies. The Jomon culture is typified as comprising sedentary fisher-hunter-gatherers, who used polished stone tools and pottery (Habu 2004; Kobayashi 2004). In contraposition to the Mesolithic of Eurasia, the Jomon have become known for their aesthetically sophisticated pottery, although many examples bear evidence of imperfections from the firing process – burn-induced blemishes. In this paper, I explore why this apparent failure to 'tame' the fire involved in pottery production was a meaningful part of the production process.

## Material: Jomon pottery

An incredible amount of Jomon pottery has been recovered from the many archaeological excavations conducted across the Japanese archipelago. From petrological and typological studies, it is clear that the majority of Jomon pottery was locally produced, used and discarded.

Most ceramic vessels of the Jomon culture show evidence of black-coring in fabric profile (Gibson and Woods 1997, 109–110), confirming their production through open-firing. The production of this pottery would have required a far more intense level of firing than is used for most general domestic purposes. To create pottery in this manner requires burning of a particular scale, duration and intensity, meaning it is reasonable to conclude that people in the Jomon period were capable of managing fire to a high degree of competence.

According to the results of experimental investigations into open-air pottery firing, pre-heating is a necessary precursor to the process (Arai 1973). This stage removes water from the clay, reducing the risk that the vessel would burst from an otherwise sudden increase in temperature due to the inner-water of the fabric material vaporising. To initiate pre-heating, the ground soil is heated by fire, which is then extinguished, so that the pots may be place on the heated floor.

After pre-heating, a new fire is started, and the main firing process is begun. Controlling the adjustment of heat in an open-air fire environment so as to avoid the discoloration of the vessel surface proves challenging even for present-day potters to manage – it is not unreasonable to assume that the same was probably true for Jomon pottery producers. Blackened discoloration and/or black patches on the vessel surfaces, caused by unstable conditions of combustion, is often recorded to varying extents on Jomon pottery, sometimes referred to as 'fire-clouding' (Shepard 1956, 92).

In terms of artefact biographies, the Jomon employed many diverse manners of disposing of their pottery after their final usage. In addition to normal discard, various forms of intentional deposition have been documented, including intensive disposal, embedment as urns or 'coffins', or as components within hearth structures, and in other manners, including forms of seemingly ritual dedication. These are all recognised traits of the Jomon period, and it is this final stage of Jomon pottery life-history that appears to bear relevance to the presence of blackened discoloration from the firing process.

To gauge the relation of these discoloured surfaces, the results of 'untamed' fire – flame beyond the control of the potters – it is necessary to have a contextual photographic record documenting the vessels *in situ*

*Figure 10.1. Map showing the location of the study area: Tochigi prefecture. All four of the archaeological sites referred to in this paper are included in this inland prefecture in the Japanese archipelago.*

once they were uncovered, within their depositional context. Further photographs were taken after excavation to provide a view of the artefacts from eight different angles, forming a composite, omni-directional photographic collation for analysis. With this photographic (and recording-drawing) database, it is possible to reconstruct the original position of particular sherds at the post-excavation stage relative to the archaeological context of their discovery by locating fracture-lines and other diagnostic markings. Through this process, it is possible to identify which way different surfaces of the vessels were oriented when deposited (Tomii 2015, 248).

## Case studies: Deposited pottery

The pottery deposition contexts examined in this paper are five pit deposits from four sites – Miwanakamachi (1), Goreimae (2), Teranohigashi (1) and Kashimawaki (1) – located within the Tochigi prefecture (Figure 10.1). All cases were radiocarbon dated to between 4400–4300 BP, or, in relative terms, the middle of the Middle Jomon period, except for one, which was dated to the Early Jomon period (Kobayashi 2008). The pits from which the Middle Jomon vessels were recovered were of a flat-bottomed flask shape. Well-preserved (if not intact) Middle Jomon pots are relatively common in features of this type within the region.

### *Miwanakamachi, Pit SK265 (Tochigi Prefectural Board of Education 1994)*

The first example (Figure 10.2) is a single vessel, although in broken pieces, recovered from the bottom layer of a pit fill. Reviewing the *in situ* photograph with the omni-directional photographic recording of the artefact, it was possible to identify the location of corresponding pieces. The surface visible in Figure 10.2 (photograph number 6) was facing upward when deposited, meaning that Figure 10.2 photograph number 2 shows the downward-facing surface. When all the eight of the photographs from Figure 10.2 are examined, we can see that it is the least blackened surface that was deposited facing upwards.

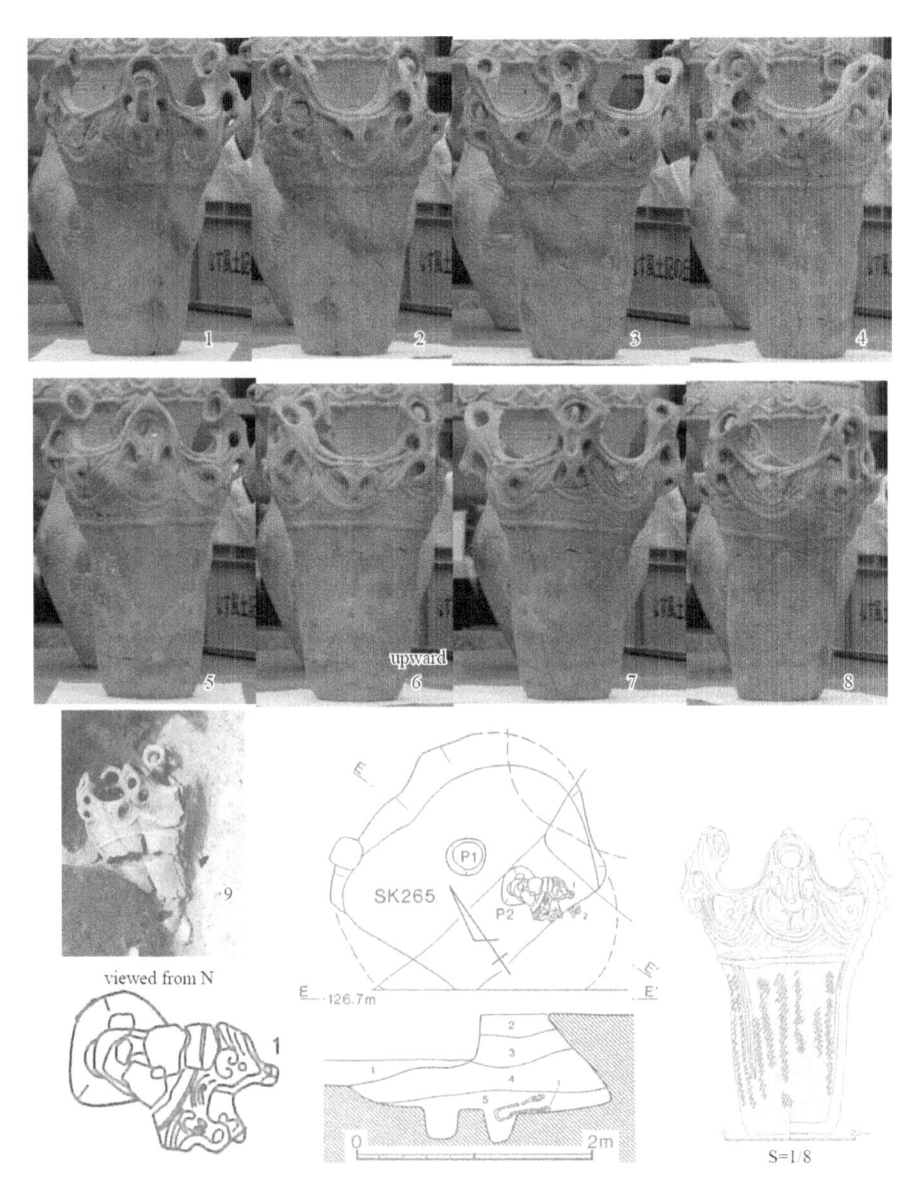

*Figure 10.2. Omni-directional photographic collation of the first vessel, from pit SK265 at Miwanakamachi (Tochigi Prefectural Board of Education 1994) – least blackened surface facing upwards.*

## Goreimae, Pit SK426 (Tochigi Prefectural Board of Education 2000)

Example 2 (Figure 10.3) is a well-preserved vessel recovered from the bottom of a heavily truncated pit. According to the contextual drawing and photograph, the surface visible in Figure 10.3 photograph number 7 faced upwards, meaning that a large 'fire-cloud' discoloration was deposited facing downwards.

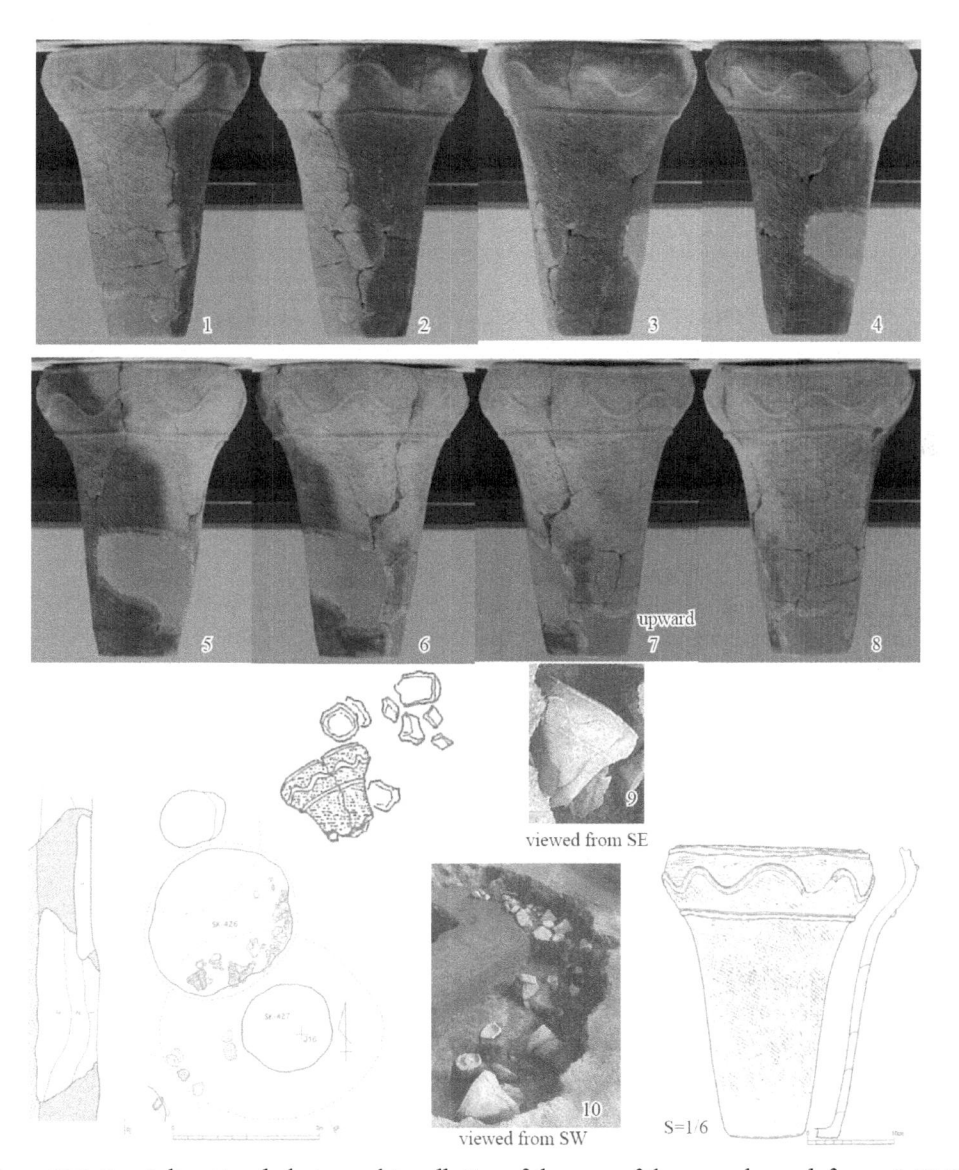

Figure 10.3. Omni-directional photographic collation of the case of the second vessel, from pit SK426 at Goreimae (Tochigi Prefectural Board of Education 2000), found in association with vessel three, and with its darkest surface facing downwards.

160                              Makoto Tomii

## *Goreimae, Pit SK426 (Tochigi Prefectural Board of Education 2000)*

The third example (Figure 10.4) is a well-preserved vessel also recovered from the same depositional context as the second example, at the bottom fill of the same truncated pit. This pit contained a number of potsherds, but only two well-preserved vessels: examples two and three. According to the contextual drawing and photo, the surface visible in Figure 10.4 photograph number 7 was placed facing upwards. This means that, as Figure 10.4 photograph number 3 shows, the only small 'fire-cloud' discoloration patch, appearing near the rim, opposite to the upward-facing surface, faced downwards.

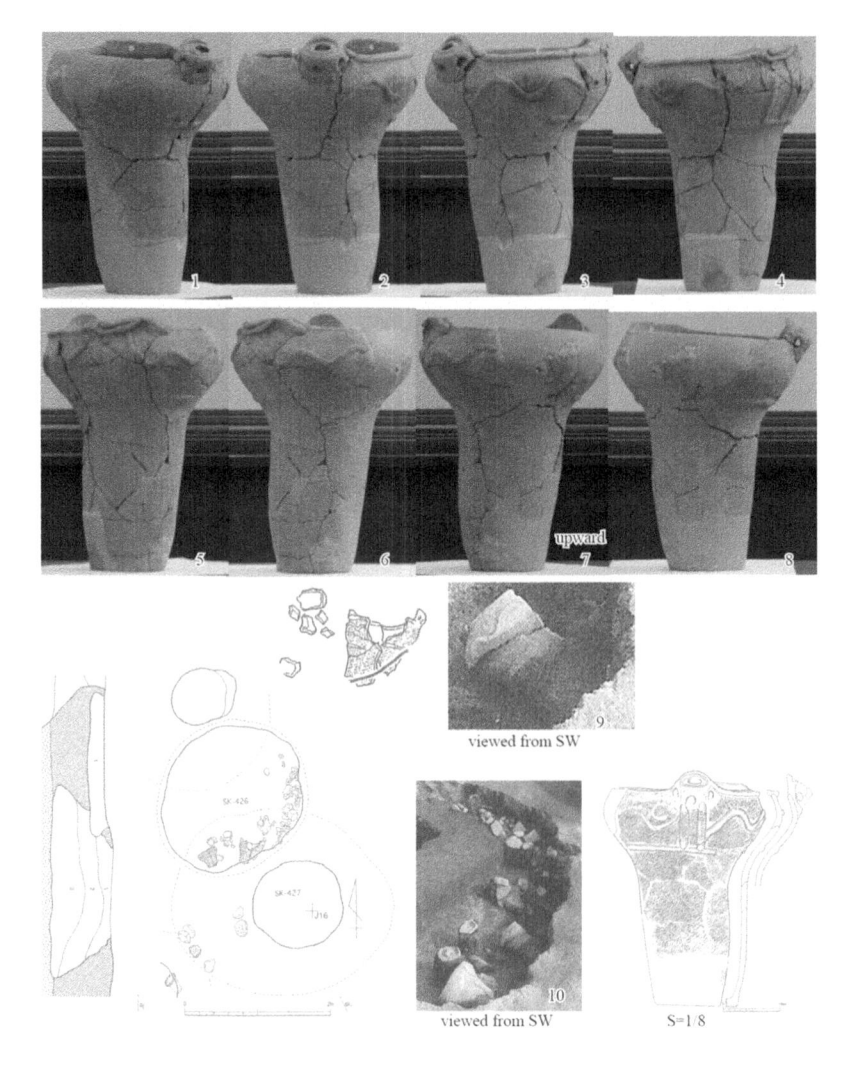

*Figure 10.4. Omni-directional photographic collation of the third vessel, from pit SK426 at Goreimae (Tochigi Prefectural Board of Education 2000), found in association with vessel two, and with its small, singular discoloration patch facing downwards.*

## *Goreimae, Pit SK45 (Tochigi Prefectural Board of Education 2001)*

The following five pots were found in association with one another in the basal fill of a single pit; seemingly a singular act of relatively intensive-scale disposal. Many potsherds were recovered from this pit, but only the following five vessels were sufficiently well preserved to merit inspection here. The first of these, example four (Figure 10.5), exhibits blackened discoloration around much of the upper circumference of the vessel. However, as shown through cross-reference to the *in situ* contextual photograph and drawing, the

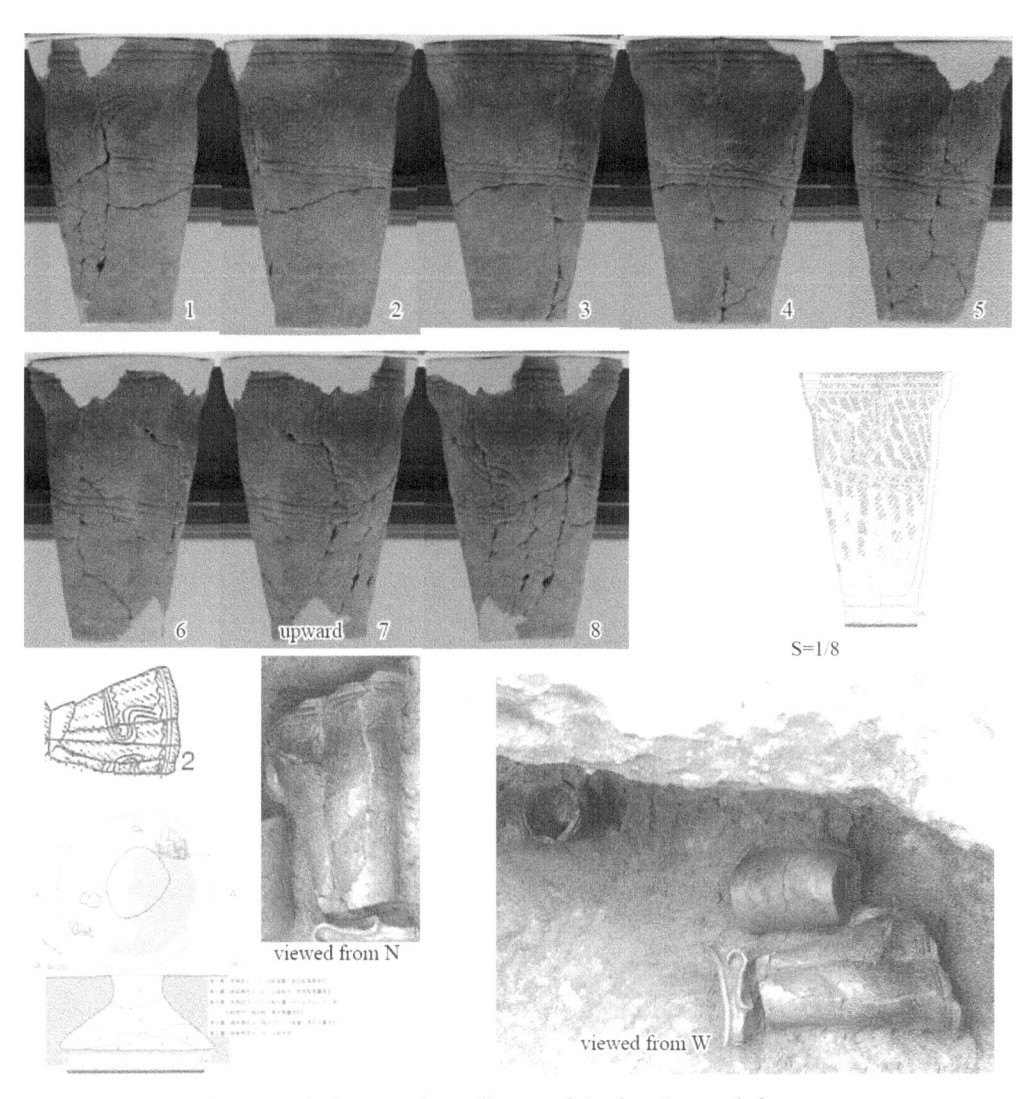

*Figure 10.5. Omni-directional photographic collation of the fourth vessel, from pit SK45 at Goreimae (Tochigi Prefectural Board of Education 2001), found in association with vessels five to eight, with its most blackened surface facing almost downwards.*

surface visible in Figure 10.5 photograph number 7 was deposited facing upwards, and this is almost opposite to the most blackened surface (Figure 10.5 photograph number 4).

## Goreimae, Pit SK45 (Tochigi Prefectural Board of Education 2001)

The fifth example (Figure 10.6) may also be characterised as being discoloured to various gradations of darkness for the entire circumference of the upper vessel. The marked fracture-line appearing on the surface present in Figure 10.6 photograph numbers 6 and 7 indicate the surface that was left facing upwards, and, accordingly, the broadly opposite facing surface of Figure 10.6 photograph 2 was left facing mostly downwards.

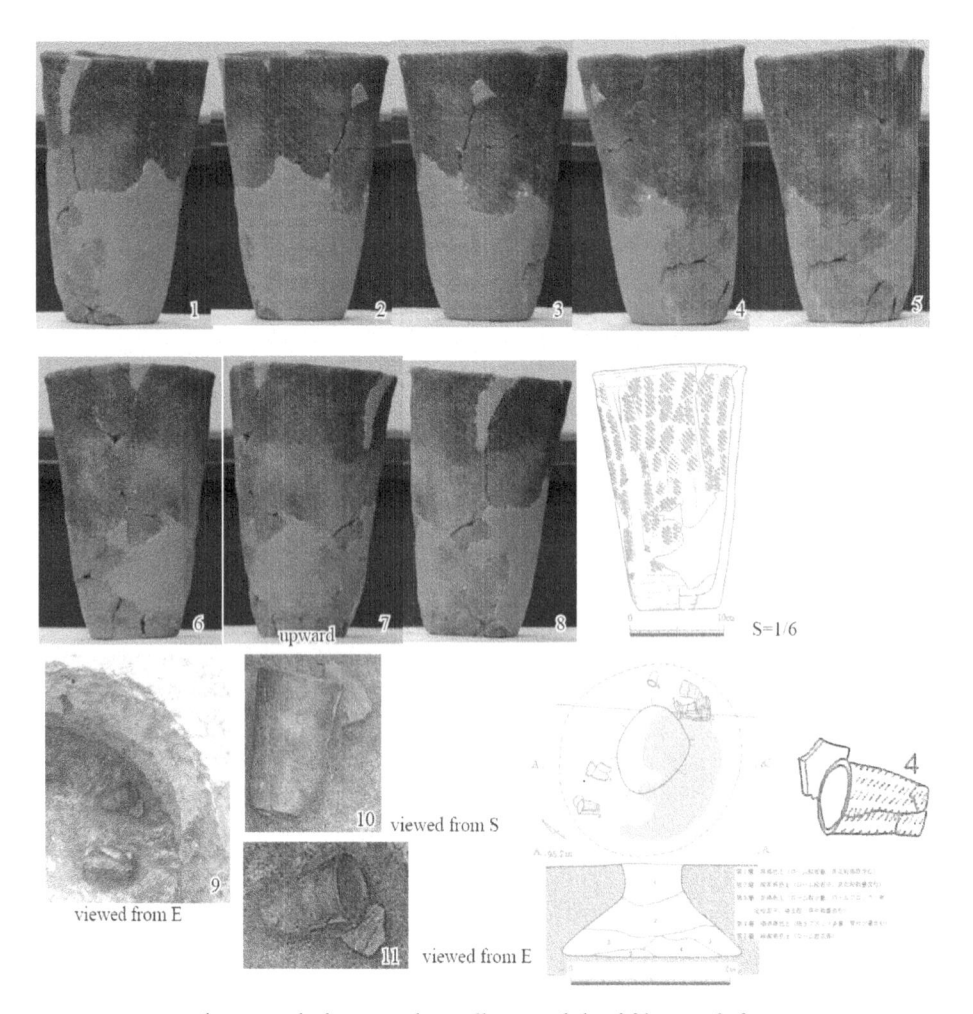

*Figure 10.6. Omni-directional photographic collation of the fifth vessel, from pit SK45 at Goreimae (Tochigi Prefectural Board of Education 2001), found in association with other four vessels four, six, seven and eight, and with its most blackened surface facing downwards.*

## 10. Concealing traces of 'untamed' fire

### Goreimae, Pit SK45 (Tochigi Prefectural Board of Education 2001)

The sixth example, as seen in Figure 10.7, bears several blemishes resulting from discoloration. However, the most significant of these, shown in the surface visible in Figure 10.7 photograph number 3, was deposited facing downwards.

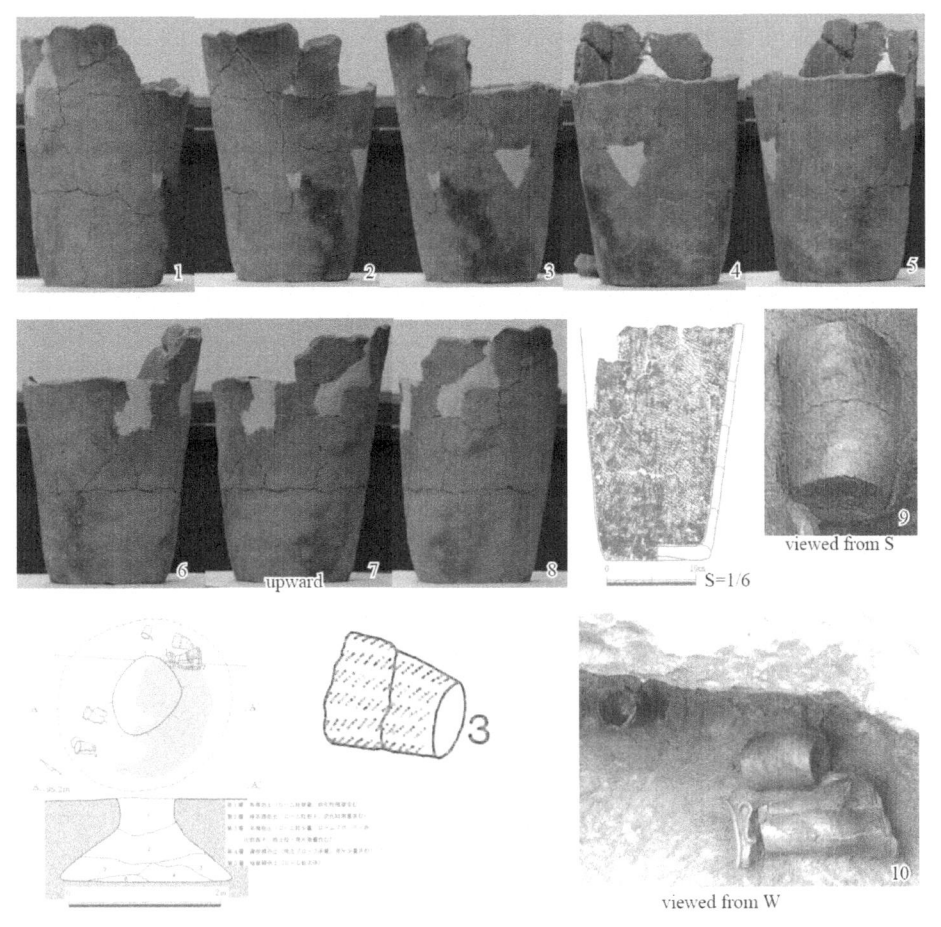

*Figure 10.7. Omni-directional photographic collation of the sixth vessel, from pit SK45 at Goreimae (Tochigi Prefectural Board of Education 2001), found at the bottom in association with vessels four, five, seven and eight, and with its most blackened surface facing downwards.*

164  Makoto Tomii

## *Goreimae, Pit SK45 (Tochigi Prefectural Board of Education 2001)*

Vessel 7 (Figure 10.8) was broken into several parts that were found separately within a discrete vertical and horizontal distribution, near the base of this pit. The largest sherd, consisting of the main body of the vessel, was found lying with its black outer surface facing downwards (Figure 10.8 photograph number 7). In contrast to the main body of the vessel, a large portion of the upper rim (visible in Figure 10.8 photograph number 5) appears unusually light in colour, probably as the result of a secondary firing process. In this case, the lighter outer surface was placed facing upwards, even though positioning the sherd in this manner would have made the fragment less stable than if the interior surface was placed facing upwards.

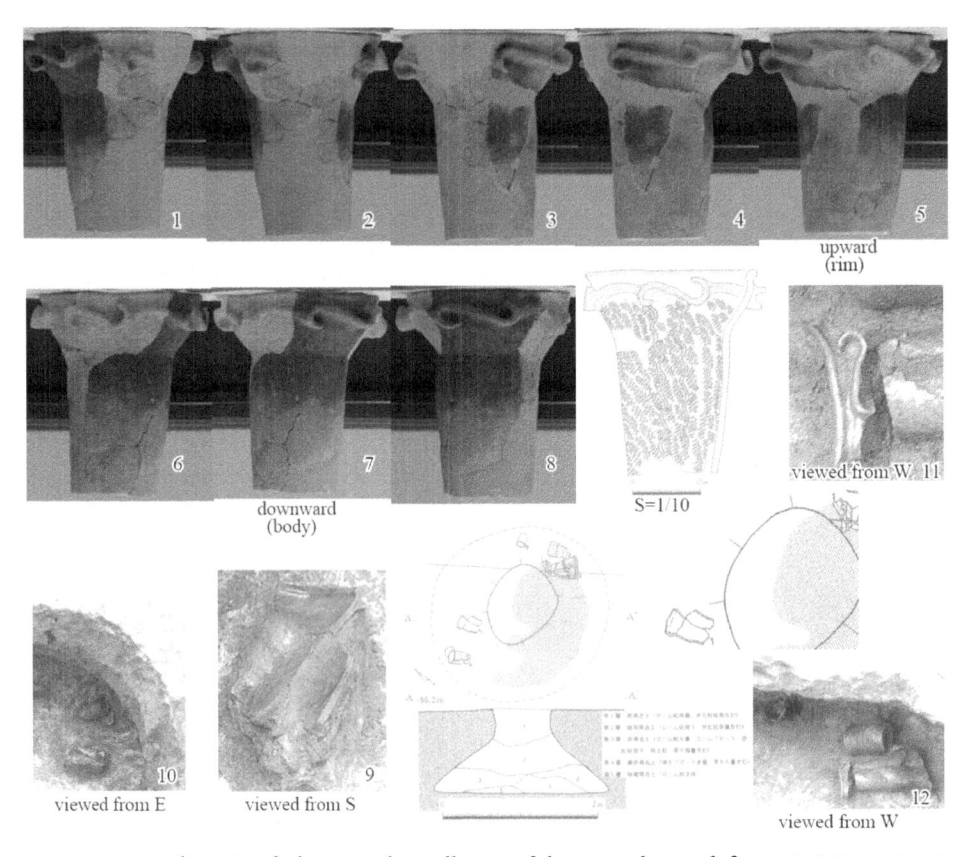

*Figure 10.8. Omni-directional photographic collation of the seventh vessel, from pit SK45 at Goreimae (Tochigi Prefectural Board of Education 2001), found in association with vessels four, five, six and eight. Note the large rim fragment, with its blackened outer surface facing downwards.*

## *Goreimae, Pit SK45 (Tochigi Prefectural Board of Education 1999)*

In the eighth and final example (Figure 10.9) from this pit, the directional placement of the blackened, discoloured surface appears to contradict that of the other vessels. Although identifying a suitable diagnostic reference for this pot proved difficult through the relative lack of obvious fracture-lines, it was nevertheless determined that it was the *most* heavily discoloured surface (visible in Figure 10.9 photograph 6) that was left facing upwards, making this example curiously at odds with the other four from this pit.

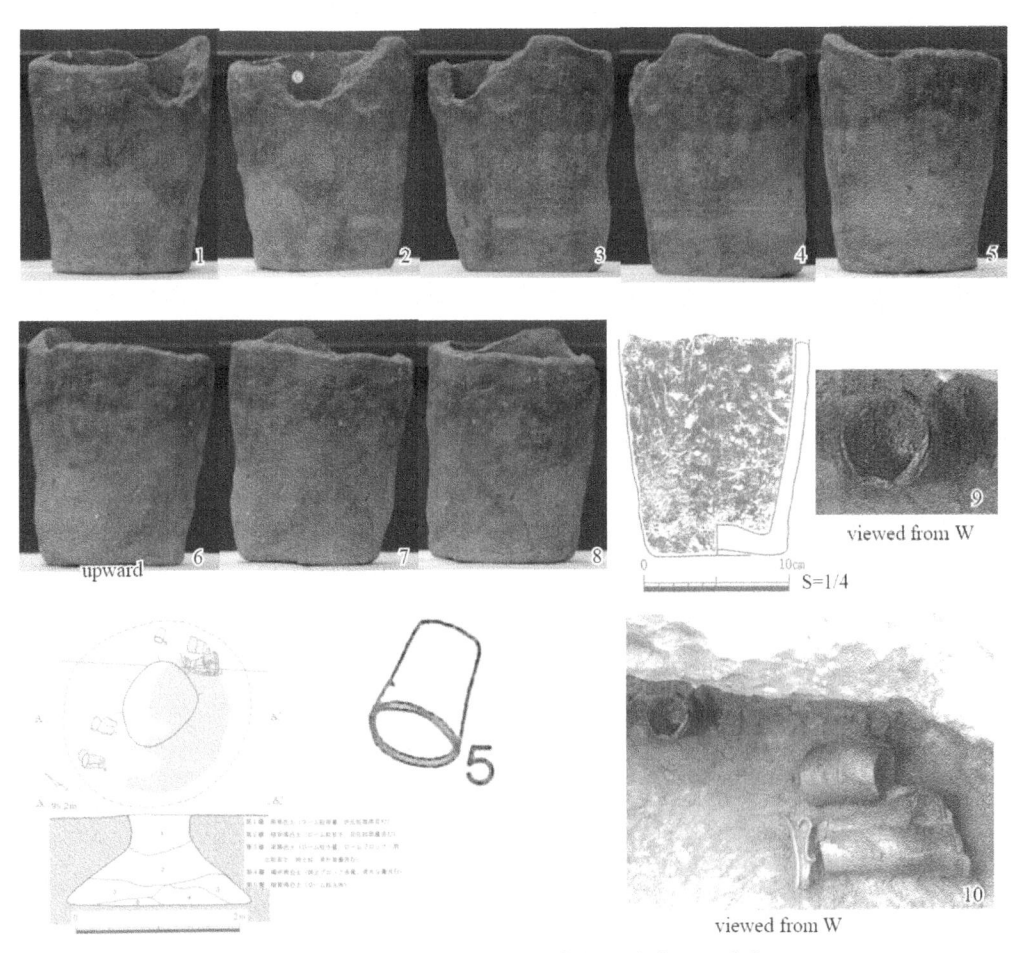

*Figure 10.9. Omni-directional photographic collation of the eighth vessel, from pit SK45 at Goreimae (Tochigi Prefectural Board of Education 2001), found in association with vessels four, five, six and seven. Note, in this case, the blackened surface was found facing upwards.*

### *Teranohigashi, Pit SK1172*

The ninth example (Figure 10.10) was complete vessel, found at the bank (or shoulder) of the pit, within the middle fill. In the excavation report, the possibility was raised that this pot had been intentionally laid down. Ultimately, however, the investigators thought it too difficult to confirm, partly because it was found in the middle fill of

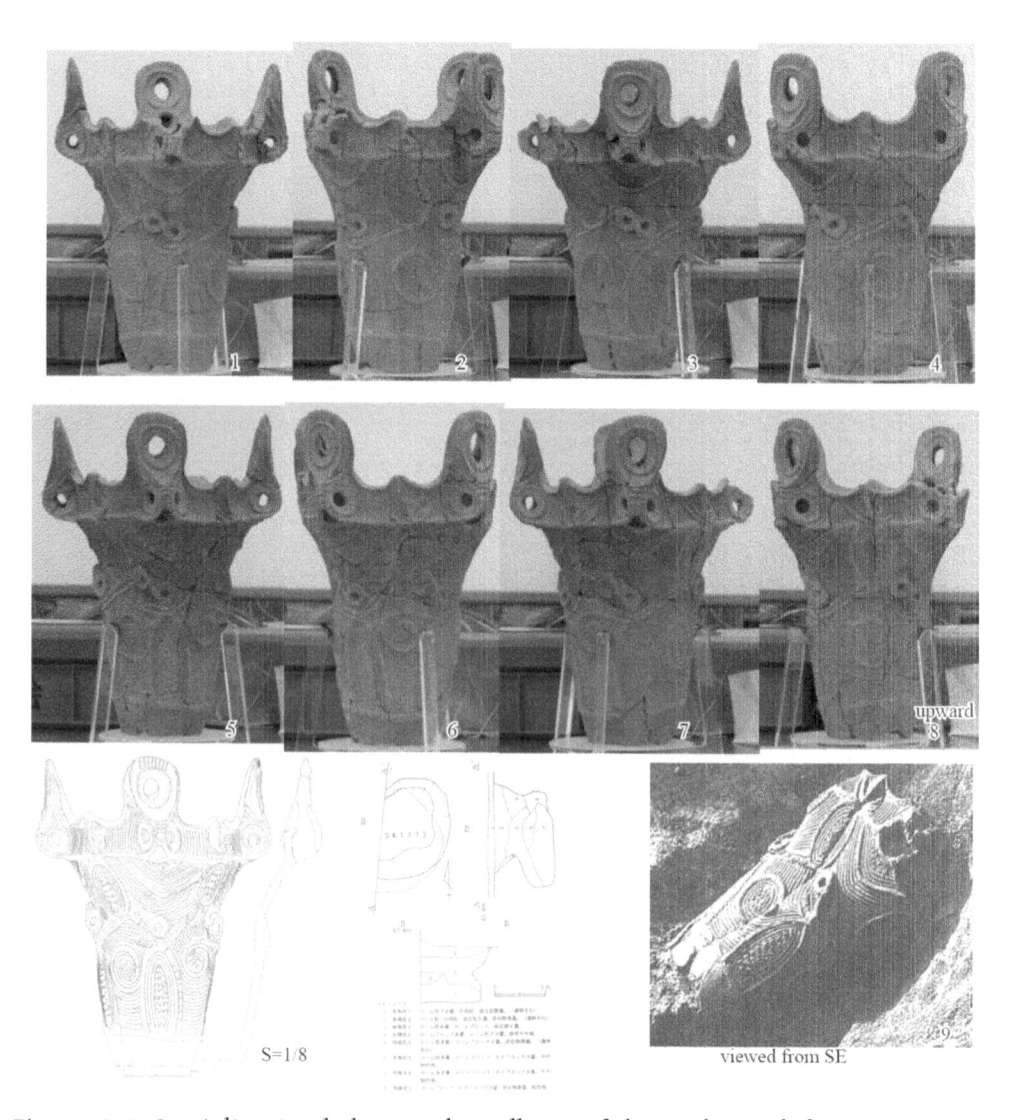

*Figure 10.10. Omni-directional photographic collation of the ninth vessel, from pit SK1172 at Teranohigashi (Tochigi Prefectural Board of Education 1999). Note that, whereas all other vessels were recovered from the basal fill of their respective pits, vessel nine was found in the middle of the fill. Its singular, small blackened surface was facing downwards.*

the pit earth, and so would presumably have necessitated an interval during infill process for this to have been an intentional act. Figure 10.10, photograph number 3 shows the surface bearing the one, and only, small discoloration, just under a handle. This surface was found facing downwards, almost perfectly opposite to the upward-facing surface, visible in Figure 10.10 number 3.

## Kashimawaki, Pit SK12 (Tochigi Prefectural Board of Education 1988)

The tenth and final example (Figure 10.11) included a saddle-quern deposited in the same pit alongside the pottery. The saddle-quern was noted, in the original excavation

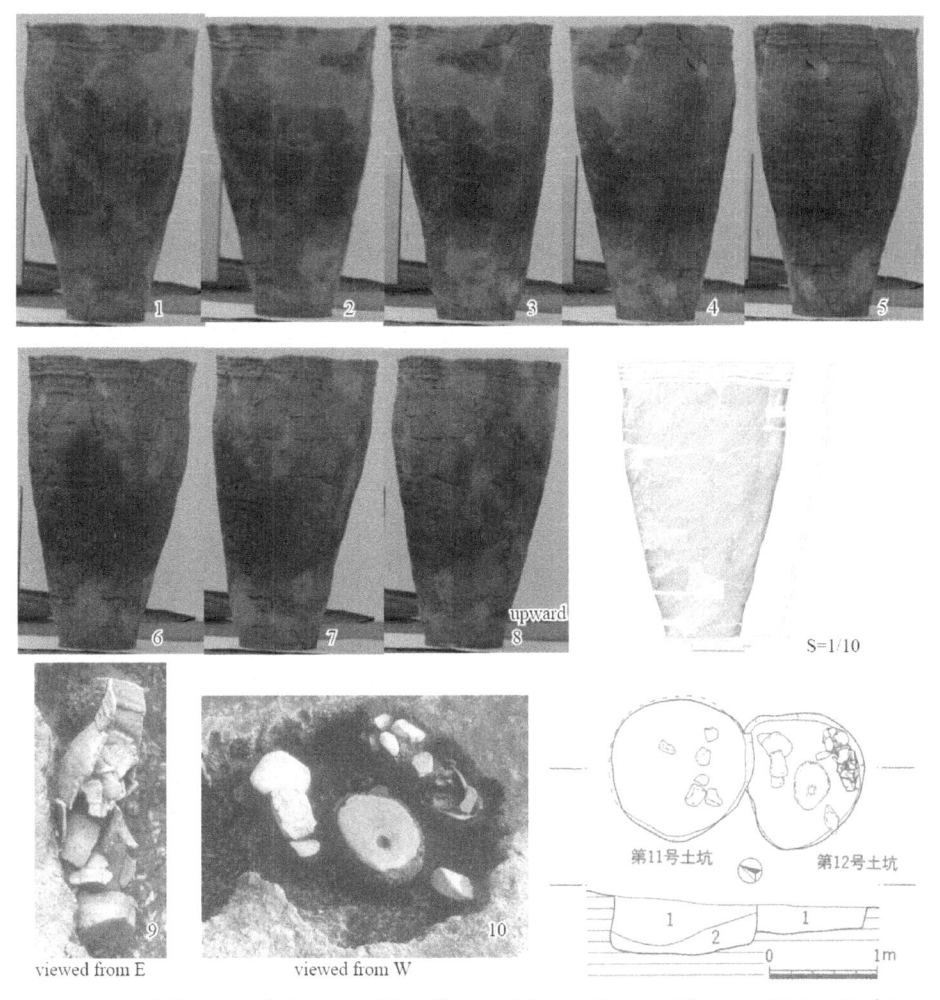

*Figure 10.11. Omni-directional photographic collation of the tenth vessel, from pit SK12 at Kashimawaki (Tochigi Prefectural Board of Education 1988), found in association with a saddle-quern, and with its least blackened surface facing upwards.*

report, as having been set in a level position – that it was sat level is used as grounds for inferring that the quern was deposited as an act of intentional placement and, by extension, that if this was indeed the case, then the associated pottery may have been an intentional deposit too. The surface visible in Figure 10.11 photograph number 8 shows the least blackened surface, and that which was left facing upwards.

## Discussion

Although the 'fire-cloud' discoloration marks from the firing process used to create these pots are irregular in character and frequency, it is nevertheless possible to draw some interesting conclusions from the ten cases presented here. These cases deserve further consideration in particular.

In the case of examples 2 and 3 (Figures 10.3 and 10.4), which were the only well-preserved vessels in a pit with many other potsherds, their association together and with these other sherds indicates that both had been deposited with the same intention, even though the black discoloration on vessel 3 is smaller and less pronounced than in many other instances.

Examples four through to eight were also notable for having been found in association with one another within the same pit (Figures 10.5–10.9). Among them, two in particular stand out. Example seven (Figure 10.8) is strongly suggestive of deliberate placement, as not only was the darkened 'fire-cloud' surface of the main vessel body seemingly positioned facing downwards, a rim piece of abnormally light colouration, probably as a result of secondary firing, was positioned seemingly with the express intent of facing upwards, even though doing so required awkwardly balancing the sherd in question to present this surface.

The second notable vessel from this series is that of pot number 8 (Figure 10.9). This vessel, unlike the others, appears to have been deposited with the blackened surface facing upwards. Perhaps this indicates that placing the pot with the most discoloured surface facing downwards was not an obligatory procedure within this community – indeed, perhaps the pottery-maker/user had greater individual autonomy in choosing the manner and nature of deposition, even if there was a broader societal norm for this practice that was favoured or followed among the community as a whole. Still another alternative is that the unusual inversion of orientation exhibited by vessel 8 may deny the unaccounted-for preservation conditions in the soil that might let the colour of the surface facing downwards become darkened. At least, this case demonstrates that the trend for darkened surfaces being placed facing downwards cannot be attributed to taphonomy or the prospect of over-cleaning in excavation or preparation for photography.

Vessel number 9 (Figure 10.10) differs from the other examples in that it was recovered from the stratigraphic midst of a pit-fill, rather than from near the base. Other than this, it was nevertheless positioned, like most of the other vessels, with the blackened 'fire-cloud' surface facing downwards. As hinted at in the original excavation report, the location of this vessel in the midst of the pit may be further strong evidence of intentional placement – this act would have required careful deposition during an interval of infilling. Vessel 9 is also unusual because of its age – it was dated to around 5500 BP (Kobayashi 2008) – which makes it late Early Jomon. This might perhaps indicate that this depositional trend was maintained for a significant stretch of time, although, on the current evidence alone, this remains a matter of speculation.

## Conclusion

In each of the cases presented here, with the exception of example 8, the pottery vessels recovered from excavation were found with their most discoloured surfaces facing downwards. Furthermore, review of the depositional context of some of these examples lends support to the idea that this trend was no coincidence, but rather a careful act of intentional deposition. The pottery-makers/users of the Middle Jomon of the modern-day Tochigi prefecture appear to have been concerned with concealing these discolorations, even in the act of their final disposal. Controlling the heat and flame of the open-firing process used to create Jomon pottery is difficult, and thus the 'fire-clouds' may have been perceived as the result of a process or power that was beyond the pottery-maker's full mastery. Although the social and cultural significance of this attitude is open to debate, it nevertheless seems that there was a desire, even in the act of final disposal, to conceal traces of this 'untamed' fire.

## Bibliography

Arai, S. (1973) *Jomon-doki no gijutsu* [*The Technology of Jomon Pottery*]. Tokyo: Chuo koron bijutsu.
Gibson, A. and Woods, A. (1997) *Prehistoric Pottery for the Archaeologists*. 2nd edition. Leicester: Leicester University Press.
Gowlett, J.A. (2016) The Discovery of Fire by Humans: A long and convoluted process. *Philosophical Transactions of the Royal Society B* 371, 1–12.
Habu, J. (2004) *Ancient Jomon of Japan*. Cambridge: Cambridge University Press.
Kobayashi, K. (2008) Jomon-doki no jitsunendai (higashi-nihon) [The Absolute Dates of Jomon Pottery in Eastern Japan]. In: Y. Taniguchi (ed.) *Soran Jomon-doki* [*Handbook of Jomon Pottery*]. Tokyo: UM Promotion.
Kobayashi, T. (2004) *Jomon Reflections: Forager life culture in the prehistoric Japanese archipelago*. Oxford: Oxbow Books.
Nagaizumi Town Board of Education (1986) *Excavation Report for Nakao, Iraune and Nodai*. Shizuoka: Nagaizumi Town Board of Education.
Shepard, A.O. (1956) *Ceramics for the Archaeologist*. Washington: Carnegie Institution of Washington.
Tochigi Prefectural Board of Education (1988) *Excavation Report for Kashimawaki and Oninokubo*. Tochigi: Tochigi Prefectural Board of Education.
Tochigi Prefectural Board of Education (1994) *Excavation Report for Miwanakamachi*. Tochigi: Tochigi Prefectural Board of Education.
Tochigi Prefectural Board of Education (1999) *Excavation Report for Teranohigashi II*. Tochigi: Tochigi Prefectural Board of Education.

Tochigi Prefectural Board of Education (2000) *Excavation Report for Goreimae*. Tochigi: Tochigi Prefectural Board of Education.
Tochigi Prefectural Board of Education (2001) *Excavation Report for Goreimae II*. Tochigi: Tochigi Prefectural Board of Education.
Tomii, M. (2015) A New Method for Contextual Analysis on Prehistoric Attitudes to Ritual Pottery. *Open Archaeology* 1, 247–257.

# Chapter 11

## Naming *neanderthalensis* in Newcastle, 1863: The politics of a scientific meeting

### Miguel DeArce

**Abstract**

*From the study of publications contemporaneous with the meeting of the British Association held in Newcastle upon Tyne in 1863, this paper observes that William King's proposition of* Homo neanderthalensis *as a new species was made in a politically fraught environment. Difficulties were caused by the interests of very large local industries monopolising the time and space available, by the turmoil in the discipline of Geology (Section C), where the new generation of geologists were challenging the established authority, and lastly because the debate over slavery divided Section E (Geography and Ethnology). King, peripheral and autocratic, read his paper in Section C (Geology) under inauspicious circumstances; on the last session of the last day, in the wrong Section and competing with popular attractions. This paper argues that King was academically unsuited to make such a proposal and therefore failed to attract the attention he sought. The public, scientists and the media were distracted away from his presentation. However, three abstracts of his paper were in print approximately one month after its delivery, which were followed shortly by reviews in academic publications. King's own interest in Neanderthals was short-lived, although he had access to good resources, particularly the Anatomy Museum in the University of Dublin, which he visited in connection with his Neanderthal work. His fundamental reasoning was not based on craniology (which was the bulk of his paper) but on a brief and dubious remark on psychology/theology. His proposal came much too early to be well founded, but it was soon supported by new findings and it stands to this day, in spite of its controvertible character.*

## Introduction

*Homo neanderthalensis* received its specific name at the 33rd annual meeting of the British Association for the Advancement of Science (BAAS) of 1863, which was held in Newcastle upon Tyne between Thursday 27 August and 2 September. BAAS meetings were popular events where a public of mixed education and interests could hear the best British scientists explain the latest developments in their discipline. The BAAS had the purpose of stimulating local interest in science in the different yearly venues where the meetings were held. The social events organised around these week-long scientific meetings were massive attractions, ensuring very generous media coverage.

Before the 1863 meeting, the Neanderthal bones, first reported in 1857, were generally accepted to be from a human (Drell 2000). They were interpreted as belonging either to a very primitive European race, possibly a Celt (Pruner Bey cited by Carter Blake 1864a, cxlix) or, as Rudolf Virchow (1821–1902) held, to a pathological human specimen of a more modern or even contemporary date. But pathologists were not unanimous in their assessment of the bones. The French physician and anthropologist Pierre Paul Broca (1824–1880) (cited by Carter Blake, 1864b) insisted that the calotte of the Neanderthal specimen was not micro-cephalic, nor did it display any congenital deformity known in humans. Although there were frequent references to the Neanderthal fossil, or the Neanderthal skull, which were non-committal as to its nature, there were also many references to Neanderthal man that were in themselves a taxonomic statement. The proposal that they belonged to a new but extinct species of the genus *Homo* as well as the taxonomic nomenclature we now use came from William King (1809–1886), then Professor of Mineralogy and Geology at Queen's College Galway (QCG). This was a bold proposition for three reasons: first, because that very year both Sir Charles Lyell (1797–1875), then the most senior British geologist, and Thomas Henry Huxley (1825–1898), the newly established authority in Comparative Anatomy and Physiology, had made lengthy contributions supporting the human nature of the specimens (Lyell 1863; Huxley 1863), second, because the genus *Homo* had been assumed to have been populated by a single species, *H. sapiens*, since its naming by Linnaeus in 1758, and third, because King's professional interests prior to 1863 had not included the human species under any aspect. King's unofficial 'nomenclatural act' in defiance of the status quo took place first as an oral presentation at the Newcastle meeting (King 1864a), for which three abstracts were published within the year (Anon. 1863b; 1863c; 1863d), but the requisite conditions of the current International Code for Zoological Nomenclature (ICZN, undated) were only met upon the publication of King's full paper, which is often called his long paper (King 1864b). Likewise, the meeting's abstract of the paper read in 1863 (Anon. 1864) does not meet the ICZN requirements, as it does not contain a substantial description of the fossil. The text of what King said at the meeting is not extant.

Here I place King's oral presentation at the BAAS meeting in a political, as opposed to scientific context, and try to answer some questions around this first unofficial naming of *Homo neanderthalensis* that, to my knowledge, have not been addressed in any other recent account of the event. For the most recent palaeoanthropological accounts, see Murray *et al.* (2015) and Schwartz (2006). For a classic account of the discovery and early interpretation, see the works of Tattersall (1995) and Drell (2000). Here I propose to follow rather the characters involved and the politics of the event, the power struggles in the midst of which William King belaboured his academic point. In his account of Victorian Anthropology, Stocking (1987) took a similar approach, but his canvas was much broader, and omitted King entirely, disposing of Neanderthal in two brief sentences (1987, 73 and 147). I also read afresh King's 1864(b) paper to try to establish the main thrust of his reasoning and his resources. I think a fresh look at King and his Neanderthal work is needed because, although it is reasonable to see his contribution as successful – the name is still in use today – and pioneering – against then current orthodoxy – particularly when further finds of Neanderthals were made shortly afterwards, it seems surprising that if he had had a positive experience in Newcastle he did not exploit his success in Anthropology after the meeting. The BAAS meeting of the following year, held in Bath (Anon. 1865), brought Neanderthals to the fore again when George Busk (1864, cited by Stringer 1999, Wood 1979 and Keith 1911, copying a letter from Falconer to Busk) exhibited the skull of what we now call Gibraltar I. King was not there and passed no remarks.

In some more detail, the questions addressed in this paper can be gathered under three headings. First, I look at the 1863 BAAS meeting itself to see if it would be possible to ascertain the most immediate reception of King's oral presentation. We would like to know details of the actual session where King gave his paper, namely what other papers were read at it, who was the Chair, who attended, whether there was any contributions from the floor in reply and who was speaking at the same time in other sections.

Second, on the broader context of the whole meeting, it cannot be ignored that it was happening just at the midpoint of the American Civil War (1861–1865), triggered at least in part by a question of race. Slavery had been abolished in the Empire by a Bill (House of Commons 1833), but this did not mean that the whole of British society had been converted to anti-slavery overnight. The point King was addressing was not unrelated to slavery; as we will see, some in Newcastle were arguing that if science could prove that *Negroes* were a species different from Europeans, this could be used as justification to hold them as slaves, thus supporting the pro-slavery faction. As a corollary, if Neanderthals were in Victorian parlance 'lower than *Negroes*', they would certainly be a species different from Europeans, thus supporters of slavery at the meeting could have been well disposed towards King's proposal. Did either King or the pro-slavery faction see this line of argument, or deploy it?

Third, the paper focuses on King himself, on his academic standing as an anthropologist and as a geologist. He was professionally, even at the time of the meeting, a controversial figure who went to Newcastle with a certain amount of baggage. First and most immediately, he intended to read a paper on the comparative anatomy of the human skull, but this subject was entirely new to him, never having published on Anthropology or Craniology before 1863, or – at his mature age of 54 – not having studied the subject under any reputable craniologist or related specialist who could assess or contrast his views. He was a complete outsider and a loner, and this brings us to the question of whether he was – in the face of an academic panel of human anatomists or professionals of related disciplines such as Craniology, Comparative Anatomy, Medicine, Phrenology or Vertebrate Zoology – an acceptable voice to challenge the current orthodoxy about the taxonomic status of the Neanderthal specimen with a reasonable prospect of being taken seriously. In framing this question we cannot forget that, partly through the action of Scientific Naturalism (Dawson and Lightman 2015, 1–24) the sciences were then becoming professionalised, making the authority of anyone without acceptable credentials questionable. None other than Sir Charles Lyell had been challenged through the pages of *The Athenaeum* in February of that year when taking part in a debate on the human brain involving Richard Owen and Thomas Huxley (Owen 1863). Lyell was respected as a geologist, but he did not have a track record in human anatomy or the brain. Soon enough Lyell's contribution to the debate was challenged, and Huxley was unmasked as his ghost-writer. With King there was no question of a ghost-writer, but could he escape being challenged? An allied question is whether we could estimate, from a fresh reading of King's 1864b, how much time had he applied to the study of Craniology or Anthropology, and what were his resources to do so. Lastly, there was the issue of King's controversial status as a geologist. For several reasons (reviewed in DeArce and Wyse Jackson 2014; Harper 1988), he was on the public record as a disputatious colleague, having had in the recent past long public arguments with other geologists with regard to matters of professional ethics that left his practices under a cloud of suspicion. Did this factor have a negative effect, eroding away the scientific merits of his Neanderthal work?

## BAAS Newcastle meeting, 1863: Section C

Under this and the following heading I have attempted to reconstruct the schedule of presentations in Sections C and E of the Newcastle meeting, because these two Sections shared interests and personnel. But before we go into the schedule we need to know more about how the BAAS meetings worked, and how they were reported.

The Newcastle meeting was attended that year by more than 2,000 people (Anon. 1863a, 9), the highest number since the first BAAS meeting in 1831. The year's President was Sir William G. Armstrong FRS, an engineer and local captain of industry (iron and coal mining, smelting and manufacturing of artillery hardware) who gave employment to many people locally. The industry was dirty and he wanted to gain the hearts and minds of the locals and public at large as well as display the accurately destructive power that his productions could have in the many armed conflicts the Empire was confronting overseas. The official proceedings of the Sectional meetings

(Anon. 1864, part 2, 1-222) merely report abstracts of papers read, but not in the order in which they were read, and although in some way the *Proceedings* encapsulate all the drama of the meeting, we can only unpack it if we know more about the characters involved.

The task of organising the programme was distributed among seven Sectional Committees (A to G) where the suitability of the papers submitted was assessed (Carter Blake 1864b, 379). We are informed that these committees could reject papers. Each Section worked under a Sectional President for the year, who in 1863 were Warington W. Smyth for Section C and Sir Roderick I. Murchison for Section E. King's submission (King 1864a) entitled 'On the Neanderthal skull, Or Reasons for believing that it belongs in the Clydian period, and that it is specifically distinct from Man' had been classed by the relevant committee under section C. It is also possible that King himself submitted it to that section directly; after all, he was a geologist. But two points suggest that either he sent it to E and was shifted to C or that no one in the Geology Committee realised that Geology was not the appropriate setting for a paper concerned primarily with the description of a (human?) skull. The first is that none of the other 38 papers in Section C referred to fossil human remains, while all other papers on human remains and on the issue of human races/species were read under section E. King's paper could fit within Ethnology, the study of human races, as well as Anthropology, the study of humans with a focus then on craniological methods, which were both part of section E. The point addressed by King in the title is clearly taxonomic not geological.

The second point – admittedly not a certainty – that King's paper was deliberately misplaced is provided by a report in the *Journal of the Anthropological Society*: 'there were several anthropological papers, which were not accepted by the Committee (NB, of Section E) simply "because they were anthropological"' (Anon. 1863h). The correspondent then proceeded to include in his report abstracts of King (1863h, 393-394) and others' papers.

To gain a detailed knowledge of the schedule we need to consult the newspapers, local and national, which reported very generously on BAAS meetings every year. However, although the reporting was generous, it was not systematic. For this paper I have concentrated on one local newspaper, *The Newcastle Journal* (NJ), and one national, *The Times* of London (TL). TL reports focused largely on social events and the more popular or dramatic presentations, while NJ talked up local figures and studies. To obtain the best information on a scientific session it is therefore advisable to check both newspapers and glance at some others as well. Usually both newspapers reported with a 24-hour delay, but other dailies could have a longer delay. TL (Anon. 1863a, 9) informs us that the different sections met in simultaneous, separate sessions in different venues around the town, except for the President's Address, which all Sections attended together. It was also deemed necessary to read *The Athenaeum* (TA), essential reading for science affairs. The Owen-Huxley debate and others about the 'ape origin of man' or the comparative anatomy of the hippocampus was reported by TA in the first weeks of 1863. Lyell, who in the context of BAAS meetings was nothing short of a popular hero, made some contributions to this debate, although the mammalian brain was not anywhere near his professional interests. The debate between Hugh Falconer and Lyell regarding the geological evidence of the antiquity of man was printed in TA following seamlessly from the Owen-Huxley debate (Falconer 1863). TA reports on the BAAS meeting had about four weeks' delay.

The 39 papers to be read in Section C and 35 in Section E were reported by TA at the rate of a day's worth of proceedings per issue. The session for Monday, 31 August, was reported on 1 September, including eight papers. Carter Blake (1864a, v) gave some additional details on this session: 'In section C most interesting discussions arose respecting the "Antiquity of Man," on papers read by Professor Phillips (NB 1800–1874) and Mr Godwin-Austen (NB 1808–1884) respectively, and on which Sir Charles Lyell and Dr Falconer offered most valuable observations'.

Phillips and Godwin-Austen were active senior figures in British Geology and spoke respectively '[o]n the deposit of gravel, sand and loam with flint implements at Acheul' (Phillips 1864) and 'On the alluvial accumulation of the valley of the Somme and Oise' (Godwin-Austen 1864). Both were very cautious regarding the assumed great antiquity of man that Lyell was proposing, saying respectively that those deposits were no more than 'a few thousand years of antiquity', and that 'it cannot be concluded that *Elephas primigenius* was contemporaneous with man'.

King's paper was read in the evening of 2 September, the last day of Sectional meetings, with the abstract appearing in TA on 3 October 1863 (Anon. 1863b). TL did not mention King or his paper. NJ gave the title and author several times; it was first mentioned in the issue of 1 September (Anon. 1863e) under the heading 'Papers to be read this day'. The session took place in the Music Hall, Nelson Street. We do not know the criterion followed by the Committee to arrange the papers in the order they were to be read, but King's is the second last. At the end of the list, NJ added a note, which read 'if the whole of these papers be not read, the Section will meet on Wednesday morning'. The following day (Anon. 1863f), NJ reports that Sir Roderick Murchison gave in this session of Section C a paper co-authored with Professor Harkness from Queen's College Cork (Harkness and Murchison 1864). Sir Roderick Murchison (1792–1871) was a very wealthy man who moved in the highest social circles in Britain and abroad, an eminent lawyer and geologist, Director of the Geological Survey as well as the year's President of Section E of the BAAS. The report on Murchison's paper in TL (Anon. 1863f) was so extensive that the impression is given of it having crowded out most of the papers that were to follow on the day. The meeting adjourned until the morning of 2 September without reaching King.

The reading of the papers in Section C could have been done at the rate of 13 per day. From Monday 31 August to Wednesday 2 September inclusive, this would have been a manageable task, starting at 11 am and allowing 20 minutes per paper. BAAS business meetings were conducted at other times or days. However, Murchison had a lot to say, as is noticeable already in the *Proceedings*, in both Sections. Newspapers did not give the same column-inches to all speakers, and many were not mentioned at all. Murchison's subject in Section C was 'Permian Rocks of the North-West of England'. Harkness, co-author, joined him as a speaker towards the end. At this session, where King must have been present as a scheduled speaker, he had the satisfaction of hearing Professor Jones read a paper by Mr J. W. Kirkby where he referred to 'The magnesian limestone worked in the Fulwell quarries (belonging) to the higher portion of the Permian System and to the crystalline Cretacean limestone of Professor King'. Limestone, as well as the Permian, was a lifelong interest of King's. However, the session went on for too long, and King had the not unexpected disappointment to hear that the last six papers, including his, were rescheduled for Wednesday 2 September in the Lecture Room, Nelson Street, with Professor Harkness as Chair. Harkness had been Professor of Geology in Cork since 1854. He was a disciple of James D. Forbes, and his main interest was the Coal period, a favourite topic in Newcastle.

The title of King's talk was repeated by the NJ the following day, 3 September (page 2, column 6, end), as having been read the previous day (Anon. 1863e). On his report on that session, the NJ mentioned *in extenso* the contents and reactions to the first papers read, but only mention the title of King's paper. This could be either because both the authors of the earlier papers and their subjects were local to Newcastle, or because a craniological paper was seen as out of place in Section C, or simply through lack of time. The last two papers, including King's, are just mentioned as having been read before the meeting was dismissed until the following year in Bath.

TA's report for Section C of Wednesday 2 September, although published about one month after the meeting (Anon. 1863b), supplies thus the earliest-dated abstract by a third party of King's paper, saying little about the other papers read then:

> 'On the occurrence of rock salt in Middlesbrough,' by Mr. John Marley. 'Description of a sea star from the mountain limestone of Northumberland, with a notice of its association with Carboniferous plants,' by Mr G. Tate. 'On some facts observed in Weardale,' by Mr C. Atwood. 'On a section of strata near Hownes Gill to Cross Fell,' by Mr T. Sopwith.

Then came

> 'On the Neanderthal skull and reasons for believing that it belongs to the Clydian period and to be specifically distinct from Man', by Prof. W. King. (437, the abstract followed, uniquely in this report)

Lastly came '"On some fish remains that have occurred in the coal measures of Northumberland" by Mr C. Athbey and Mr J.W. Kirkby', also without abstract. In view of the three papers on the Carboniferous, Harkness' choice as Chair was appropriate, but the inclusion of King's paper was less so. King could not expect much informed or authoritative feedback from the speakers at this session.

In his abstract, King said that the deposits in the cave in the Neander valley 'occur ... under the same ancient physical-geography conditions as the caves in the Meuse valley', thus agreeing with Lyell rather than Phillips or Godwin-Austen on the antiquity of man, but his reasoning was not very forceful. To sum up, a series of coincidences left King in Section C not only as the second-last speaker of the last science session of the meeting, but also speaking in the wrong Section.

## Slaves, races and species: Section E

A glance over the schedule for Section E brings up new circumstances working against the unfortunate King. The possibility of a schism hung over the meetings of Section E since James Hunt had resigned his position in the Ethnological Society of London (ESL) to found and head the Anthropological Society of London (ASL) in May 1863 (Sera-Shriar 2013). The ESL had been founded by James Prichard (1786–1846), and favoured the linguistic method to study the origin of races. Its members were mostly monogenists and conservative, but they included also Huxley, a scientific reformer who was seeking to carve out an academic niche for his discipline and needed to put space between his research and Hunt's ideas (Sera-Shriar 2013). In 1863, the ASL were seeking to have their own subsection within E. Ethnologists and Anthropologists debated not only matters of method. Hunt despised Prichard's methodology and dependence on Religion, and supported polygenism, and Craniology as a method of study. Both groups also differed on the question of slavery, with the anthropologists, Hunt in particular, in favour of it. Hunt used the Newcastle meeting in an attempt to provide scientific support for the slavery of the *Negro* in the US, seeking to prove that they were a species different from Europeans. For details on Hunt's thinking see Rainger (1978), and see Sera-Shriar (2013) for a comparison between his and Huxley's observational practices.

A great show was made in this Section about the staged confrontation between Mr Crawfurd and Mr Craft, as mentioned above. Prichard had been a lifelong active Quaker, and Sir Roderick Murchison, the current president of Section E, while not being overtly religiously motivated, took pride in the Society's anti-slavery work (Murchison 1862–1863), but had a paternalistic view of the *Negro*, agreeing with Hunt in some respects. Hunt presented two papers; 'On Anthropological classification' (Hunt 1864a, 139), where he reviewed the systems of different authors to classify human races, concluding that language was not a valid principle of classification, giving greater value to religion or art. In 'On the physical and mental characters of the Negro' (Hunt 1864b, 140), he underlined the many physical differences between Europeans and Negroes, defending the idea that the psychological development of the mature *Negro* was comparable to that of the adolescent European.

John Crawfurd, an eminent linguist who was initially part of the ESL, gave four papers (Crawfurd 1864a, 135; 1864b, 135; 1864c, 136; 1864d). The first went against previous craniological observations among the tribes of the Americas. The second went directly against Prichard's (1831) essay, entitled 'The Eastern origin of the Celtic nations proved by a comparison of their dialects with the Sanskrit, Greek, Latin and Teutonic languages'. The title brings to mind Revd Edward Casavon, George Eliot's tragic character in 'Middlemarch' (Eliot 1871). Crawfurd's late response was 'On so-called Celtic languages in reference to the question of race'. Crawfurd also attacked

Lyell's proposal for a much older age of humanity in the third of his Newcastle papers, an amplified version of which had appeared as a review of Lyell's 1863 book, published in the ASL journal a few months earlier, where the professional ethics of the most senior British Geologist (Lyell) was dealt a considerable blow. Crawfurd read his paper on (or rather, against) Lyell on Friday 28 August, which was reported in TL on Monday 31 August (Anon. 1863h). It was not just that in Crawfurd's view Lyell was incorrect in his science, but also that there were persistent allegations that he had plagiarised the views of others.

Knowing that the touchstone test for two individuals being of different species was the reduced or nil fertility of their hybrids, Crawfurd, in the fourth of his Newcastle papers, entitled 'The commixture of races as affecting the progress of civilization', proposed that marriages among mulatos were less fertile or vigorous than those among two Europeans or two Negroes. Hunt saw in Crawfurd a possible ally for the ASL and eventually succeeded in recruiting him to his cause (Ellingson 2001, 201–271).

Revd Richard Lee had a paper on 'The extinction of races' (Lee 1864, 140), where he predicted the extinction of all other races except Europeans. Lastly, A.R. Wallace attracted attention with his paper on the Malay Archipelago (Wallace 1864, 147). Alfred Russell Wallace, who had co-authored with Darwin the first publication on the origin of species by natural selection (Darwin and Wallace 1858), was attending the BAAS after 13 years of fieldwork away from England (Vetter 2010), exciting great curiosity. His paper (see below) was read on 1 September. NJ reported fully on the session (Anon. 1863e), and TL on 3 September (Anon. 1863g) mentions a second discussion on the antiquity of man, this time in Section E. Carter Blake commented, 'the most valuable (NB ethnological paper) without exception, was that contributed by Mr Wallace on the "Ethnology of the Malay Archipelago," in which the questions relating to the antiquity of man were discussed in the most philosophical aspect ... in which Sir Charles Lyell, Prof Jukes, Dr Falconer, Mr Godwin-Austen and Prof Wilson (NB as well as Hunt and Wallace himself) took part, were often of the most interesting nature'. Jukes said that at least 20 years earlier he had held informally the opinion that the age of humanity was at least 100,000 years, and probably much more. Hunt made similar but wilder remarks, mentioning 9 million years. Absolute dating of human remains was impossible at the time.

While King read his paper, Section E were cramming their venue for a presentation by William Craft, a native of Dahomey and former slave in the US, who had managed to escape to England with his African wife Ellen, also a slave. Craft had an exciting story to tell, covering a recent visit he had paid to his native Dahomey: dancing Amazons mingled with human sacrifices, as he described the natives as being of a generally backward state (Craft 1864, 135), playing thus into the hands of his sponsors, the anthropologists. *The Times* of 3 September, page 7, column 3, said, 'The only section which possessed any very special interest yesterday was ... Section E ... it was unusually crowded to hear Mr. Craft ...'. The report, one of the longest in the TL for a single speaker, went on for two full columns.

To conclude, attitudes to slavery were a cause of major division among scientists in Section E, where the ASL had mounted a many-pronged campaign to discredit the humanity of Sub-Saharan Africans, turning to biology for reasons to consider Negroes as inferior to Europeans and forming a different species. We have no record of King's personal stance on slavery, but he concluded, using the craniological method favoured by the ASL, that Negroes, Australians and even the 'degraded Andamaner' with their high forehead and use of speech were as much *Homo sapiens* as the European. Beyond this, he tried to prove that the differences between Neanderthals and all extant human races were too large to consider them as one species, or even one genus. None of the scientists present put forward the view that, if that was the case, Neanderthals could be considered a precedent for different species within the genus *Homo*. Further, no one remarked on whether the projected extinction of Negroes (see Lee above) could be part of the same phenomenon as the factual extinction of Neanderthals. Thus slavery and the Neanderthal question as posed in Newcastle had potential for mutual reinforcement, but on the day they only touched indirectly.

## King's professional status and independent character

King was an intelligent man. In 1863, he was a professor with dozens of publications, including specialised monographs. He was also the father of a large and successful family (Harper 2004), with his older children well married and holding good official jobs overseas. He made a modest income and was of unsophisticated appearance and manner. He also was very autocratic and independent, which had made some see him as a troublemaker since well before 1863. Without a doubt, he was viewed by some colleagues with caution. He had had disputes with Richard Howse over who held priority on publishing a catalogue of Permian fossils from Durham (Howse 1848; King 1848), he confronted the management of the Hancock Museum over the ownership of Permian fossils that he had collected locally, which he took with him when moving to Galway in 1849 (Pettigrew 1979), and in 1861–1863,King had been busy corresponding with George Wallich in the pages of *The Nautical Magazine* where Wallich accused King of plagiarising his report on the materials obtained in the soundings of the North Atlantic sea-bed by HMS *Porcupine* off the west coast of Ireland (Wallich 1863; King 1863). This pattern of venting professional arguments in public would remain a feature of King's life. While forceful debates were not uncommon among Victorian scientists, a lifelong, systematic antagonising of colleagues was less so.

One of King's colleagues who must have been aware of these earlier disputes was Murchison. He shared with King an intense interest in the Permian period, and, since he occupied prominent administrative posts in British academic and field Geology, he was well informed of the various geologists working in Great Britain at the time. He was also, as we have seen, a key man in the organisation of the Newcastle meeting. The early debate on the taxonomic status of the Neanderthal fossil was thus conducted with Murchison in the background who knew aspects of King's personality. Given the gravity of the situation, one of Murchison's main roles was to keep a balance in Section E between Ethnologists and Anthropologists. One way to do this was to shunt King to Section C. Other circumstances helped to keep King away from controversial discussions in this occasion.

The Neanderthal debate of 1863 was clearly premature, occurring in the absence of much information on the Neanderthal skeletal specimens and associated cultural artefacts. The suspicions among the diverse groups of scientists who read King's Newcastle paper about his gentlemanly character exacerbated the situation. Was the adoptive Galway-man made to feel an outcast or a redneck among sophisticates, a scientific pariah among the London elite? An indication that something like this was what happened is found in some of the reports of King's speech in Newcastle (Carter Blake 1864a; 1864b), indicating that King was put in his place – as if asking the reader whether anything of interest to science could be expected to come from Galway. On several occasions the reporter, after mentioning King's name, wrote in brackets, as if in a theatrical aside, 'Professor King (from Galway) said'. There was no other King at the meeting, and no other speaker received such treatment, so we can only interpret this as an ironic reference to King's provincialism. Another effective way of ostracising King would have been simply to ignore him, in a form of scientific boycott, something that King would have been justified in feeling in Newcastle.

After his disputes with Carpenter (which occurred later, reviewed by O'Brien 1970 and Adelman 2007), King used to refer in private to the members of the Royal Society as 'the Society for the preservation of scientific pride'. But now, in Newcastle, he approached the dilemma (race or species?) by indulging both the ASL and the ESL, but satisfying neither. King's point of view was based decisively on his assumption that Neanderthals must have possessed a primitive brain, the rude, ape-like social behaviour favoured at the time, to match their lowly skull.

King's entry into the field of Anthropology/Craniology was characteristically daring, well informed and iconoclastic. He was going directly against the then orthodox interpretation of Neanderthals as an extinct human race, proposed over the years by Schaafhaussen, Fuhlrot, Lyell, Huxley and Busk.

Since King used a craniological method to support his proposition, we need to ask how much he knew about skull anatomy. The description of the fossil skull in his long paper (1864b, 91-96) indicates that he was well informed. The fine observations in his paper – the reasons why it was selected as the landmark definition of *H. neanderthalensis* – convey competence and, if anything, excessive confidence in his knowledge about human and animal skulls. However, there is a big objection to his inference of 'simial' behaviour from the simian appearance of the skull; he did not (could not) elaborate from scientific principles on the nexus between a superficially 'simial' skull and the supposedly 'simial' behaviour that he attributed to Neanderthals. Carter Blake picked up this objection later (Carter Blake 1864b);

> Whilst the question of the mental endowments of the Neanderthal man must remain for a long period unanswered, I am afraid that the speculations of Professor King as to the precise theological belief professed by the individual must remain in abeyance.

In one respect the skull was not as 'simial' as he made it to be. Darwin and Huxley, with Schaafhausen, were impressed by the large cranial capacity (commensurate with brain volume) of the fossil – in the mid ranges of human variation – that was more than the capacity of any extant primate, facts that had been known since Schaafhausen's report (Schaafhausen was translated into English by Busk 1861). King did not seem to have reflected on the disparity between a very simian outer aspect of the Neanderthal crania and its large brain volume. Neither did he reply to Huxley (1864) when, after the Newcastle meeting, he commented on the similarity of the endocasts of Neanderthal and Australian (Huxley 1864).

From King's 1864b publication, we can estimate how much time it would have taken for him to do the required research as well as analyse the craniological resources at his disposal. With regard to the time requirements to acquire the knowledge necessary, we need to acknowledge that he was describing a relatively simple object, the outer aspect of a calotte. In this author's opinion, there is no particular aspect of King's 1864 longer paper that would have required years of intense laboratory or intellectual work. In comparison, until at least a decade or so ago, pre-medical students learned the full anatomy of the human head and neck (including vasculature, innervation, muscles and bones, and facial bones) in about one term in their first or second year.

After his move to Galway in 1849, King was on the lookout for new topics of research that his new location would favour (DeArce and Wyse Jackson 2014). The record of his geological research of the early 1860s suggests how he was led to think of the Neanderthal fossil. In 1862, King wrote a memoir attempting to correlate the glacial and post-glacial deposits in the British Isles to determine their mode of succession (King 1862). He called this succession the Clydian period, which was mentioned in the title of his Newcastle presentation (King 1864a). For his long publication, he removed the reference to the Clydian period from the title and moved it to the body of his paper (King 1864b, 88), obviously seeking to underline the anthropological – as opposed to geological – nature of the work. This was a move away from the Permian and such a move would lead him to the first point he made in his paper on the Neanderthal skull (1864b, 88) that the associated geological deposits in the cave in the Neander Valley were the same age as the human remains in caves near the Meuse. The age of these deposits could then be known from the associated faunas as the same as his Clydian period or, in modern terms, the end of the Wurm glaciation. Once this was accepted (and, as we saw, neither Phillips nor Godwin-Austen would accept it), the rest of his paper, the actual anatomical comparisons, would take just a few months' work to complete, if the resources were available.

Let us consider his craniological resources. Only one resource of those listed by King (1864b) was large enough to enable him to say that he had acquainted himself with the skulls of 'the principal races of man' (King 1864b, 91 n. 4). This comment is most likely referring to the collection in the Museum of Anatomy in the University of Dublin, the closest and most comprehensive craniological resource available to King that has not been mentioned before (other than by King himself – see King 1864b, 94-95). This collection is largely *in situ* to this day, although not for public viewing. An examination of its old catalogue shows that many of the skulls date from after 1863, but since there are several hundred of them (the author estimates 500-600) from a range of provenances throughout the five continents, including some ancient North Europeans, and since additions to the collection began in the eighteenth century, it is quite possible that some of the specimens we see today were there at the time of King's visit in early 1863 or late 1862. Several physicians with positions in the School of Medicine in the College, such as James McCartney MD (Professor 1813-1837) or Sir William Wilde MD (1815-1876), whose collection in the Museum of Anatomy Trinity College Dublin contains several Australian skulls, had had an interest in gathering skulls before the date of King's study. I have been able to retrace the *Kaffir* (donated 1852), *Australian* and *Andamaner* (donated 1808) skulls mentioned by King (1864b). If even a small part of this collection was seen by King, his statement about the range of his observations would be fully justified and it is reasonable to conclude that King had a good idea, from direct observation, of the ethnic variability of the human skull. However, his paper did not attempt to be a detailed comparison of the extant human races among themselves or with the Neanderthal calotte.

Although his interest in Neanderthals was very likely aroused through his geological work, judging from his written output King's engagement with the subject of the Neanderthal skull did not have to have been very long. It was probably a very brief departure from his abiding interest up to 1863, which had been and continued to be the rocks and fossils of the Permian in England, Germany and Ireland. His primary subject of study then was quite removed from primate fossils of the last European glacial period or the comparative anatomy and pathological variations of their skulls. After his Neanderthal study, King returned to more traditional Geology, producing with Professor Rowney, of the Department of Chemistry in QCG (King and Rowney 1881) a masterpiece on the chemical changes associated with geological metamorphism, in one of the first books ever to be printed with colour illustrations.

The year 1863 provided several external triggers that could have galvanised King's decision to research the Neanderthal fossils. Professor John Cleland (1835-1925) had been appointed Chair of Anatomy in QCG in late 1863, and could have had an effect on King's choice of subject for his next piece of research. Cleland had himself an interest in craniology lasting well beyond his appointment to Galway (Cleland 1877), specifically from his first publication on the subject in 1861 until the last in 1877 while still in Galway, which he continued after a subsequent appointment at Edinburgh. This appointment to Galway, in December 1863, of a real human anatomist with a good track record and an interest in craniology could explain why King did not consider it politic to return to the subject again. February that year saw also the first edition of Lyell's *Geological evidence of the Antiquity of man* (Lyell 1863, quoted by King in his 1864b paper) and Huxley's *Evidence as to man's place in nature* (Huxley 1863, also quoted by King), both of which contained extensive commentary on what they called 'Neanderthal man'. I suggest that King's involvement with human skulls, the Neanderthal calotte in particular, might have only spanned from February 1863 to the BAAS meeting in August–September that same year, or at most from his publication on the Clydian period (King 1862) until the publication of his Neanderthal paper, January 1864. He never wrote on the subject again.

What was the heart of King's reasoning to establish *H. neanderthalensis* as a new species, which had not been seen by keener eyes before him? His craniological observations on the fossil led him to conclude that it was more *simial* than human, but, being aware that this may not be enough to make his case, he introduced a psychological or even metaphysical argument. He said that the Andamaner, 'who without a doubt is the human race closest to the animal' (King 1864b), ought to be classified as a member of the human species, because of his having speech and a tall frontal bone without the supraciliary ridges so obvious in Neanderthal, and because even they make a reference to the godhead in their practices, he concluded that Neanderthals could not do any of those human things, particularly the latter, because their skull was so low compared to the European:

> Why may there not have been a Pliocene, or a Clydian species, possessed of no higher faculties than such as would enable it to erect a protecting shed, fashion a stone for special purposes, or store up food for winter; but like the gorilla, or chimpanzee, be devoid of speech, and equally as unconscious of the existence of a Godhead?
>
> The distinctive faculties of Man are visibly expressed in his elevated cranial dome, a feature which, though much debased in certain savage races, essentially characterises the human species. But, considering that the Neanderthal skull is eminently simial, both in its general and particular characters, I feel myself constrained to believe that the thoughts and desires which once dwelt within it never soared beyond those of the brute. (King 1864, 96; also quoted in Anon. 1863g, 393)

Thus King had established language and religion as species-specific traits, and decided, exclusively in view of the low frontal bone and massive supraciliary arches, that Neanderthals did not possess those traits. To summarise, reading into what King did and did not say (or write) about the Neanderthal skull, it can be concluded that his involvement with the subject had been short and that his knowledge of the surface of human skulls was as detailed as it could possibly have been at the time, but that he took a step too far from Anatomy to Psychology or Philosophical Anthropology that was hardly warranted.

King's understanding of evolution as applied to man was perhaps more penetrating than Huxley's. King clearly saw the possibility of several species of *Homo*, each having developed certain skills useful in their survival, while Huxley and other Darwinians at the time had a more uni-linear idea of human evolution. Thus the human evolutionary tree in King's mind would have several short branches and only one lasting to the present, including several races.

Unfortunately, King also left clear evidence that he was hesitant about the definitive value of his own proposition in that he thought he had not gone far enough. The differences that he perceived between *neanderthalensis* and *sapiens* were too large in his view to consider them within the same genus. However, inconsistently with this concluding remark, which he repeated at least twice, he abstained from proposing a new generic name for the fossil.

## Conclusion

From observations about the 1863 BAAS meeting, this paper shows that the meeting in Newcastle was a watershed for the established authority on the science of man in Britain. The authority of Lyell, Prichard and Huxley was respectively challenged by Crawfurd, Hunt and King, King himself unwittingly contributing to the establishment of the new science of Anthropology.

Section E of the BAAS was fraught with divisions among the attending men of science, following political and social fault-lines. Among the former, they differed greatly on their attitudes to slavery. This clearly shows that science is rarely untrammelled by other issues of human interest that affect scientists as members of society. Power struggles among scientists and ideological issues unrelated to 'pure science' are inevitable companions and even guides in the direction science takes at a given time.

A reconstitution of the meeting's schedule indicates that King's presentation overlapped with a popular presentation on slavery in Section E. Wallace had also made ethnological contributions to this session that attracted some of the best-known names to the discussion.

With regard to King's personality and social standing, it is concluded that he brought to Newcastle a history of professional disputes, and his colleagues and seniors, especially Murchison, must have been well aware of this. However, in Section C, King did not encounter any substantial opposition, but neither did he find support.

The allocation of King's paper to an unproblematic Section C could have been partly because he was known as a geologist and not as an academic anthropologist (or related). But there could have been also an element of trying to avoid a troublesome man in an arena (Section E) that was more suitable for King's presentation, but was already quite troublesome as it was without King. Any discussion about the scientific merits of his paper had, in practice, taken place at the committee stage when he had not been denied the opportunity of speaking. Nevertheless, he had been given a soft, nearly irrelevant forum.

In this occasion, which was as far as it is known the first time that King confronted a potentially large meeting, he showed himself less disputatious than usual, but, given his audience on the day, a confrontation was unlikely. Although Hunt or Crawfurd could have capitalised on King's paper to show that it was not just the ASL that proposed other *Homo* species, but that a geologist from Galway reported a similar idea, albeit involving a species now extinct, they did not do so. Neither did they coin any names for their proposed new species.

With regard to King's involvement in the disciplines of Human Anatomy, Anthropology and Craniology, I conclude that it need not have been very long and that it could have lasted just months rather than years. It is proposed that his interest in the subject was triggered by academic events (publications) occurring in February 1863, and that he had, within Ireland, in the Museum of Anatomy of the University of Dublin, enough resources to acquaint himself extensively with the science of Craniology, such as it was. In view of his colleague John Cleland's curriculum vitae (Cleland 1877) up to then, it would seem that he would have had much better prospects than King of attracting serious attention among his peers on the matter of Neanderthals, and King effectively retired from the subject.

It is observed that, ultimately, King's reasoning for creating a new species for the Neanderthal fossil was more psychological or theological than craniological, and since in the same breath he said that he had not gone far enough, as not just a species but a whole new genus should be created to accommodate Neanderthal, (King 1864b), he undermined his own proposition of a new species. However, 150 years of uninterrupted usage make the specific name so venerable as to fix it permanently.

## Acknowledgements

I am grateful to Siobhan Ward for guiding me through the skull collection at the old Museum of Anatomy, in Trinity College Dublin, a very little-known resource for the study of Craniology through the nineteenth century. Nicola Morris from Online Research Ireland Ltd obtained the newspaper references and transcribed some of them.

## Bibliography

Adelman, J. (2007) Eozoon: Debunking the dawn creature. *Endeavour* 31, 94–98.
Anon. (1863a) *The Times*, London, 26 August.
Anon. (1863b) *The Athenaeum*, 3 October 1857.
Anon. (1863c) British Association Meeting, *The Geologist* (October), 391–392.
Anon. (1863d) (probably Charles Carter Blake). Professor King on the Neanderthal Skull. In 'Anthropology at the British Association', *Journal of Anthropology* 1, 393.
Anon. (1863e) *The Newcastle Journal*, 2 September, 3. Also, *Caledonian Mercury*, same date, 2.
Anon. (1863f) *The Newcastle Journal*, 3 September. Also, *Caledonian Mercury*, 3.
Anon. (1863g) *The Times*, London, 3 September.
Anon. (1863h) *The Times*, London, 31 August.
Anon. (1864) *Report of the Thirty-Third Meeting of the British Association for the Advancement of Science held in Newcastle upon Tyne in August and September 1863*, 81–82. London: John Murray.
Anon. (1865) *Report of the Thirty-Fourth Meeting of the British Association for the Advancement of Science held in Bath in August and September 1864*. London: John Murray.

Busk, G. (1861) Translation with Comments of 'On the crania of the most ancient races of man' by D. Schaaffhausen. *The Natural History Review: A Quarterly Journal of Biological Science* 1, 153–176.

Busk, G. (1864) Pithecoid Priscan Man from Gibraltar. *The Reader* 4, 109.

Carter Blake, C. (1864a) On the Alleged Peculiar Characters, and Assumed Antiquity of the Human Cranium from the Neanderthal. *Journal of the Anthropological Society* 2(5), 139–167.

Carter Blake, C. (1864b) Report on the Anthropological Papers Read at the Newcastle Meeting of the British Association for the Advancement of Science, in August and September, 1863. *Journal of the Anthropological Society of London* 2, 153–154.

Cleland, J. (1877) Testimonials in Favour of John Cleland, M.D., F.R.S., L.R.C.S.E., Professor of Anatomy and Physiology in the Queen's College, Galway: candidate for the Chair of Anatomy in the University of Glasgow. Available online: https://archive.org/stream/b24930751/b24930751_djvu.txt.

Craft, W. (1864) On a Visit to Dahomey. In: Anon. (ed.) *Report of the Thirty-Third Meeting of the British Association for the Advancement of Science held in Newcastle upon Tyne in August and September 1863*, p. 135. London: John Murray.

Crawfurd, J. (1864a) On the Origin of the Gipsies. In: Anon. (ed.) *Report of the Thirty-Third Meeting of the British Association for the Advancement of Science held in Newcastle upon Tyne in August and September 1863*, p. 135. London: John Murray.

Crawfurd, J. (1864b) On the So-called Celtic languages, in Reference to the Question of Race. In: Anon. (ed.) *Report of the Thirty-Third Meeting of the British Association for the Advancement of Science held in Newcastle upon Tyne in August and September 1863*, pp. 135–136. London: John Murray.

Crawfurd, J. (1864c) A Few Notes on Sir Charles Lyell's 'Antiquity of man'. In: Anon. (ed.) *Report of the Thirty-Third Meeting of the British Association for the Advancement of Science held in Newcastle upon Tyne in August and September 1863*, p. 136. London: John Murray.

Crawfurd, J. (1864d) The Commixture of Races as Affecting the Progress of Civilization. In: Anon. (ed.) *Report of the Thirty-Third Meeting of the British Association for the Advancement of Science held in Newcastle upon Tyne in August and September 1863*, p. 135. London: John Murray.

Darwin, C.R. and Wallace, A.R. (1858) On the Tendency of Species to Form Varieties, and on the Perpetuation of Varieties and Species by Natural Means of Selection. Communicated by Sir Charles Lyell, J.D. Hooker. *Journal of the Proceedings of the Linnaean Society of London, Zoology* 3, 45–50.

Dawson, G. and Lightman, B. (ed.) (2015) Introduction. In: G. Dawson and B. Lightman (eds) *Victorian Scientific Naturalism: Community, identity, continuity*, pp. 1–44. Chicago: University of Chicago Press.

DeArce, M. and Wyse Jackson, P.N. (2014) The Alternative Geologist: William King (1809–1886) and his scientific controversies. *Journal of the Galway Archaeological and Historical Society* 66, 100–124.

Drell, J.R.R. (2000) Neanderthal: History of interpretation. *Oxford Journal of Archaeology* 19, 1–24.

Ellingson, T. (2001) *The Noble Savage*. Berkeley: University of California Press.

Eliot, G. (1871) *Middlemarch*. London: Penguin.

Falconer, H. (1863) Primeval Man. *The Athenaeum*, 4 April, 459–460.

Godwin-Austen, G. (1864) On the Alluvial Accumulation of the Valley of the Somme and Oise. In: Anon. (ed.) *Report of the Thirty-Third Meeting of the British Association for the Advancement of Science held in Newcastle upon Tyne in August and September 1863*, p. 64. London: John Murray.

Harper, D.A.T. (1988) The King of Queen's College. William King DSc, first Professor of Geology at Galway. In: D.A.T. Harper (ed.) *William King, a Palaeontological Tribute*, pp. 1–24. Galway: Galway University Press.

Harper, D.A.T. (2004) King, William (1809–1886). In: L. Goldman (ed.) *Oxford Dictionary of National Biography*, online edn. Oxford: Oxford University Press.

Harkness, R. and Murchison, R.I. (1864) Observations of Sir R.I. Murchison upon the Permian Group of the Northwest of England, in Communicating the Outline of a Memoir Thereon by Prof. R. Harkness and Himself. In: Anon. (ed.) *Report of the Thirty-Third Meeting of the British Association for the Advancement of Science held in Newcastle upon Tyne in August and September 1863*, pp. 83–85. London: John Murray.

House of Commons. (1833) *A Bill for the Abolition of Slavery Throughout the Colonies etc.* Available online: http://parlipapers.chadwyck.co.uk.elib.tcd.ie/home.do.

Howse, R. (1848) *A Catalogue of the Fossils of the Permian System of the County of Northumberland and Durham.* Newcastle upon Tyne.

Hunt, J. (1864a) On Anthropological Classification. In: Anon. (ed.) *Report of the Thirty-Third Meeting of the British Association for the Advancement of Science held in Newcastle upon Tyne in August and September 1863*, pp. 139–140. London: John Murray.

Hunt, J. (1864b) On the Physical and Mental Characters of the Negro. In: Anon. (ed.) *Report of the Thirty-Third Meeting of the British Association for the Advancement of Science held in Newcastle upon Tyne in August and September 1863*, p. 140. London: John Murray.

Huxley, T.H. (1863) *Evidence as to the Place of Man in Nature.* London: Williams and Norgate.

Huxley, T.H. (1864) Further Remarks upon the Human Remains from Neanderthal. *Natural History Review* (2nd series) 1, 429–446.

ICZN International Code for Zoological Nomenclature (undated). Available online: http://www.iczn.org/iczn/index.jsp.

Keith, A. (1911) The Early History of the Gibraltar Cranium. *Nature* 87, 313–314.

King, W. (1848) *A Catalogue of the Organic Remains of the Permian Rocks of Northumberland and Durham.* Newcastle upon Tyne.

King, W. (1862) Synoptical Table of Aqueous Rock-Groups, Chiefly British, Arranged by their Order Superposition and Chronological Sequence. *The Geologist* 5, 194–198.

King, W. (1863) The Porcupine's Soundings, or Professor William King's Reply to Dr. Wallich's Statements. *The Nautical Magazine* 32, 132–135.

King, W. (1864a) On the Neanderthal skull, Or Reasons for Believing that it Belongs in the Clydian Period, and that it is Specifically Distinct from Man. In: Anon. (ed.) *Report of the Thirty-Third Meeting of the British Association for the Advancement of Science held in Newcastle upon Tyne in August and September 1863*, pp. 81–82. London: John Murray.

King, W. (1864b) The Reputed Fossil Man of the Neanderthal. *Quarterly Journal of Science* 1, 88–97.

King, W. and Rowney, T. (1881) *An Old Chapter of the Geological Record with a New Interpretation of Rock Metamorphism (especially of the methylosed kind and its resultant imitations of organisms).* London: Van Voorst.

Lee, R. (1864) On the Extinction of Races. In: Anon. (ed.) *Report of the Thirty-Third Meeting of the British Association for the Advancement of Science held in Newcastle upon Tyne in August and September 1863*, pp. 140–141. London: John Murray.

Lyell, C. (1863) *Geological Evidence as to the Antiquity of Man.* London: John Murray.

Murchison, R.I. (1862–1863) Address. *Proceedings of the Royal Geographical Society of London* 7, 123–202.

Murray, J., Nasheuer, H.P., Seoighe, C., McCormick, G.P., Williams, D.M. and Harper, D.A.T. (2015) The Contribution of William King to the Early Development of Palaeoanthropology. *Irish Journal of Earth Sciences* 33, 1–16.

O'Brien, C.F. (1970) Eozoon canadense, the Dawn Animal of Canada. *Isis* 61, 206–223.

Owen, R. (1863) In Ape Origin of Man. *The Athenaeum*, February–April.

Pettigrew, T.H. (1979) William King, a Biographical Note. *Newsletter of the Geological Curators Group* 2, 326–329.

Phillips, J. (1864) On the Deposit of Gravel, Sand and Loam with Flint Implements at Acheul. In: Anon. (ed.) *Report of the Thirty-Third Meeting of the British Association for the Advancement of Science held in Newcastle upon Tyne in August and September 1863*, pp. 85–86. London: John Murray.

Prichard, J.C. (1831) *The Eastern Origin of the Celtic Nations Proved by a Comparison of their Dialects with the Sanskrit, Greek, Latin and Teutonic Languages.* London: Houlston and Wright.

Rainger, R. (1978) Race, Politics and Science: The Anthropological Society of London in the 1860s. *Victorian Studies* 22, 51–70.

Schwartz, J.H. (2006) Race and the Odd History of Human Palaeontology. *The Anatomical Record Part B: The New Anatomist* 289B, 225–240.

Sera-Shriar, E. (2013) Observing Human Differences: James Hunt, Thomas Huxley and competing disciplinary strategies in the 1860. *Annals of Science* 70, 461–491.

Stocking, G.W. (1987) *Victorian Anthropology*. London: Collins MacMillan.

Stringer, C. (1999) Editorial. *Journal of the Linnean Society* 15, 1–2.

Tattersall, I. (1995) *The Last Neanderthal: The rise, success and mysterious extinction of our closest human relatives*. Peter N. Nevraumont book. New York: MacMillan.

Vetter, J. (2010) The Unmaking of an Anthropologist: Wallace returns from the field, 1862. *Notes and Records of the Royal Society of London* 64, 25–42.

Wallace, A.R. (1864) On the Varieties of Men in the Malay Archipelago. In: Anon. (ed.) *Report of the Thirty-Third Meeting of the British Association for the Advancement of Science held in Newcastle upon Tyne in August and September 1863*, pp. 147–148. London: John Murray.

Wallich, G.C. (1863) Letter to the Editor on Professor King's Preliminary Remarks on the *Porcupine* Soundings of December 1862. *The Nautical Magazine* 31, 26–31.

Wood, B.A. (1979) The 'Neanderthals' of the College of Surgeons. *Annals of the Royal College of Surgeons* 61, 385–389.

# Chapter 12

# George Busk and the remarkable Neanderthal

*Paige Madison*

## Abstract

*George Busk was a scientist with many research interests. Although he began his scientific career studying surgery and sea mosses, he developed expertise in a collection of subjects that, although at first glance may seem random, in fact, placed him in a unique position at a formative period in the history of anthropology. When a strange skull was discovered in a cave in Germany, Busk's work on human variation and prehistory allowed him to formulate some of the first hypotheses about the fossil. Tracing Busk's research interests throughout his career allows us to obtain a clearer picture of both Busk as a scientist, and the new field of science he was exploring: that which eventually became palaeoanthropology. Thus, the story of Busk and the first Neanderthal is essentially a story of the formulation of early palaeoanthropology, viewed through the eyes of one of the discipline's original leaders.*

## A strange human skull

'Remarkable', Busk commented as he turned the plaster skull cast over in his hands, a cranium that he believed would certainly prompt the 'utmost interest' (Busk 1861, 161). It was 1860, and George Busk was examining a replica of a strange fossil that had recently been found in the Neander Valley, Germany (Figure 12.1). Busk, a retired surgeon living in London, was preparing a paper on the skull. This paper would be a translation of the original German manuscript on the fossil, followed by a section detailing Busk's own impressions. Having obtained a rare cast of the skull from Germany, Busk was eager to make his own pronouncements on this extraordinary object.

It was unlike anything Busk had ever seen. The skull was discovered four years earlier: the fossils were unearthed accidentally, hastily shovelled out of a cave in a quarrying operation (Schmitz and Thissen 2000). In addition to the partial skull

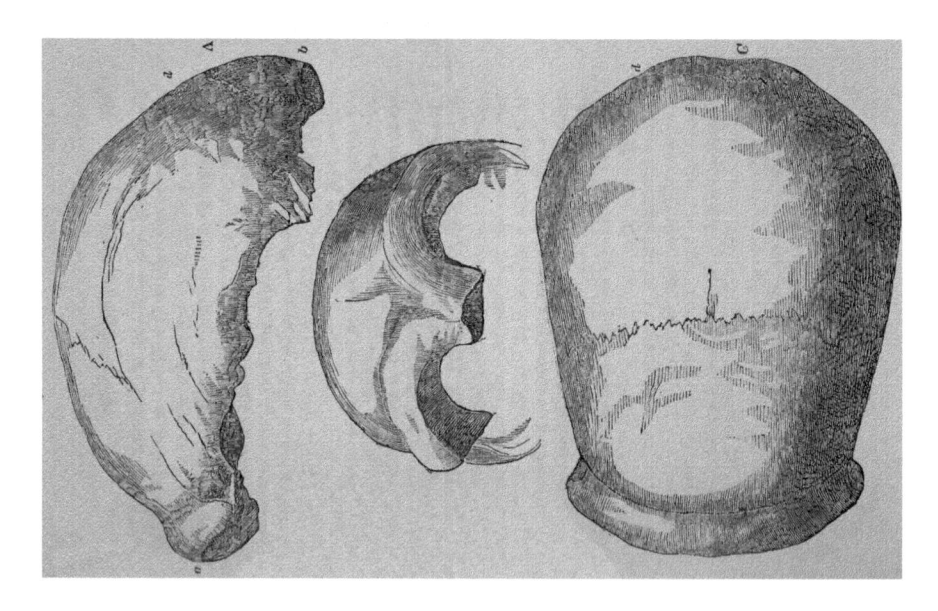

*Figure 12.1. The Neanderthal skull viewed from three angles, drawn by Thomas Huxley and George Busk, from* Evidence as to Man's Place in Nature *(Huxley 1863, 161).*

fragment, a number of various postcranial bones had been discovered, including some ribs and bones of the arms and legs. The creature's skull suggested a large brain, leading scientists to believe it was human (Madison 2016). However, this human exhibited unique traits that began to attract scientific interest, and Busk tasked himself with making sense of it.

The question was made increasingly challenging by the fact that the idea of what constituted being 'human' was radically changing (Goodrum 2012). At the time at which Busk was preparing his remarks on the fossil, scientists were uncovering evidence that humans had a longer history on Earth than previously imagined, and that human populations exhibited enormous diversity in form (Grayson 1983; Stocking 1991). Both these ideas placed the concept of being 'human' on shifting grounds. Scientists wondered how long humans had been around for, and how diverse they were. As a fossil that was both potentially ancient, *and* a mix of human and less conventionally human traits, the Neander skull had the potential to factor significantly in these conversations (Bowler 1986).

Today, over 150 years after Busk held the remarkable cast, the skeleton from the Neander valley is known as the type specimen for *Homo neanderthalensis*, known as Neanderthal 1 (Figure 12.1). In the century and a half since the discovery, much has been learned about our most closely related species of hominin. The fossils have moved through a variety of interpretations, ignited controversies about intelligence and culture, and even yielded DNA (Krings *et al.* 1997). The long history of these fossils, combined with their continued importance can, however, obscure our understanding of their history. It is sometimes difficult to separate modern views of the fossils from the views of the scientists who studied them centuries ago. This separation of ideas is especially difficult for the Neander fossils because they were studied during a pivotal moment in the history of biology, when evolutionary concepts were taking shape (Bowler 1989). Thus, some histories have suggested the fossils – discovered at such an auspicious time – were crucial pieces of evidence for debates about human evolution (Trinkaus and Shipman 1993). A closer look at the study of the Neander fossils, however, reveals a different story.

The study of hominin fossils in the nineteenth century was a novel scientific endeavour; a burgeoning field of research that occupied the crossroads of a range of other disciplines (Goodrum 2012). Scientists like Busk borrowed ideas from geology, archaeology and any other branch of science that could potentially illuminate the human past. This paper seeks to get a clearer picture of that intersection, asking how the bones from the Neander valley were understood in the early years after their discovery, and in particular, why did Busk form the views he held on the matter? What questions were asked about the fossils, and what issues were raised in their interpretations? The conversations that emerged around the bones were many and diverse, but Busk was a central figure in discussions of both interpretations of the fossil, and the broader concept of human prehistory at the time. Therefore, the works of Busk between 1860 and 1861, during this critical development, reveal a sharp picture of the early study of the fossils.

Examining Busk's work reveals that, because the Neander fossils were interpreted as human, the bones were subjected to the two major concerns in the study of humans at the time. The first was the question of antiquity: how long had humans been on Earth? The second was that of variation: how much did human skulls truly vary, and what did those variations mean? For Busk, the study of the Neander fossils was intertwined with these questions. Seeing the Neander fossils through Busk's eyes – years before they became *Homo neanderthalensis*, and decades before the scientific discipline of palaeoanthropology fully emerged – reveals a chapter in the history of Neanderthal studies that is quite different from our understanding as is popularised today.

## George Busk: Surgeon and sea moss expert

At first glance, George Busk would not appear to be an obvious candidate for the role of bringing news of the remarkable Neander fossil to the English-speaking world. He was not a particularly radical scientist, one to ruffle feathers or loudly champion revolutionary ideas, nor is he remembered as an expert in the field of human palaeontology. When Busk is remembered in historical literature, it is usually for his role as a British naval surgeon and his research on marine moss (Cook 1997). He is described as having been reserved, averse to public speaking and cautious about making scientific conclusions (Thomas 2008). So how did he end up studying the strange human from the Neander Valley?

In the years before his work on the Neander fossil, Busk had had a long and varied career. A surgeon by training, he had been educated in medicine, first at Dr Harley's School in Yorkshire, and later at St Thomas's Hospital. Busk spent most of his working life as a surgeon on the hospital ship *Dreadnought* and was a member of the Royal College of Surgeons England (Thomas 2008). During his time on the ship, Busk had become an expert on a phylum of marine invertebrates known as moss animals, Bryozoa. His work on Bryozoa led him to become especially interested in microscopy, and he had founded the Microscopical Society and edited journals such as the *Quarterly Journal of Microscopic Science* (now known as the *Journal of Cell Science*).

In the early 1850s, Busk began branching out beyond the small circle of scientists interested in microscopes. He was honoured by a number of elite scientific bodies, becoming a fellow of the prestigious Royal Society and a secretary for the Linnean Society. He then resigned from the *Dreadnought* to fully devote himself to natural history (Thomas 2008).

## Hunterian professor and craniologist

By the late 1850s, Busk (Figure 12.2) had become a central figure in Victorian science. He gained esteem as the Hunterian Professor at the Royal College of Surgeons, despite his disdain for public lecturing (Thomas 2008). He also edited papers for scientific journals and translated German texts, including one on human histology (Kölliker 1853). Busk played important roles behind the scenes in these scientific societies; as a Secretary for the Linnean Society, he was instrumental in orchestrating what have come to be regarded as monumental moments in the history of science, including the first reading of both Charles Darwin's and Alfred Russel Wallace's papers on natural selection in 1858 (Gardiner 2000). Indeed, Busk was so influential that, shortly after *The Origin of Species* was published, Darwin wrote to Thomas Huxley, a mutual friend, to confirm whether Busk was 'on our side' with regard to his theory, claiming that if he was 'it would be very good' (Darwin 1859).

Within such societies as the Linnean, Busk met scientists with similar interests. It was shortly before embarking on a study of the Neander fossils that Busk befriended the young surgeon Thomas Henry Huxley, who would ultimately become his colleague in the study of the Neander fossil. Like Busk, Huxley was fascinated by microscopic marine life, and their research interests largely overlapped (Desmond 1997). Over the next few years, their work together would shift away from marine life.

In the late 1850s, Busk shifted his gaze from marine organisms to humans. He was exposed to many of the major debates that were occurring about humans at the time; and, serendipitously, his scientific training meant he was, in some cases, uniquely positioned to address them. First, Busk began to weigh in on questions about the age of the human species: how long had humans been around and how could scientists know? Second, he became fascinated with the growing field of craniometry, the science of measuring human skulls. Craniometry sought to quantify skull variations, measuring features including prognathism, length and width. Scientists wondered how those characters changed in humans from different parts of the world and attempted to understand the significance of those changes (Gould 1996). Were humans all one species, scientists wondered, despite these differences? If humans differed in many respects, where should the line be drawn between humans and other creatures?

These questions – the age of the species, and the boundaries that distinguished species – were central to interpretations of humans at the time, and because the Neander specimen was considered human they came to figure prominently in discussions of antiquity and variation. When Busk first encountered the Neander fossils, he was not only engaging with both of these debates, but also overseeing excavations, examining evidence and providing expert opinions. His study in all these realms resulted in the Neander fossils becoming intertwined with questions of both the human past and our place in nature.

*Figure 12.2. George Busk, from* The Thomas Henry Huxley Collection *(Imperial College London, 1825–1895). Identifier 11.219 Box Number 11 Series 1b.*

## The Man from the Neander Valley

Before news of the Neander fossils reached Busk, the bones had been passed through a number of hands and had become known as the Man from the Neander Valley, or the Neanderthal Man (thal meaning valley). A few scientists in Germany saw the creature as an ancient race of humans, while others thought it to be a modern, deformed 'idiot' (Mayer 1864). Only one scientist, however, had prepared a detailed examination of the fossils, though, and the translation that opened the account to scrutiny from the English-speaking world came courtesy of Busk. The scientist who Busk translated was Hermann Schaaffhausen, a Professor of Anatomy at the University of Bonn, Germany. Schaaffhausen had been working with a schoolteacher, Johann Carl Fuhlrott, who had obtained the bones from the quarry, and together they argued that the Neanderthal was of an ancient European human race (Schaaffhausen 1858).

It is unclear how exactly Busk became interested in the Man from the Neander Valley. He most likely became aware of the fossils through his friend and neighbour, the geologist Charles Lyell. Lyell had been summoned to the valley in the late 1850s by Fuhlrott and Schaaffhausen, who were having trouble substantiating their claims that the bones were indeed ancient (Lyell 1863). Fuhlrott called on Lyell, hoping the geologist would study the cave sediments and settle the issue of antiquity, proving the bones were ancient. Lyell returned from the valley in 1860, bringing with him a cast of the skull given to him by Fuhlrott (Lyell 1863). Lyell himself was not qualified to study the skull in detail, so he gave it to Huxley and Busk to prepare a more detailed analysis.

Busk seems to have immediately embarked on this analysis, while simultaneously preparing a translation of Schaaffhausen's work. Although he translated Schaaffhausen's words on the entire skeleton, Busk's own analysis focused on just the skull, as it was the sole part of the skeleton to which he had access. Busk's paper appeared in April 1861, in the *Natural History Review*; it was titled 'On the Crania of the Most Ancient Races of Man, a Translation with Comments by D. Schaaffhausen' (1861). Following the translation, Busk described his impression of the skull under a section labelled 'Remarks'. In addition to his comments, Busk included illustrations of the skull, as well as various other human and ape skulls for comparison. Reflected in both Busk's observations, as well as in his illustrations, was a concern with the issues central to the study of humans: antiquity and variation.

## Human antiquity

In early 1863, Charles Lyell noted that 'no subject has lately excited more curiosity and general interest ... than the question of the Antiquity of the Human Race' (1863, 1). This curiosity resulted in the potential overturning of the previously popular idea that humans had only been around for a comparatively short time – maybe a few thousand years or so (Rudwick 2005). For centuries, the geological record had substantiated this theory – while the bones of extinct creatures such as mammoths could be found in ancient strata, human skeletons appeared only in recent strata. But this reasoning began to fall apart in the mid-nineteenth century when discoveries of crude human-made stone tools were uncovered alongside mammoths and extinct cave bears (Van Riper 1993).

The discovery of these stone tools, associated with mammoth remains, opened up the possibility of a previously unimagined stretch of time in the human story, a 'pre-history', that took place before metalworking, writing and any known civilisations (Goodrum 2012). This was, initially, a controversial idea, and one that needed substantial evidence to back it up. Scientists had to prove that the tools and mammoths were truly associated with one another – *i.e.* that they had been deposited at the same time. As early as the 1830s, naturalists such as Philippe-Charles Schmerling, working in Belgium, began claiming they had found such materials associated, but their statements were dismissed (Grayson 1993). It was possible, Lyell and other experts argued, that the sediments had been mixed, and that the stone tools and mammoth bones had actually been deposited at different times.

In the late 1850s, however, evidence that humans did have an extensive prehistory was beginning to amount. One site became critical to solving this controversy: a cavern near Torquay, in England, known as Brixham cave. As had been claimed of other caves, stone tools and extinct animal fossils were discovered in association

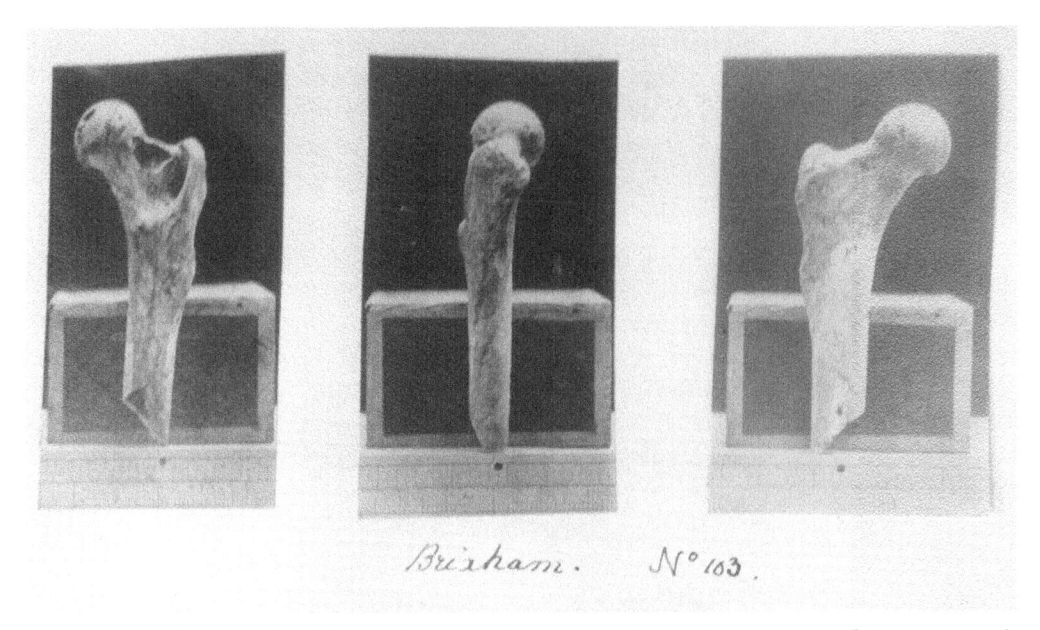

*Figure 12.3. Photograph of fauna from Brixham Cave, from* The Papers of George Busk *(Archives of the Royal College of Surgeons England, 1812-1876).*

at Brixham. But, unlike the others, Brixham was carefully excavated by scientists who documented the position of each object and the stratigraphic layer from which they it was recovered (Gruber 2008). Busk and other leading scientists oversaw the organisation of the excavation, calling themselves the Brixham Cave Committee. Additionally, Busk helped present the findings at scientific meetings and studied the extinct fauna of the cave for years to come (Pengelly *et al.* 1873; Figure 12.3).

The excavations at Brixham proved that stone tools had indeed been deposited alongside ancient creatures, thus settling the debate of human antiquity by 1859 (Grayson 1993). Busk reminded his readers of this in his opening sentence of his remarks on the Feldhofer cranium, stating 'the fact of the geological antiquity of Man ... has apparently been fully established' (Busk 1861, 172). Victorian scientists came to envision a vast human prehistory, one known only by stone tools. They refused, however, to believe that each instance of stone tools and mammoth remains found in close geological proximity to one another were necessarily contemporaneous, rendering it crucial that each case be examined individually.

By the time Busk received the Neanderthal cast, he had helped settle the larger issue of antiquity. Accordingly, however, assessing the antiquity of individual cases required case-by-case scrutiny. This question was particularly pressing for the Neanderthal discovery, as the fossil had not been found through organised excavation, but was instead recovered by chance. It is difficult to imagine circumstances further from those of the Brixham excavation: instead of deliberate excavators, the Feldhofer specimen had been uncovered by uninterested workers, who had mindlessly tossed the fossils downslope. This raised a problem for interpreting the Neanderthal find; how could antiquity be proven in this individual case?

Busk admitted that the circumstances of the Neanderthal's discovery were 'not altogether demonstrative of their real geological position' and therefore age (Busk 1861, 172). While this was problematic, Busk himself ultimately trusted that the Neanderthal was old. This decision was probably due to conversations with Lyell, who had ultimately labelled the fossil as ancient (Lyell 1863). Other scientists, however, were not convinced. Without evidence of antiquity, the Neanderthal was just an odd human skull, they claimed. Some scientists argued that it was just a deformed modern human, a diseased 'idiot', for example (Carter Blake 1862). Others went so far as to argue that the creature was a recent Mongolian soldier, whose skull had been deformed because he suffered from chronic pain, which caused him to furrow his brow in agony (Mayer 1864).

Seeing the Neanderthal through Busk's eyes requires recognising the importance of its antiquity. Indeed, much of the translation was devoted to attempts to ascertain its age (Busk 1861); as with many human skeletons discovered at the time, the question of antiquity was paramount. If one was to imagine – as Schaaffhausen suggested – that the Neanderthal was a member of an ancient human race, there needed to be proof that the fossil was indeed ancient.

## Human variation

The realisation that humans had a deep history had given rise to another important question: who were these early humans? Answering this question was even more problematic. According to Busk, the fossil's antiquity had been proven from 'man's works rather than ... his actual remains', because scientists knew nothing of the humans who made these stones tools (Busk 1861, 172). Did these mammoth-hunters differ from the humans who presently inhabit the earth, and if so, what did those differences mean? To understand humans of the past, it became clear that scientists needed to understand humans – and their differences – in the present. This turned out to be a complicated endeavour. British scientists had only recently become aware of the vast differences between human populations around the globe, and they were unsure how to categorise and make sense of those differences (Stocking 1991).

Confronted with humans from Africa and Asia of different skin colour, technology and customs, scientists turned to measuring variations in skulls. These variations were discussed in terms of different races of humans, although what exactly 'race' meant was still a highly contentious debate (Goodrum 2016). The task of describing the human species and documenting its variations was one Busk took great interest in. During the time in which he was overseeing the Brixham cave excavations, serving as secretary of the Linnean society, and examining the Neanderthal cranium, Busk was also working on a massive project documenting human variation. He was measuring, tracing and cataloguing human crania from all over the world to better understand how they differed and what those differences meant.

Busk's project was meant to culminate in a giant text called *Crania Typica*, but the book never saw publication. Other scientists had undertaken this endeavour; Busk was following in the footsteps of men who had produced books that illustrated and examined different skull variations (*e.g.* Morton 1839). Busk wanted to know how long each cranium was, how wide, how big the eye sockets were and more. These comparisons could help him understand the particular ways skulls varied, and draw conclusions about varieties within the human species. He illustrated the crania, showing each skull in multiple views, allowing others to see how facial angles and the lengths of the crania differed. He compared skulls from Europe, Asia, Tasmania and more, noting how foreheads and skull lengths differed in each case (Busk 1812-1876).

The Neanderthal added urgency to the task of understanding human variations, because the shape of its skull and size of its brow was more divergent than in most humans. Busk's *Crania Typica* addressed this in a section focusing on priscan (ancient) humans. This section was unlike other craniometry texts, which only examined recent human skulls. In his anatomical tables filled with measurements, he included entries for his priscan skulls to assess whether they resembled or diverged from recent human skulls in various ways, and the Neanderthal was included as one such priscan skull (Busk papers). Though *Crania Typica* was never published, Busk drew heavily from it in his 1861 publication on the Neanderthal.

Busk's work on human skull variation was ongoing, and he was unable to use it to make any definite conclusions in his 1861 remarks on the Neanderthal fossil. He admitted 'no satisfactory opinion can be offered' with regard to the Neanderthal's resemblance to any other known human skull. Instead, Busk stressed that many 'diversities of form' existed in human skulls, and the Neanderthal was just an extreme example of these forms (Busk 1861, 174).

## Concluding remarks: Studying the Neanderthal as a human

After his initial conclusions were published in 1861, Busk continued to study the Neanderthal for the next two years. He laboured alongside his friend Thomas Huxley, providing illustrations of the skull and building upon his work on variation. Their study culminated in Huxley's book *Man's Place in Nature*, in which they concluded that it was indeed on the extreme end of human variation, but definitely human. Their examination of the Neanderthal was part of a larger discussion about 'the question of questions for mankind, the problem which underlies all others, and is more deeply interesting than any other ... the ascertainment of the place which Man occupies in nature and of his relations to the universe of things' (Huxley 1863, 71).

Years would pass between Busk's initial examinations of the Neanderthal and the moment when the fossil became labelled the separate species *Homo neanderthalensis*

(King 1864). For the next century and a half, the Neanderthal would continue to weigh on this 'question of questions'. But, as Busk's study of the Neanderthal fossil shows, mid-nineteenth-century ideas surrounding the place of humans in nature were very different to the ideas of today. Comprehending that this nature had a prehistory was vital, and understanding how humans varied was equally important. This picture of the Neanderthal's study diverges from the general historical narrative that has been propagated of the science at the time. Generally, histories have assumed that Neanderthal examinations were shaped by evolutionary beliefs, but this paper has argued that concept of evolution was arguably not yet as vital for interpretations as the idea of prehistory itself (Goodrum 2012). The story of Busk and the Neanderthal, then, sheds light on an early chapter in the story of Neanderthal interpretations. It is a chapter framed by extinct cave bears and 'races' of humans, the first in many chapters of scientists seeking to use Neanderthal fossils to understand humans and their past.

## Bibliography

Blake, C.C. (1862) On the Crania of the Most Ancient Races of Men. *The Geologist* 5, 205–232.
Bowler, P.J. (1986) *Theories of Human Evolution. A century of debate 1844-1944*. Baltimore: Johns Hopkins University Press.
Bowler, P.J. (1989) *Evolution: The history of an idea*. Berkeley: University of California Press.
Busk, G. (1812–1876) *The Papers of George Busk*. Archives of the Royal College of Surgeons England. Available online: http://surgicat.rcseng.ac.uk/Details/archive/110004600.
Busk, G. (1861) Translation with Comments of 'on the crania of the most ancient races of man' by D. Schaaffhausen. *The Natural History Review: A Quarterly Journal of Biological Science* 1, 153–176.
Cook, G. (1997) George Busk FRS (1807–1886), Nineteenth-Century Polymath: Surgeon, parasitologist, zoologist and paleontologist. *Journal of Medical Biography* 5, 88–101.
Darwin, C. (1859) Letter addressed to Thomas Henry Huxley, Darwin Correspondence Project, 'Letter no. 2582'. Available online: http://www.darwinproject.ac.uk/DCP-LETT-2582.
Desmond, A. (1997) *Huxley: From devil's disciple to evolution's high priest*. Reading, MA: Addison-Wesley.
Gardiner, B.G. (2000) Darwin and Seemann. *The Linnean* 16, 10–12.
Goodrum, M.R. (2012) The Idea of Human Prehistory: The natural sciences, the human sciences, and the problem of human origins in Victorian Britain. *History and Philosophy of the Life Sciences* 34, 117–145.
Goodrum, M. R. (2016) The Beginnings of Human Palaeontology: Prehistory, craniometry and the 'fossil human races'. *British Journal for the History and Philosophy of Science* 49, 387–409.
Gould, S. J. (1996) *The Mismeasure of Man*. New York: W.W. Norton.
Grayson, D.K. (1983) *The Establishment of Human Antiquity*. New York: Academic Press.
Gruber, J.W. (2008) Brixham Cave and the Antiquity of Man. In: T. Murray and C. Evans (eds) *Histories of Archaeology: A reader in the history of archaeology*, pp. 13–45. Oxford: Oxford University Press.
Huxley, T.H. (1825–1895). *The Thomas Henry Huxley Collection*. London: Archives of Imperial College London.
Huxley, T.H. (1863) *Evidence as to Man's Place in Nature*. London: Williams and Norgate.
King, W. (1864) The Reputed Fossil Man of the Neanderthal. *Quarterly Journal of Science* 1, 88–97.
Kölliker, A. (1853) *Manual of Human Histology*. Trans. G. Busk and T. Huxley. London: Sydenham Society.
Krings, M.S., Schmitz, R.W., Krainitzki, H., Stoneking, M. and Pääbo, S. (1997) Neandertal DNA Sequences and the Origin of Modern Humans. *Cell* 90, 19–30.

Lyell, C. (1863) *The Geological Evidences of the Antiquity of Man: With remarks on theories of the origin of species by variation.* London: John Murray.

Madison, P. (2016) The Most Brutal of Human Skulls: Measuring and knowing the first Neanderthal. *The British Journal for the History of Science* 49, 411–432.

Mayer, F.J.C. (1864) Über die fossilen Überreste eines Menschlichen Schädels und Skeletes in einer Felsenhohle des Düssel-oder Neanderthales. *Müllers Archiv* 29, 1–26.

Morton, S.G. (1839) *Crania Americana: Or a comparative view of the skulls of various aboriginal nations of America.* Philadelphia: J. Dobson.

Pengelly, W., Busk, G., Evans, J., Prestwich, J., Falconer, H. and Ramsay, A. (1873) Report on the Exploration of Brixham Cave, Conducted by a Committee of the Geological Society, and under the Superintendence of Wm. Pengelly, Esq., FRS, Aided by a Local Committee; with descriptions of the animal remains by George Busk, Esq., FRS, and of the flint implements by John Evans, Esq., FRS Joseph Prestwich, FRS, FGS, &c., Reporter. *Philosophical Transactions of the Royal Society of London* 163, 471–572.

Rudwick, M.J. (2005) *Bursting the Limits of Time: The reconstruction of geohistory in the age of revolution.* Chicago: University of Chicago Press.

Schaaffhausen, H. (1858) Zur Kenntnis der ältesten Rasseschädel. *Mullers Archiv* 24, 453–478.

Schmitz, R.W. and Thissen, J. (2000) *Neandertal: die Geschichte geht Weiter.* Heidelberg: Spektrum Akademischer Verlag.

Stocking, G. (1991) *Victorian Anthropology.* New York: Simon and Schuster.

Thomas, K.B. (2008) Busk, George. In: C. Coulston Gillispie, L. Holmes and N. Koertge (eds) *Complete Dictionary of Scientific Biography* 2, pp. 616–618. Detroit: Charles Scribner's Sons.

Trinkaus, E. and Shipman, P. (1993) *The Neandertals: Changing the image of mankind.* New York: Alfred A. Knopf.

Van Riper, A.B. (1993) *Men Among the Mammoths.* Chicago: University of Chicago Press.